Kate Hill was born in London in 1965 and went to school there. At Lady Margaret Hall, Oxford, she graduated in philosophy, politics and economics. She worked with children on an after-school project, and at the International Centre for Child Studies in Bristol on research into child development. Having begun this book after her brother's death, she completed the text while working on research into young people and suicide at the University Department of Psychiatry, Warneford Hospital, Oxford. She also edited the SIBBS (Support in Bereavement for Brothers and Sisters) quarterly newsletter and contact network of The Compassionate Friends, and put together a Bereavement Information pack for The Samaritans.

Kate Hill died of a brain haemorrhage in 1994.

THE LONG SLEEP

Young People and Suicide

Kate Hill

A *Virago* Book

First published by Virago Press 1995

Reprinted 1995, 1996

Copyright © The Estate of Kate Hill 1995

The moral right of the author has been asserted

A CIP catalogue record for this book
is available from the British Library

ISBN 1 85381 589 6

Printed and bound in Great Britain by Clays Ltd, St Ives plc

UK companies, institutions and other organisations wishing
to make bulk purchases of this or any other book
published by Little, Brown should contact their local
bookshop or the special sales department at the address below.
Tel 0171 911 8000. Fax 0171 911 8100.

Virago
A Division of
Little, Brown and Company (UK)
Brettenham House
Lancaster Place
London WC2E 7EN

For John Hill
1969–1990
with love

Contents

FOREWORD

Suicidal behaviour in young people today is causing great concern. This is because of the dramatic increase in suicide that has occurred in the past 10 to 15 years in young men and the fact that non-fatal suicidal behaviour (attempted suicide) is particularly common in young people in the United Kingdom, especially in young females. The explanations for both of these tragic phenomena are at present unclear.

Research is essential in order to understand suicidal behaviour, whether it be in terms of its causes, consequences, treatment or prevention. The findings from research investigations can answer such questions as who is most at risk, what social, economic and other environmental factors seem to be associated with the behaviour, and how effective are preventive efforts. To fully understand the problem of suicide, however, one must also develop an appreciation of the human issues, by talking to people who have survived suicide attempts and to relatives and friends of both survivors and people who have died by suicide. To integrate both approaches to this problem is in practice extremely difficult, yet this is exactly what Kate Hill has done in this remarkable book. Thus in addition to reviewing the relevant literature and speaking to researchers in the field, she took the painful step of contacting and interviewing people who had experienced the aftermath of a close relative's suicide or had themselves survived suicide attempts. I know that this is difficult enough when such interactions happen within the relatively safe setting of clinical practice. But to conduct interviews of this kind in an entirely different and unstructured context was a brave move, one that has undoubtedly contributed to the success of this book. I also know that her interviews were often a source of considerable support and help to those she met.

In reviewing the findings of research Kate Hill has managed to present even the most dry statistics in an interesting and engaging fashion. Her knowledge of the research literature has clearly been extensive. But most importantly she has enriched the book throughout with summaries of cases and quotes from her interviews. This is perhaps her book's greatest strength. The combination of the two components provides the reader with a rich and full exploration of the problem of suicide and attempted suicide in young people. When I was asked by Kate Hill to read the manuscript in draft form I found that after reading the first chapter I was eagerly awaiting further chapters. I also found myself in envy of the quality of her writing style and her ability to present even the plainest detail with an interesting flourish.

I first met Kate Hill when she was in the early stages of preparing this book. I was immediately impressed by the extent of background research that she had already done. I was particularly struck by her concern to produce a book that would not just be an account of the problem of suicide and attempted suicide in young people but one that would be a significant step forward in both understanding this problem and conveying this understanding to other people. This stemmed in part from her own painful experience of her brother's death, but was also a reflection of the concern she felt for other people. Thus the book constantly leans in the direction of what can be done to prevent suicidal behaviour and to help those who have suffered its consequences.

When I obtained a research grant for an in-depth study of young people who had died by suicide I immediately realised that Kate Hill was the person I wanted to involve in this project and I was delighted when she agreed to participate. Her influence on the project was considerable as she rapidly demonstrated her skills as a research worker.

Tragically, in July 1994 Kate Hill died suddenly and unexpectedly from a brain haemorrhage at the age of 29. We can only be thankful that she was able to complete this important book before her death. She was unable to prepare the references and I am sure she would have wanted to thank Aslög Malmberg, Sue Simkin and Annette Erlangsen who joined me in doing this, although we regret that we have been unable to complete them to the standard she intended.

This book is a masterly exploration of one of the most important and pressing problems of our time. Kate Hill wrote it primarily for the lay person who has interest and concerns about this problem. It will, however, be extremely valuable for people working in this field, especially those trying to help young people with emotional problems. This includes both professionals and members of voluntary agencies. I recommend this book to this wide and varied audience with firm encouragement to experience and make the most of a very carefully and thoughtfully prepared work.

Keith Hawton
Oxford University Department of Psychiatry

Notes on interview material

This book draws on interviews conducted with two groups of people: young suicide attempters and relatives bereaved by youth suicide. In one case an interview was given by a close friend of a young man who died. All the young people concerned were under-25 at the time of their suicide attempt or death. To protect their privacy the subjects of the interviews have been given pseudonyms. For young suicide attempters *only*, age is specified in brackets, underneath quotations. This indicates how old he or she was at the time of the suicide attempt being referred to. Since some interviewees made more than one attempt, over a number of years, the age may vary.

Acknowledgements

I am deeply grateful for the help of all those who have talked to me: young people who have attempted suicide in the past and parents, siblings and friends bereaved by youth suicide.

I would also like to thank all those who provided research interviews, sent me papers and data, shared their ideas and commented on drafts of the book. In particular my thanks are due to Dr Keith Hawton, Dr Steven Platt, Steve Beswick and The Samaritans Youth Outreach Team, Hereward Harrison of Childline, The Compassionate Friends, Anna Motz, Jan Bridget of the Lesbian Information Service. Thank you to Ruth Petrie, Melanie Silgardo and Rebecca Swift at Virago Press for all their encouragement. I am very grateful to the Society of Authors whose grant helped to complete this book. And finally, my love and thanks to all those who were a little too close for comfort to the writing of this book, in particular Anna, Claire and Don Hill.

PREFACE

When the present feels intolerable or the future inconceivable, death can seem to offer a solution. It is a 'solution' which growing numbers of young people have chosen in recent decades. In the UK, the male suicide rate has escalated dramatically among the under-25s and young women now attempt suicide in enormous numbers. This is a book about these acts and why they happen.

It is also about our responses to the young and suicidal. A collective commitment to save lives creates suicide prevention policies, and these I look at. Yet as individuals – particularly as individuals with no special training or understanding of suicidal crises – most of us find we have only intuition to guide us when faced with the hint or half-conscious dread that someone close to us may be *that* desperate. Unfortunately gut reactions to the suicidal are often unreliable, sometimes tragically so. Whilst young people may not survive despair without a human lifeline, few of us are naturally equipped to throw one.

The field of research calling itself 'suicidology' offers a wealth of work by psychiatrists, psychologists and sociologists, much of it inaccessible to non-professionals. Since the point of this research is to help prevent suicides, this is a pity. This book draws on that research, on the practice and perspectives of professionals and volunteers who work to help the suicidal, as well as interviews with those who have been directly affected by suicidal crises. Two groups of people agreed to be interviewed for this book: young people who had survived suicide attempts, and parents, siblings and friends bereaved through youth suicide. Those who had survived a suicide attempt often described difficulties in making others 'see' that they could not cope with their feelings and problems. For the bereaved, an understanding of just how desperate and unhappy their child, sibling or friend was feeling often grew with hindsight after their death. I hope the personal views and experiences shared by those who spoke to me may help, a little, to close this gap in understanding.

Each part of this book may be read in its own right. Part I sets the crises of individual children, adolescents and young adults in their broader social context. The scale of recent increases in suicide and attempted suicide among the under-25s is described in Chapter 1, and those groups of young people who have proved most susceptible in Chapter 2. Grim suicide statistics inevitably raise questions about the social pressures and changes that are hurting the young (Chapter 3). Suicide prevention has become a more urgent necessity and Chapter 4 considers the feasibility of saving young lives.

Part II maps the experience and needs of young people struggling with suicidal feelings. Some readers may want to refer directly to it, particularly if they are concerned about a young person close to them. The suicidal process, during which self-destructive feelings and thoughts of dying develop and intensify, is traced in Chapter 5. The fears, defences and misconceptions that often leave the suicidal isolated are considered in Chapter 6. Responses which, on the other hand, diffuse tension, kindle hope and encourage communication are the subject of Chapter 7. The ambivalent feelings that prevent many young people from seeking help with their feelings and problems are explored in Chapter 8 and Chapter 9 provides information about sources of help that are available in the UK.

Current rates of self-inflicted injury, poisoning and death among young people suggest crises of hope are far from rare. This book is for anyone who would like to know more and would prefer – should the need arise to help a suicidal young person – not to be taken by surprise.

PROLOGUE

No Hope: Dead Ends

Ashley

Home life was pretty heavy. My dad's an alcoholic. When I was about 13 he was in a local mental hospital, chilling out. It was for alkies. I didn't really understand anything except he had a drink problem. He never showed any sign of affection. I was always in fear of his moods. I lived in this world where kids were just ignored. My mum had a really difficult job. She had four kids and we weren't at all wealthy. She used to do clothing alterations. She had a hard enough time herself. She was on tranquillisers and just wanted to keep the peace between me, my dad and the other kids.

I hated school. It didn't seem right, the authoritarianness of the teachers. It was a comprehensive – a boys' school. I was somebody that was classed as a loser. Basically I never trusted any teachers because all I ever received from them was punishment. I used to love winding them up. We could really push them and they couldn't handle it. They used to lose their rag and we'd feel good.

I got into misbehaving and hanging about with idiots and druggies and pissheads. There was about seven of us and we were the hard kids. We ended up being quite respected. We were seen as the people you wouldn't mess with but we were all very insecure. We all feared being the next one to be ridiculed.

We were into drugs and being pissed. I got into drugs and glue-sniffing and taking mushrooms from 13 upwards, just out of boredom. There wasn't really anything going on. I needed kicks. I needed something. So drugs gave me a buzz. I didn't know what the bloody hell we were taking. I'd have took anything. And I was drinking all the time. I couldn't handle being straight at all. A few drinks and I could relax, I could be a laugh, I could feel good about myself.

When I was 13 I was sexually abused by a woman. She was in her forties and she was into young lads. We needed an adult to go to the off-licence for us and she used to go. She'd touch us up and stuff. It was really fucked-up stuff – we were all dead young. She said she wanted to go out with me, which was ridiculous. Because I was young I'd never really had any sexual experience. Basically she took me to bed. It was total nightmarish stuff. A lot of the time I was pissed but it was repeated. My life was so horrible. I remember being outside her house, just hanging about on this estate, thinking, 'Fucking hell, is this life? Is this it?' It was something I always felt bad about and it fucked up my view of women. I thought all women wanted sex and she was the only one brave enough to come out. So when I was drunk and my defences were down I copped off with [so many] people and had ridiculous relationships.

I really did feel a need to fit in. I didn't fit in at home, I didn't fit in at school and I wanted to fit in with some criminal underclass – that's who I identified with. I was always in trouble with the cops. I'd been arrested maybe seven or eight times before I was 15 – just stupid things like putting a window in, being drunk and disorderly. The first time I was arrested the CID officer came into my cell and roughed me up. I left the cells with bruises. It was a shock more than anything. I wasn't used to being treated in that way. It created a great deal of hatred in me. I got quite rebellious. I felt anger toward society. I hated my life. I got into a real negative thing with authority. The lives of the adults I saw around me just didn't really count for much, so how could I take notice of people whose lives were fucked? When the police came along there was an enemy that I could get back at. I ended up in juvenile court. For my birthday and Christmas quite a few times my mum just paid the fines.

At 16, I left school and got kicked out of home. I went on a YTS scheme for a day. It was just the same as school. All the kids from school were there and the bullying was still there. When I was 17, a gang of us got together and squatted a school. We tried to live communally. I didn't want any controlling hands on me. I wanted to do my own thing.

Then everything just got out of hand and I lost perspective. I had this desire to change things. I was a squatter. I was involved in animal rights and anti-Fascist Action. I was like a headless chicken – involved in all this bloody stuff. I used to be frustrated because I'd see people around me that were so laid back about things. I couldn't understand that. To me it was all so immediate. And I got in with a lot of middle-class feminists and I ended up taking on this idea that men are crap. I swallowed it all. I was keen to learn. I didn't like my past. I'd come from this really heavy, working-class, shit estate. I was a regular in a pub when I was 17 and all of that rubbish. I wanted to change. I wanted to step into this new world. But a lot of what I was coming through, I couldn't articulate at the time. And I suddenly realised I was different. There weren't that many working-class kids around me. They were mostly middle-class liberal kids – quite a few students. I just began to feel guilty, because of the way they spoke, because of their snide remarks. I was scared, because where I'd come from wasn't where they had come from. I just had such a low opinion of myself from the past that I thought I was a shitty bloke.

And I gave people reasons to not like me because I was drinking a lot. I was an alcoholic. I'd get up in the morning and drink Special Brew, I'd go to bed at night and drink Special Brew. I'd be pissed all day. I was having really crap relationships and making people mistrust me. I'd sleep with people I didn't really want to sleep with. I was just pissed all the time.

I wanted a way out but I didn't have anywhere to go. I never thought I had a future. I thought either I'd be dead or I'd be in prison. Things had gradually got worse. I didn't like any part of my life and I couldn't see a way forward at all. Suicide had always flashed through my mind. It had become a day-to-day thing. There was always that option. Quite a few times I went on top of the flats but I couldn't handle jumping and all that painful stuff. There were all these silly attempts. Well, they weren't silly but they didn't work. One time I put a rope round my neck in a cellar but the floor was too high. There was not much of a place to swing. I didn't really fucking care either way.

I was having a relationship with this woman. We went out together for about a year and I really, really liked her. But I basically wore her out. I drained her of energy. The night I tried to top myself we had an argument. But it wasn't that. That was just the last straw. It was the whole fucking thing. I just couldn't handle it any more. I couldn't do anything right. Everything I did, I fucked up. I felt so bad about the way I was treating people. I'd pissed all my friends off so I didn't really matter to a lot of people. There wasn't much to lose. I felt a million miles away from my family. I'd ring my mum, crying. I was alienated – isolated – fucked-up – guilt ridden. I was unemployed. Wherever I turned I had the police after me. And I wasn't a very well man. My nervous system was knackered through the drink. I was paranoid and hallucinating. *Everything* got on top of me and I didn't have any way out.

I can remember it all very clearly. After the argument she [Ashley's girlfriend] went to bed. I was very calm, when I did it. It was not really an impulse because I was over an hour and a half deciding to do it. I'd been drinking but I wasn't pissed. Everything was quiet and still. It was about two in the morning. I just felt calmer than I'd felt in years and years. I went to the bathroom, broke a razor and slashed my wrists. I really did mean business. I cut them really, really deep.

Elaine

I used to think to myself that Elaine wasn't quite as emotionally mature as the others, perhaps. She just seemed that little year or

4

so behind. Perhaps it was because she was my youngest child. I just felt she was still very much a child. And yet on another level she was incredibly mature. She had a very deep interest in other people. She was somebody who really cared very much. As she got older and a little more patient, she became very, very loving and demonstrative. She was always interested and kind and supportive.

She was very energetic, always. She walked at ten months and she climbed out of her cot at a year. She was like a monkey. Very wiry and slim and athletic – full of beans. And she was very good at sport. She couldn't sit still for long. That was real penance to have to sit still.

I was always very conscious that I needed to reassure her, because she had dyslexia. She had her confidence demolished so many times, mostly by teachers denying that she had a problem. They would say, 'She doesn't try. She doesn't concentrate.' But in spite of all her problems she loved school. She never was unhappy at school. She liked going. She liked her friends – she was a very sociable girl. In a tiny village like this there was not the company once the others had all left home. I was always happy to have her friends over, although latterly she didn't really. But she did enjoy her own company. Elaine wasn't a girl who appeared lonely. She was very industrious – drawing, painting, listening to music, doing her keep-fit.

I think Elaine would have been helped had she not been dyslexic and could see herself getting herself a good job. The options are much less if you are dyslexic. It would have helped if she could have seen a way out that she could strive for on her own. But she was still very dependent in many respects on other people helping her find her goal in life. She was foundering with regard to her career. I think I sensed that she wasn't quite ready to face it, so we tended not to bring it up. We didn't want to pressure her into having to face it before she was ready. If people said to her 'What are you going to do when you leave school, Elaine?' she would say, 'Oh, I don't know.' And I'd always make a point of saying, 'She hasn't decided.' Because I didn't want her to feel pressured. I was always very conscious of this being something that upset teenagers.

Perhaps I answered for her too much. I just felt she needed that little bit of protection for that little bit longer. I wasn't afraid to let her go. It's a terrible dilemma. If we had taken the opposite attitude and she had still killed herself we'd be saying, 'God we drove her into it.' I feel so grieved that the worst possible thing could have happened, in spite of all my efforts. I never consciously thought I must make all these efforts to stop Elaine from committing suicide, but I did make all these efforts to make sure she had a happy transition from being a child to an adult. This was my priority as far as Elaine was concerned. And the fact that the worst happened in spite of all my efforts – I still find that really hard to take. I remember saying, 'If my love couldn't keep her safe then anything can happen to anyone. If the amount that we loved her couldn't make the difference then I just don't understand what it's all about.'

But you see I haven't touched on the other things that we know about now, that we didn't know about before Elaine died. She had this teacher at school – Liz. Elaine developed a crush on her, which she saw as the only thing in the world worth worrying about. Apparently Elaine confided in her that she'd got a crush on her and that she was very worried about her future, she was very mixed up and she thought she was gay.

That was what was bothering her and I didn't know anything about it. Obviously I understand now why Elaine didn't feel she could talk to me. Well I don't understand, because Elaine could have talked to me about it. I value people, not their sexuality – it doesn't make any difference. I would have understood. I searched and I cannot think what I could possibly have done in our past relationship that would ever have given Elaine the idea that I would have rejected her in any way because she was gay.

I bitterly regret that I didn't twig. Elaine liked to do her own thing. She didn't like interference by me. She didn't like girlie clothes and never ever had. Right from when she was very little she thought they were absolutely ridiculous. She liked dungarees and jeans and sporty clothes. But I'm not a very conventional person and never have been. There was no pressure on Elaine to be conventional. She had never had a boyfriend. She was such an attractive girl and so this was all the more surprising. That was one of the things that was starting to register with me. She was only just 17 and some girls don't have boyfriends until they're older, but it was just starting to register with me that perhaps she wasn't interested in boys. She certainly confided in friends at school that she thought she was gay. God, I wish she had told me about it. I've dreamt since that she has talked to me about it and that we've sorted it out. Obviously Elaine was becoming conscious that there were people who didn't approve. I guess Elaine could see choices coming ahead. She was going to have to make serious choices.

Plus the fact that Liz wasn't available to have a relationship with anyway. Poor Elaine – perhaps Liz said to her, 'Look Elaine, this is an impossible situation. You're going to have to face the fact that there isn't going to be a relationship.' Elaine may have thought: that's it, that's the end of my world. A month after she died Liz told me that Elaine had rung her and said, 'I'm worried about being on my own. I'm afraid I may do something stupid.' Liz was sufficiently worried and had made an appointment for her to see a psychotherapist. They had tried to ring [a counselling service] but there was a three-month waiting list before they could get her an appointment.

Elaine took matters into her own hands so quickly, before anybody had a chance to do something about it. She was a very private person. Her friends were actually worried about her when they broke up for the school holidays. Just before the holidays I was saying, 'I still haven't got my finger on what is stressing Elaine.' It's clear she wasn't all right. She hadn't been all right for a while. But it wasn't the message we were getting. She had obviously been fighting it, but we knew nothing about it. She was not as communicative as usual. There was, I think, probably just a sense of withdrawal. But as a mother I know that

7

that's part of the growing-up process. You've got to give them their space. I didn't see it as anything other than that – growing away. They grow away and then come back again. Children do have to make that sort of break.

Something came to a head very quickly that day. It was a very spontaneous thing she did – I think she did it in a fit of anger. Elaine did ring Liz just before she did it. She just cried and said that she wouldn't be available to go out on the Saturday. That lunchtime it must have built up into something totally overpowering. She came in and went straight up to her room. She was so angry about something. We still don't know what. Something must have triggered it – some remark – unless it was a general anger against life.

I went up to see what on earth was wrong. And she said, 'I'm livid.' And she wouldn't look at me. And I remember putting my hand under her fringe and said, 'Oh what's up? Come on, it's not like you to be in a bad mood.' She said, 'I'm not in a bad mood. I'm very, very angry.' I said, 'Well, what are you angry about? Please tell me.' She said, 'No, I don't want to talk about it . . .' I thought, I'm not going to get any sense out of her like this. I'll let her simmer down a bit and then I'll come back.

We sat and had lunch and then I nipped up to see her again and she wasn't in her room. I went looking for her and she wasn't anywhere. I was absolutely mystified. I thought perhaps she'd cheered up. I happened to look out of the window and saw the garage block door was swinging in the wind. I thought – perhaps she's over there knocking the hell out of her bike or changing her tyres.

So I just went across to say, 'Elaine, are you going to come and have some coffee?' I called and there was nobody there. I thought – what's the door doing open? I went in, just to look. And there she was, hanging in front of me. I thought – God, it looks like Elaine. It was a nightmare, an absolute nightmare. I looked at this dummy. I looked at this thing. I thought this had got to be a joke. I walked across to her and looked up at her and I knew this was a dead person. It registered that this was a dead person and it was Elaine. It looked like Elaine, so it must be Elaine. I put my arms around her and just held her close. I tried to lift her, but she was so heavy I couldn't. I remember thinking – 'Elaine, what have you done?'

Patricia, Elaine's mother
Elaine died, aged 17.

—— PART I ——

Youth Suicide:
A Recent History

CHAPTER 1

Numbers

Statistics may all too easily engulf their subject. As Al Alvarez suggests, in his study of suicide *The Savage God*, the suffering of the suicidal has little in common with the numbers they may become: 'All that anguish, the slow tensing of the self to that final, irreversible act, and for what? In order to become a statistic.'[1] Despite this dissonance, numbers do of course matter. Statistics provide vital insights into the scale, evolution and circumstances of suicidal behaviour. They record its social impact. A grim epitaph to recent decades, statistics remind us that suicidal behaviour has flourished amongst the young under contemporary conditions. Inevitably, though, suicide statistics require careful handling. Their source is the highly sensitive transfiguration invoked by Alvarez – the translation of individual deaths into suicide data. It is a process which encounters special difficulties, and many youth suicides are lost in translation.

The Problem with Statistics

I thought the coroner would say Tommy committed suicide but he never said that. He said Tommy killed himself.

(PHYLLIS, TOMMY'S MOTHER)

They put it down to 'Misadventure'. But it's impossible to pull a trigger of a shotgun and put it in your mouth accidentally. You just don't put guns in your mouth, do you?

(JANICE, MARK'S SISTER)

Most people feel able to distinguish a suicide from an accident. A suicide is intentional; an accident is not. Equipped with a modicum of information about how someone died, and their circumstances at the time, the pieces fall into place. A deliberately self-inflicted death tends to be perceived as a suicide. Most would surmise that Tommy (above) who died from an overdose of drugs prescribed for depression, and Mark, who shot himself, died through suicide. Both had talked about suicide in advance and acted to end their own lives. However, neither made the official UK suicide statistics for the year in which they died. In the eyes of the law, the evidence surrounding their deaths was circumstantial. Official suicides are far rarer than people who kill themselves.

Shrinkage in official suicide statistics can be traced to the way in which deaths are classified. Suicides, like all deaths from unnatural causes, warrant legal investigation in order to rule out foul play and supply death data for posterity. The inquiry sets out to establish a cause of death, and duly transforms the dead into statistics, although under Scottish and English law the procedures involved differ.

In England, Wales and Northern Ireland the painful and intimate circumstances of each self-inflicted death unfold at a public inquest. With press, witnesses and relatives in attendance, a coroner hears evidence and delivers a verdict of suicide, homicide, accidental or undetermined death accordingly. In some cases juries are involved. Inquests are inevitably charged occasions. Witnesses, post-mortem reports and suicide notes paint grim portraits of the dead, and the presence of bereaved relatives adds to the potency of the event. In Scotland the identification of suicides is a subtler affair. The Procurator Fiscal – the nearest equivalent to the English coroner – investigates suspicious deaths in a procedure hidden from public view.

A private report to the Scottish Office suggests whether or not a suicide has occurred. No public statement is made about individual deaths and the press are not involved. Unfortunately, given the distribution of the population, this discreet system processes only a minority of UK suicides.

The differences between the English and Scottish systems reflect anomalies in legal tradition. Never a felony in Scotland, suicide is not fettered by old criminal associations, but under English law it is. Suicide and attempted suicide remained crimes in England and Wales until 1961, and the suicide verdict still reflects its innocent-until-proven-guilty criminal heritage. The coroner's definition of suicide is a strict one. Suicide requires an intention to die, and the law requires this intention to be beyond any doubt.[2] For a suicide verdict to be delivered, in the words of one coroner's officer, 'The same weight of evidence has to be supplied as for a murder.'[3] A suicide cannot be merely suspected or presumed.[4] Fatal intentions must be clear, supported by evidence and not too befuddled by alcohol or drugs.

Since a dead person's intentions are not easy to prove, doubt is often inevitable. The legal search for a cast-iron intention is, in any case, ill-matched to the often ambivalent nature of suicidal crises. Suicide notes, or clear evidence of preparation for death, may be available to help the coroner reconstruct the feelings and thoughts of the deceased. The choice of suicide method is also considered important. Different methods allow for different degrees of doubt, and active means, such as hanging, are most likely to receive a suicide verdict.[5] Other methods appear more ambiguous. Since few people have a sophisticated understanding of the toxicity of drugs, overdosing is often regarded as a gamble with the unknown, and intentions are harder to determine. Consequently self-poisoning deaths are least likely to be labelled suicide.[6] The effect of this accumulated uncertainty is that suicide is substantially under-reported. A study of coroners' verdicts in London found that the real number of suicides may have been double that registered.[7] And as if to emphasise that a 'commonsense' view of suicide is not at home in a coroner's courtroom, another found that 60 per cent of those who died under trains in north London did not receive a suicide verdict from a coroner's jury.[8]

These difficulties are compounded in the case of children and adolescents, who are least likely to receive a suicide verdict.[9] In part this reflects a sparsity of proof. Young suicide victims leave fewer clues. Clear evidence of suicidal planning tends to be unusual and suicide notes rarer than for adults. Neither can it be assumed that a child or adolescent had a reliable understanding of the relative dangers of different suicide methods. Coroners' verdicts show that self-inflicted deaths by the most unequivocal methods are often regarded as ambiguous when the victim is young. Between 1980 and 1990, 33 per cent of 10–14-year-olds, 75 per cent of 15–19-year-olds and 89 per cent of 20–24-year-olds who hanged themselves in England and Wales were given a suicide verdict.[10] The lethality of the method was not, in the case of child suicides, equated with a clear intention to die, as would generally be the case for adults. Where death is by overdose, the balance of misfortune and suicidal motivations may be particularly unfathomable. Suicide verdicts were given for only 14 per cent of 10–14-year-olds, 34 per cent of 15–19-year-olds and 39 per cent of 20–24-year-olds who died from drugs overdoses.[11] Whilst this figure includes overdoses from 'street drugs' as well as pharmaceutical products, it suggests the proportion of self-inflicted deaths omitted from the official suicide figures.

The burden of legal proof within the English system makes the under-reporting of suicide common practice. The youth suicide rate is also eroded by tactful coroners. The inquest highlights how a system for gathering suicide data can become choked by stigma and private grief. The public exposé of the details of individual suicides bears heavily on the bereaved and the inquest's legalistic tone and setting may exacerbate their vulnerability:

It's in a court for a start. There's witnesses. There was a pathologist, a psychiatrist and the guy who was holding the inquest, who was in the position of judge . . . I felt that people

were passing judgement on me, because I was grieving some-
one who had destroyed themselves.

(CAROL, JAKE'S SISTER)

The evidence, as well as the surroundings, can be extremely distressing:

> *They brought the gun out which Mark had killed himself with.*
> *I just blanked out then. I can't remember anything.*
>
> (JANICE, MARK'S SISTER)

Neither can the press, for whom inquest coverage is bread-and-butter work, be relied upon for discretion. In Patricia's case the local paper misrepresented her testimony:

> *In the paper that night it said that I'd said: 'Elaine was a very*
> *private girl and had a very poor social life.' I never said any*
> *such thing. They had totally misinterpreted it. And it wasn't*
> *true. It was so awful because it sounded as if she was without*
> *a friend in the world.*
>
> (PATRICIA, ELAINE'S MOTHER)

So close to her 17-year-old daughter's suicide this misattribution felt searing. In circumstances like these, coroners naturally wish to minimise the impact of the drama on those implicated in it.

One way they seek to do so is by sparing families a suicide verdict. In the view of one London coroner, 'the reluctance of relations of the deceased to accept a verdict of suicide is well known'.[12] The assumption that the bereaved will necessarily feel stigmatised by a suicide verdict has been challenged, but it seems likely to remain the coroners' rule of thumb. To some the coroners' liberal use of discretion to avoid a suicide verdict may come as a surprise and, to the uninitiated, an element of absurdity can creep into inquest pronouncements. Janice (above) regarded her brother Mark's death as an unmistakable suicide, and could not discern the logic behind the legal ruling. Phyllis was simply bemused that her depressed son's fatal overdose was not proof enough of suicide: 'That's what he died from. He didn't die because of anything else.' Yet the self-inflicted death of a child is an excruciatingly punishing loss for a parent, and for some a suicide verdict would undoubtedly exacerbate anguish. 'I didn't want to believe that he had done that,' said one mother of a 15-year-old suicide quoted in the *Independent*. 'I felt I had failed him so miserably.' The 'open verdict' passed at her son's inquest was a relief to her. It was also a finding she helped secure: 'I told the coroner that I didn't believe he meant to do it, but I think he did want to.'

A reluctance to acknowledge self-destructive desires in the very young infiltrates youth suicide statistics.[13] For every suicide recorded in the 1980s among 10–14-year-olds in the UK three other children died from 'undetermined' causes or 'accidental' drugs overdoses.[14] Although a relatively rare occurrence, childhood suicide is most likely to be masked.[15] Early deaths invite discretion, and confused motives may be readily inferred. The attribution of mixed-up motives to young suicide victims must to some extent reflect the confusion and horror these deaths arouse in adults. The self-inflicted death of a young person disturbs our fiercest taboos: 'A tendency towards minimising, denying and mythologising suicide occurs in most cases of suicide, but even more so in children and adolescents.'[16]

Willingness to deny youth suicide, combined with strict legal dictates, throws a half-light over the numbers of self-inflicted deaths occurring annually in the UK. The soundbite figures quoted in public discussions of youth suicide – 318 under-25s dead in 1970, 430 in 1980, 615 in 1990 – are deflated numbers. Far more casualties of self-destruction passed through the mortuaries in those years and the first task of the suicide researcher is to find out how many.

The Hidden Face of Youth Suicide

She drove straight into this wall. The car was a total wreck and she had to be cut out. The police said she didn't have a safety-belt.

(ANDREA)

Some suicides cannot be detected. The unknown numbers who die each year in road traffic 'accidents' similar to Simone's exemplify this. Whilst the inaccuracy of official suicide figures is widely recognised by suicide researchers, it is impossible to correct these distortions completely. But most suicides are traceable, and to provide more realistic estimates of lives lost, researchers now identify 'probable' suicides.[17]

Most of these are disguised as 'undetermined deaths'. The details of all deaths in the UK are registered according to a standard international system for classifying causes of mortality.[18] In 1968 this system introduced a new category which became instantly popular in dealing with less clear-cut suicides: 'Injury undetermined whether accidentally or purposely inflicted'. The 'undetermined' death, designated by an 'open verdict' in the English inquest system, provided the perfect pseudonym for unproven suicides. It allowed the psychological causes – or intentions – behind a self-destructive act to remain oblique, while recording physical causes. Certain deaths – from self-asphyxiation, self-poisoning or gassing – imply suicide, whether or not the legal label sticks. Since 1968 'undetermined deaths' and officially recorded suicides have looked remarkably alike, and throughout the 1970s and 1980s fluctuated in tandem.[19] Occasionally unproven murders and unidentifiable corpses stray into the 'undetermined' category, but it is now widely recognised to very largely comprise self-inflicted deaths. When these less overt suicides are added to the official tally the total number of suicides in all age groups increases by about 50 per cent.[20] For children and adolescents the increase is higher: 77 per cent for 15–19-year-olds in the UK during the 1980s and 240 per cent among 10–14-year-olds.[21]

Deciphering suicide statistics is not a purely academic necessity. Unless all suicides are taken into account, misinformation can leak into public debate. A local example was provided by media coverage of suicides at Oxford University in 1992–3. Three young students killed themselves at the university within as many months. Media inquiry pursued the suspicion that in the shadow of the dreaming spires intense academic pressure and social stresses left students vulnerable to suicide. Official suicide statistics supported this proposal. The suicide rate among Oxford students was found to be 30 per cent higher than among other 18–25-year-olds – headline news.[22] Yet when probable suicides were added to the calculation the difference disappeared.[23] It seemed students were more likely than others their age to receive a suicide verdict, but no more of them were dying self-inflicted deaths. None of which proves that Oxford University does not have peculiar environmental hazards, nor that concern about student suicides is unwarranted. What it does suggest is that official and probable suicide rates can tell very different stories and that the 'facts' of youth suicide may turn out, on closer scrutiny, to be artefacts of classification.

For practical purposes officially recorded suicide figures are defunct. The UK Department of Health's own calculations confirm this. In 1992, Virginia Bottomley, the Secretary of State for Health, made a commitment to reduce the suicide rate in England and Wales by 15 per cent by the end of the century (see Chapter 4). The 'suicide rate' in question turned out to be the combined death rate from suicide and undetermined causes.[24] A footnote in a government handbook for health professionals explained: 'Coroners vary in their criteria for recording a suicide verdict. Including the category of undetermined deaths reduces the variation considerably. Most undetermined deaths are suicides.'[25]

Yet more suicides are classified neither as suicides nor as undetermined deaths, but as accidents. Mark's fatal 'Misadventure', referred to in the previous section, was one. Ultimately there is no clean division between suicides and other deaths resulting from risk-taking behaviour. The complexity of self-destructive impulses and their myriad interpretations mean that innumerable young deaths might be judged to have a 'suicidal' component. Numerous self-inflicted deaths each year in the UK are classified as accidental, in particular those involving overdoses of pharmaceutical drugs, judged to have been back-fired 'cries for help'. Again, suicide researchers sometimes include these deaths in estimations of 'probable suicides'.[26] In the last 25 years many youth suicides will have been classified as accidents, but erring on the side of caution the estimates that follow exclude them. Over 6,000 10–24-year-olds have died 'undetermined' deaths in the UK since 1968 and these are combined with official youth suicides in the picture that follows.

Youth Suicide – the Last 25 Years

The United Kingdom has seen sharp increases in youth suicide since the 1960s. Suicide and undetermined death claimed 53 in every million 15–24-year-olds in 1970. Ten years later the toll was 73 per million and by 1990 the death rate had reached 112; a 110 per cent increase in 20 years.[27] Yet this general figure masks dramatic sex differences. The rate of youth suicide has, in fact, been driven up by rising numbers of deaths among young men. Between 1970 and 1990 their suicide rate increased by a huge 160 per cent, swamping a 14 per cent rise among young women. Suicide currently kills around 70 young people (aged 15–24) a month in the UK, at least 55 of them male.[28]

For all ages the recent history of British suicides corroborates a story of growing sex differences. These are traditional in the UK – more men than women kill themselves, and have always done so – but their respective suicide rates have tended to run on parallel lines.[29] When male suicide rose or fell, so too did female. This was the case after the Second World War when suicide increased, peaked in the early 1960s and then sharply declined.[30] The pattern then changed. Suicide among men began to pick up in the mid-1970s but female suicide did not, falling instead from the early 1980s. For the first time on record suicide trends between men and women in the UK are now diverging.[31] As men become more vulnerable to suicide, women have appeared increasingly resilient and, extraordinarily, the

UK is unique among European countries for this growing gender gap.[32] Some peculiarly home-grown social conditions appear to be feeding an increasing discrepancy in the fate of the sexes.

Youth suicide confirms this story, but with its own twist. Recent decades have seen a startling divergence between the sexes, as the lethal trend towards self-destruction picked off a growing proportion of young men. Male (15–24) suicides outnumbered female by 2:1 in 1970, by nearly 3:1 in 1980, and by 1990 the scale of self-destruction witnessed among young men in the 1980s had pushed the ratio up to 6:1. Eighty per cent of youth suicides in the UK are now male.[33] The twist in the tale, unique to youth suicide, concerns young women. Wavering, rather than decreasing in recent decades, the suicide rate among them is not on a safely downward trend as it is amongst older women. Whatever is protecting women in general from self-destruction appears to be offset in the under-25s by other pressures. The failure of young women to keep in line with their sex reiterates the glaring evidence of young male deaths: being young at the present time involves some special pressures and dangers.

The UK is not alone in having a problem with youth suicide. Throughout the Western industrialised world youth have shown an increasing vulnerability, in recent decades, to self-destruction.[34] This susceptibility to suicide has been more striking because suicide in older people has not increased at the same pace, or has fallen. As a result the young are now more prominent among the casualties of suicide. By the mid-1980s one-fifth of suicides in the Western world were adolescents, compared with between one-eighth and one-ninth in the 1950s.[35] Whilst the old have always been, and still are, at greater risk of killing themselves than the young, the gap between them has narrowed. The elderly have become better able to stand living as the young become less able. Suicide in older age groups decreased sharply in the UK during the post-war years, as youth suicide has increased.[36] An increasing proportion of lives struck out by suicide are just commencing.

The escalation of youth suicide has naturally spawned fears for children. For reasons already discussed, their suicides are well concealed and slip easily through the epidemiological net: On the basis of official statistics, at any rate, suicide in childhood is almost unknown in England and Wales.[37] Children's suicides do not escape the notice of the media so easily. Intensive publicity surrounded a handful of deaths, in the early 1990s, among children as young as 12 who had reportedly been bullied at school. These high-profile suicides disturbed the public imagination; concern was widely expressed and coincided with a rethink of school policies on bullying. The suicide of a child sends out strong social shock-waves, but it remains a relatively rare event.

Since 1968 official suicides have averaged only six a year among 10–14 year-olds in the UK and suicide among the under-10s is virtually unheard of. This of course is a substantial underestimate. When suicides, undetermined deaths and accidental drugs overdoses among 10–14-year-olds are considered, a more realistic estimate of child suicide emerges, averaging 22 deaths a year since 1968.[38] It has been argued that increases in child suicide have been disguised since the 1950s by the way in which suicides are classified.[39] In the last 25 years numbers have increased but, given fluctuations in the UK population of 10–14-year-olds, these numbers are so small as to make talk of trends unreliable. Two features of childhood suicides are clear. More boys kill themselves than girls but the growing gender gap seen in youth suicide has not been replicated in younger children. If anything it has shrunk slightly. Secondly, whilst the numbers of probable suicides among 10–14-year-olds rose in the 1970s, child suicide did not continue to rise in the 1980s. In the 1990s the suicide of a child is still an exceptional event and, since rarity mystifies, child suicide remains a poorly understood phenomenon.

Clearly the risk of suicide increases rapidly through adolescence and into early adulthood, where it looms large in relation to other mortal threats. Suicide is now the second biggest killer of 15–34-year-olds in the UK,[40] claiming fewer lives than road traffic accidents, but more than cancer. Yet suicide, a leading cause of death at an age when natural stamina and physical health should make death a distant prospect, has a low profile as a public health problem. One remedy for this lack of interest, in a resource-minded culture, has been to highlight the economic impact of so much wasted life.

Suicide, like any major public health problem, has a price. It accounts, a recent government document pointed out, for eight per cent of all working days lost through death in the work-age population.[41] The cumulative loss of life and skills through suicide is substantial. During the 1970s youth suicide destroyed 300,000 years of potential life in the UK. In the 1980s this rose to around 440,000 years. The personal catastrophe of youth suicide is also a social and economic travesty; the worst possible return on a society's investment in its young. The devastating sense of waste evoked by youth suicide at the individual level has far wider implications. So too does the staggering cost to the National Health Service of suicidal behaviour in young people. In 1992, the costs of treating a mere 316 paracetamol overdoses at a Leeds hospital was estimated to be £750,000. The annual bill for treating young people who are so desperately unhappy that they want to die, or inflict damage on themselves, clearly runs into millions.

The full meaning of the growth of youth suicide is not yet clear. If the increased suicide risk of today's young men remains with them as they grow older, higher rates of self-destruction will be seen, in years to come, among older men. The prospect, as this vulnerable generation proceeds through life, is a disturbing one. Alternatively, youth suicides may currently be reflecting stresses and conditions particular to the 1980s and 1990s. If this is the case, the suicide rate can be expected to drop again if and when conditions improve. There is, of course, no way of knowing which scenario fits the future.

As the costs of youth suicide – human, social and economic – mount in the UK, the causes of this deadly trend demand investigation. The factors that may have contributed to a boom in youthful self-destruction are discussed in Chapter 3.

24

However, one is inextricable from suicide itself. Influencing rates of self-destruction, and the sex of its victims, is the choice of the suicide method itself.

Methods

I remember writing lists – slit your wrists or jump off a bridge – writing up the pros and cons of each one. It was really logical the way I thought about it. I wanted a way that would work, a way that is the least messy to find and a way that's the least painful.

(DEBBIE)

For some the choice of a suicide method is a meticulously considered decision. Others reach spontaneously for the nearest available means when desperation hits. In either case the suicidal are unlikely to use a method that is not already on a commonly known and culturally accepted list of possibilities. Improvisation, with unusual suicide methods, is rare. Someone may have clear ideas about how they would prefer to die – in Debbie's case without pain, mess or the chance of 'failure' – but these are framed by an awareness of established and easily available suicide methods.

Suicide methods divide roughly between active and passive. Active means such as hanging, shooting or jumping tend to be relatively abrupt and effective. Leaving little room for afterthoughts or interruption once an attempt is under way, these methods are often fatal. Active methods may require some preparation and are often equated with a determination to die. Elaine died by hanging. As her father remarked, 'It's such a final thing to do. You don't get a second chance, do you?' Passive methods tend to involve less overtly violent acts, with more gradual effects. The overdose is the modern mode of passive suicide, popularly perceived as a 'gentle' option, offering a narcotic, painless route to oblivion. Overdosing is often associated with ambiguous intentions, because it leaves time for intervention: 'Pills are time capsules. You're not actually going to die as soon as you put them in your mouth' (David).

Effectiveness is one consideration in choosing a suicide method; fear is another. For many the fear of a painful death may be prohibitive: 'I'd been on top of the flats quite a few times, but I couldn't stand jumping and all that painful stuff' (Ashley). For this reason the emergence of a suicide method that is at once lethal and painless can have dire social consequences. When poisonous coal gas was introduced into British homes at the turn of this century, its inhalation became, within decades, the nation's most popular suicide method. The gas oven enticed the despairing with the prospect of gentle cessation. It was responsible for half of male and female suicides in 1960.[48] The detoxification of British domestic gas between 1963 and 1971 eliminated this popular and accessible way of dying, and the British suicide rate dropped accordingly. Deprived of a favoured way of dying the suicidal did not, it seemed, simply turn to other means. Instead the 'Coal Gas Story' suggests that available suicide methods may affect the suicide rate, curbing or facilitating self-destructive impulses according to the nature of the death they offer.

The suicide methods most often used by young people since 1968 are shown in Tables 1 and 2. Among 15–24-year-old men hanging (30 per cent), car exhausts (23 per cent) and overdosing (14 per cent) are currently the most common suicide methods in the UK (see Table 1). Amongst young women overdosing is most common (44 per cent), then hanging (15 per cent) and death by car exhaust (10 per cent (see Table 2)). More young men (6 per cent) than young women (2 per cent) use guns or explosives for suicide, although the proportion jumping to their deaths is about the same (6 per cent). These choices immediately throw some light on the paradox that whilst young men *attempt* suicide less often than women, far more of them die in the process. When attempting suicide, young men use more deadly means.

Suicide methods clearly make a difference. The last 25 years have seen some significant changes in the way young

Table 1 Methods used in suicides & undetermined deaths in the UK in 15–24 year old males, 1968–1992

	1968–1972 No. = 1,610	1973–1977 No. = 1,856	1978–1982 No. = 2,440	1983–1987 No. = 3,012	1988–1992 No. = 3,793
Overdoses	31.4%	34.2%	24.8%	14.4%	14.4%
Domestic Gas	11.9%	1.3%	0.6%	0.5%	0.2%
Car Exhaust	6.8%	8.2%	12.0%	17.9%	23.0%
Hanging	16.8%	19.6%	20.8%	26.1%	29.6%
Jumping	4.5%	7.8%	7.9%	8.2%	6.6%
Firearms	6.9%	7.0%	8.1%	8.6%	5.6%
Drowning	10.4%	9.0%	6.3%	5.1%	3.8%
Other (incl cutting)	11.4%	12.9%	19.5%	19.2%	16.8%

Sources:
General Register Office for Scotland
General Register Office, Belfast
Office of Population Censuses and Surveys (England & Wales)

Table 2 Methods used in suicides & undetermined deaths in the UK in 15–24 year old females, 1968–1992

	1968–1972 No. = 681	1973–1977 No. = 865	1978–1982 No. = 922	1983–1987 No. = 824	1988–1992 No. = 922
Overdoses	63.7%	67.3%	53.0%	43.2%	43.7%
Domestic Gas	9.0%	0.4%	0.3%	0.0%	0.4%
Car Exhaust	1.6%	2.0%	2.9%	6.7%	10.1%
Hanging	7.5%	8.6%	9.3%	10.8%	15.4%
Jumping	5.7%	6.9%	8.0%	10.3%	6.3%
Firearms	0.9%	1.4%	1.8%	1.6%	1.4%
Drowning	4.8%	6.0%	5.1%	3.5%	2.1%
Other (incl cutting)	6.7%	7.5%	19.4%	23.9%	20.6%

Sources:
General Register Office for Scotland
General Register Office, Belfast
Office of Population Censuses and Surveys (England & Wales)

people kill themselves. At the close of the 1960s the gas oven still accounted for one in ten youth suicides. As domestic gas poisoning disappeared, overdoses increased. More popular among young women, these caused 68 per cent of female and 34 per cent of male youth suicides by the mid-1970s. Given that these figures exclude 'accidents', the real proportion of fatal overdoses is likely to have been higher. Since the 1970s overdosing has claimed a declining proportion of young lives, but still accounts for nearly half of suicides in young women. The drug paracetamol, which can cause a slow and harrowing death from liver failure, has accounted for a growing proportion of these young deaths in recent decades.[43]

The decline in overdosing has seen a dangerous move towards more active methods of self-destruction amongst the young. A disastrous innovation has been the use of car exhausts for suicide, made possible by the post-war growth in car ownership. Young people's growing access to cars, combined with publicity and imitation, has helped the new method to catch on.[44] This method now claims one in every four suicides in 15–24-year-old men and one in every ten among young women. Hanging has also increased steadily among the young since 1968. Traditionally used by males, this notorious suicide method is being ruled out less readily by young women today. Two decades ago overdoses outnumbered hanging among 15–24-year-old female suicides by 8:1; today the ratio has shrunk to 3:1. Female preference for the 'passive' suicide methods is being eroded with time. Young women still choose very differently to young men, but less differently than two decades ago.

The years between 1968 and 1992 showed a move towards more active or violent suicide methods. Regardless of suicidal intentions, certain means are more deadly than others. As the chosen methods of the young become more dangerous, they leave themselves fewer 'second chances'. Additionally, it seems probable that the methods favoured by the sexes help to accentuate or equalise differences in the male and female suicide rates, differences which at the current time need some explaining. The recent history of youth suicide clearly poses essential questions concerning sex roles and differences. So too does the type of suicidal behaviour not yet considered: that which falls short of death.

Suicide Attempts among the Under-25s

I'd put aftershave down under the door, so people wouldn't be able to smell the blood. I couldn't move because whenever I moved my arm would open. The day after I wrapped a sheet around it and went to Boots to get some bandages and TCP. I had to go and buy a new duvet. I had to make sure the rubbish people wouldn't open this bag with a duvet covered in blood, or the police would be round. I thought if somebody saw me like this I'd be put away. My room just stank of TCP for five or six months. For a year my arms ruled me – everything I did revolved around making sure I was clean.

(GARETH)

There was no way I was going into casualty. I couldn't handle it. Although I was scared, going to casualty felt scarier.

(KAREN)

As many as 44,000 young people under the age of 25 are admitted to general hospital each year in the UK having deliberately taken overdoses or injured themselves.[45] The harm done ranges from the potentially deadly through to relatively minor injuries, and the motives and impulses behind these crises are diverse. Some young people want to die, some definitely do not and others are confused. The feelings and motives that lie behind suicide attempts and self-harm are explored more fully in Chapter 5. For simplicity's sake, these actions are here described as 'suicide attempts'.

Attempted suicide is an elusive subject. No country in the world keeps national records of it and what is known about this prolific social problem is usually pieced together from general hospital records or special hospital-based studies.[46] Yet many young suicide attempters steer clear of hospitals. Shame, stigma and fear can make the prospect of asking for help appear insurmountably daunting. Rather than having the deep wound in his arm stitched up, Gareth (above) bound it himself, withdrew socially, relied on alcohol to dull both physical and emotional pain. The prospect of hospital provoked more dread in Karen, who became frightened after taking an overdose, than the risk of being poisoned. It is impossible to know how many young people tell no one about incidents of self-harm.

Neither are hospitals the first stop for many who do seek help. Nearly a third of suicide attempters, according to one study, receive physical first aid from GPs, friends or relatives. In another study a third of teenagers being treated in hospital after overdosing reported a previous attempt. Only 40 per cent of these had visited hospital as a result.[47] Even when young people do reach hospital casualty departments they may slip away before talking to a doctor, or explain what happened as an 'accident'.[48] Still more young attempters are confined in prisons or psychiatric hospitals, where they will be treated for their injuries.

Inevitably general hospital records underestimate attempted suicide, but they provide a good idea of how suicidal behaviour fluctuates over time. Commemorated in medical longhand as the 'adverse effects of medicinal agents', the overdose accounts for 90 per cent of modern suicide attempts.[49] Overdosing – or self-poisoning – has increased calamitously since the early 1960s in most Western industrialised nations. The UK is no exception; in fact its rates of attempted suicide have soared well above the European average.[50] Hospital records in England and Wales provide some sense of the virulence of this self-destructive trend. In 1961, 24,000 people were admitted for 'adverse effects' of medicines. The numbers doubled within five years and tripled within ten. By 1977, a year in which 106,000 were admitted to hospital and £20 million was spent on rescuing them, an exorbitant 350 per cent increase in medicinal overdosing was complete.[51] Self-poisoning was by now the most common reason for the emergency admission of women to hospital, and the second most common for men.[52] Its prevalence was such that doctors not only began to talk of an epidemic, but ruminated on what would happen when hospital beds ran out.

The rise of the overdose has threatened certain social groups more than others. In striking contrast to suicide itself – which becomes more probable with age – attempted suicide is a behaviour predominantly encountered in adolescence and young adulthood.[53] Throughout the 1970s and 1980s UK studies have reiterated the unusual vulnerability of the under-25s to overdosing and self-injury. The most dangerous ages of all are 15–19 for women and 20–24 for men, although the upsurge in suicidal behaviour has also taken its toll on children.[54] In a study of Oxford adolescents in the late 1970s the most marked rise in overdosing was among 12–15-year-olds.[55]

Heightening the contrast with suicide itself, suicide attempts are far more common among women than men. This reversal of the sex difference seen in fatal acts is most decisive among the under-25s. Young female suicide attempters out-number their male counterparts more than at any other age.[56] Teenage girls are most ready to swallow dangerous doses of pills, and their suicide attempts have outnumbered boys' in proportions which range, in different studies, from 2:1 to 9:1.[57] In Edinburgh by 1975 one in every 100 15–19-year-old girls made a suicide attempt which led to hospital admission – a 250 per cent increase since the late 1960s.[58] Not only are girls in greater danger of self-harm, but they appear to become suscep-tible at an earlier age. The risk that they will harm themselves increases steadily from 12 years of age upwards with 16 their most vulnerable year.[59] For boys the risk is slightly more delayed: the likelihood of a suicide attempt increases through-out their teenage years, to a high-risk period in their early twenties.[60]

The overdosing epidemic peaked in the UK in 1977.[61] From then on through the early 1980s it began to wane.[62] Yet it was a spectacle that had raised uncomfortable questions about the free flow of 'therapeutic' drugs – notably tranquillisers and sedatives – from doctor to patient, and the decline in self-poisoning has often been associated with more cautious prescribing by doctors since the late 1970s.[63] However, stemming the supply of prescribed drugs proved inconclusive. Since 1985 attempted suicide has shown signs of increasing once more, but with a peculiar nuance. Although women still attempt suicide more often than men, the 1980s eroded the sex differences of the 1970s not only in the UK, but across Europe.[64] Young men who take overdoses are now less atypical of their sex. Young women aged 15–19 remain the highest risk group at present in the UK, but young men are catching up.[65] In the 1990s the gender gap in attempted suicide is the narrowest yet.

Unfortunately this crucial evolution is becoming harder to follow in the UK. The closure of monitoring facilities in Edinburgh – which along with Oxford has kept track of attempted suicide in recent decades – has obscured understanding of the British suicide attempts in the 1990s. The sources of information that remain are sending out ominous signals. Rates of attempted suicide in Oxford in 1990 were again extremely high, and whilst not necessarily typical, this city's experience cannot be fortuitous.[66] Projected for the UK as a whole, suicide attempts among young people in Oxford suggest an annual total of 29,400 female suicide attempts and 14,530 male, among the under-25s.[67] Suicidal behaviour is flourishing in the 1990s, with the young, and young women in particular, its most common casualties.

Any crisis in which a young person attacks him- or herself reflects a potent mixture of emotions, and a hard collision with despair. Its personal meaning is loaded and, in retrospect, a suicide attempt becomes a reference point with considerable symbolic significance. Its inherent danger lies not only in the physical injuries sustained, but in the psychological damage that such a personal low point represents. In the words of one young attempter, 'I look back and think I was so near. I could not have woken up. And that scares me. It just scares me to think what a mess I was in' (Karen). Such fear can linger, threatening a precarious equilibrium. For Cheryl her first suicide attempt at 13 became part of a threatening personal legacy: 'There was always this sense of unfinished business. Because I'd tried when I was younger it had become an option as a young adult.' Every suicide attempt harbours the ultimate threat that, unless underlying problems can be resolved, a fatal suicide attempt will follow.

Suicide after Suicide Attempts

He made several attempts in that year. There was his wrists. There was the time in the car. And then when he died . . .
(JOAN, JASON'S MOTHER)

Jason's final and fatal suicide attempt was his third. In the first he slashed his wrists after an argument with his girlfriend, to whom he was engaged. The relationship subsequently broke up, a fact he blamed on this incident. 'If I hadn't done that,' he told his mother, 'I'd still have her.' Working as an electrician, but preoccupied with the loss of his girlfriend and disorientated after leaving the army, which he had joined at 16, he became increasingly depressed. To dampen his feelings and escape sleeplessness he began to drink alone at nights. Some months after his first attempt, with his wrists still festering, Jason was picked up by the police while trying to kill himself in his car. Held overnight in the cells, he was ordered to get help and went along willingly to a local hospital. Here he talked to a psychiatrist for an hour, but refused the antidepressant pills she offered, believing them to be addictive. No return visit was arranged. Jason struggled on, his state of mind much the same as before his suicide attempt, only now he wept occasionally. Living in a bedsit near to his sister Nicole, and in regular contact with his mother, Jason's only other visitors during the last months of his life were Jehovah s Witnesses. When he last saw Nicole his mood seemed to have improved. That night, leaving his family a suicide letter and some photographs, he killed himself in his car, aged 22.

Suicide frequently, though by no means always, pulls its victims from a pool of vulnerable people with previous attempts behind them. A suicide attempt is a crucial omen of the possibility of future suicide. About half of all people who die through suicide have previously attempted.[68] One per cent of the many thousands admitted to hospital each year following overdose or self-injury will die within a year, 5 per cent within five years.[69] People who attempt suicide are therefore extremely vulnerable – one hundred times more likely to end their lives in suicide than other men and women – and to trivialise a suicide attempt is, quite simply, dangerous.[70]

Yet the relationship between suicide and attempted suicide is a complex one, a complexity suggested by their different profiles. Suicide is more common in men; attempters are predominantly women. Suicide becomes more likely as people grow older; attempted suicide afflicts mainly the young. Most suicide attempters take overdoses; those who kill themselves use more varied methods. Nor are the two kinds of suicidal behaviour necessarily synchronised. As fatalities mounted in the early 1980s, suicide attempts dipped. Geography also shows up differences. Suicide rates in the UK are below the international average, but the British are more prone to attempt suicide than other nationalities.[71/72] Viewed from a distance the two social phenomena have a number of jarring features.

This has a lot to do with the heterogeneity of the actions loosely labelled 'suicide attempts'. The diversity of self-harm and suicidal behaviour suggests why 'suicide attempters' in general are not typical of the minority who go on to kill themselves. Some individuals want to die more than others; some have a keener sense of how to go about it. Suicidal impulses and lethal know-how combust in suicide attempts with very different end results. And self-harm may express many things other than a wish to be dead. This also suggests why sensitive interpretation of these actions is so essential. The sheer numbers of young people who harm themselves or act on suicidal feelings places tremendous pressure on those concerned with their protection. In youth, suicide attempts outnumber suicides on a large scale. For every young person dying through suicide or undetermined death each year in the UK, it may be estimated that about 45 are admitted to general hospital following suicide attempts. Many more engage in self-harm which does not lead to hospital attention.[73] Gauging accurate ratios of suicides to suicide attempts is in fact impossible but what is easily gleaned from the information available is that only a tiny fraction of suicidal acts in young people are fatal. And because attempts are most likely in the young and suicide least likely, suicide attempts outweigh actual deaths most heavily in youth.

Deeply shocked following Jason's second suicide attempt, his family were unprepared for the routine nature of the local hospital's response: 'He spent about an hour talking to the psychiatrist. She said he was all right – there was nothing to worry about. Then we all just came home' (Joan, Jason's mother). His sister felt her brother's attempt on his life was treated with an inexplicable lack of urgency: 'I couldn't believe they'd said he was all right. He'd just tried to kill himself' (Nicole). Large numbers of young suicide attempters require protection and help. This task has fallen to modern medicine, notably the psychiatric doctors and nurses assigned to deal with crises in our mental life: 'Among the many skills that psychiatrists must acquire, the ability to assess the risk of patients killing themselves is probably the most important and demanding.'[74] The incidence of suicide following suicide attempts, and the frequency of suicidal behaviour in young people, suggest why. The figures show that whilst relatively few of the young and suicidal end up dead, the casual assumption that suicidal young people are rarely in real danger for their life is not tenable. Suicide attempts may well be, as they were for Jason, crucial markers on the way to suicide.

CHAPTER 2

Vulnerability

Social Patterns, Personal Pain

The recent history of youth suicide in the UK tells a story of growing sex differences, an ironic footnote to a cultural agenda which pioneered sexual equality in recent decades. In the 1990s, 80 per cent of youth suicides are male. Other patterns of suicidal behaviour among British youth are also unmistakable. Research consistently suggests that some young people – belonging to certain social groups or sharing difficult experiences or problems – are more susceptible to suicide than others. Patterns of vulnerability suggest who is at higher risk of suicide and depict the social and personal circumstances of their despair.

Since mental distress has a complex mix of causes, patterns of risk inevitably overlap. Some pressures on young people appear to reflect social and cultural factors, such as class or race. Others cut across social groups. Childhood sexual abuse, for example, occurs equally in all classes and ethnic groups.[1] Mental health problems identify other vulnerable groups of young people. Finally, individual sensitivity and personality traits will affect the way individual young people cope with life. Lisa observed that her sister, Emma, who killed herself at 24, found the world a more hostile and painful place to inhabit than she did:

At first it seemed as if she was too weak to exist under the same pressures as everybody else – she was weak and therefore buckled under. But then you start to develop some insight. You realise different pressures have different effects on people. I've never had problems sleeping. I can switch off straight away. But she couldn't ever switch off. She could never sleep. She could never turn the switch off. She lay there with all this stuff going through her mind – the world, the world, the world and all its problems. She must have had a threshold where it all spilled over and had a devastating effect that she couldn't cope with.

Adolescence

Being that age we didn't think he was depressed. We thought, typical young person – up and down.

(ANGELA, TERRY'S MOTHER)

Rates of self-inflicted poisoning, injury and death among young people relentlessly suggest that contemporary adolescence involves some peculiar stresses. The relative security of youth appears to have diminished. Located somewhere between the ages of 12 (or less) and 25, adolescence spans the years in which a child's identity makes way for an adult one.[2] Rapid physical, intellectual and emotional development makes this a precarious time. Hereward Harrison, Director of Counselling at Childline, observes that children and adolescents who call for help can be divided into two groups. First, there are those facing long-term problems caused by, for example, sexual abuse or a parent's mental illness. The second group comprises adolescents who simply seem overwhelmed by the pace of recent change in their lives.[3]

Change starts with the physical onset of puberty. To an adolescent who dislikes his or her 'new' body – its height, weight, shape – the loss of a familiar and comfortable child's body will be mourned. Kaye's self-image plummeted during adolescence: 'It was all mixed up with my sexuality – becoming aware of my body and disliking the changes. I was really skinny and had horrible hair.' Dan's agonies of self-doubt were focused on his genital size: 'I went to the local GP and told him that my penis was too small. I was convinced that I had a hormone imbalance. He looked at me and said: "There's nothing wrong with you."' A misfortune like acne may seem a catastrophic blight on a young person's confidence, as sexual attractiveness gains social significance with age: 'It's just impossible not to be disgusted by endless greasiness, pus, scars . . . I just wish I could do something about this acne which hurts me so much.'[4]

The emotional and intellectual developments of adolescents are also highly charged. As children outgrow the conditions of childhood nurturing, the familiar and regulated world of their parents begins to pinch. A growing desire for autonomy and a distinct identity makes a degree of separation from parents inevitable. It is no longer enough to be dependent, to mimic habits and reflect values. Adolescents begin to reach into the wider social world of their peers for emotional sustenance and affirmation. Yet this distancing process is shot through with ambivalence. Adult life offers freedom; childhood offers security. The yearnings of adolescence swing between the two. A future full of imminent choices and tests – leaving home, earning a living, going to college, establishing relationships – is an exhilarating prospect, yet one which may mutate suddenly into an unnegotiable burden.

As intellectual faculties mature during adolescence and young people develop a critical eye, their parents – and the adult world in general – fall naturally into its line of vision. Tensions often emerge as the conformity of childhood is superseded by adolescent self-assertion. For Susie, questioning the teachings of a fundamentalist Christian upbringing clearly threatened the conditions of parental approbation: 'I really began questioning the Faith and what my parents had told me. I began to think of all the inconsistencies in it. That was really hard because I had nothing to cling on to.' In search of inspiration for adulthood, Ashley's disenchantment with his inheritance was unequivocal: 'The lives of the adults I saw around me didn't really count for much. So how could I take notice of people whose lives were fucked?' If adults are unnerved by the critical onslaughts of adolescence, the critics themselves are as often bereft.

Adolescence may also be a poorly synchronised transition, with young people disorientated by the different pace of physical, intellectual and emotional change. Puberty starts early. The average girl begins to menstruate at eleven and a half, and the physique of the 'early developer' may bring expectations of emotional maturity which are ill-founded. Later, the tension between emotional and intellectual maturity is often overlooked. An adolescent's critical faculties may race ahead of his or her ability to cope emotionally with the insight these can bring.[5] For this reason, it has been suggested, bright adolescents may be more susceptible to suicidal behaviour. The imperfections of a tarnished world may suddenly be illuminated with devastating clarity. As conceptual doors open, notions of life and death, religion and politics, faith and ideology, belief and meaning may be daunting. Social problems too – hunger, sickness, poverty, the environment – may leave impressions which are painfully deep.

A sense of powerlessness is not uncommon: 'I used to get down about things that were happening in the world and I used to get annoyed with myself that I couldn't do anything about them' (Carrie). If changing the world hardly seems feasible, an air of moral culpability may be associated, as adulthood beckons, with joining in. Yet time cannot be arrested and the exit from childhood is compulsory: 'since a return to being a child, to ignorance, is no longer possible, some adolescents pull out, banish themselves to death as the only hope for a better world, this being no world at all'.[6]

Sex differences

At a very early age you pick up on the rules and the very subtle role-plays. The only way that men can actually touch each other publicly is either in violence or sport. Anything else is misconstrued. They're trapped. They can't show their emotions and they can't show they're vulnerable.

(BARRY)

Restrictions on male expressions of vulnerability are enforced early on. Research suggests that parents tend to encourage emotional control in their sons more than daughters, with 'feminine' traits in boys feared more than tomboyishness in girls.[7] Boys learn to avoid behaviour that will earn them the cissy's ignominy and to achieve status through competition with one another. In contrast, girls develop an affiliative social life, learning early to sustain and develop relationships through intimacy.[8] Over time, making oneself vulnerable becomes a more threatening and alien prospect for boys than girls. This begins to suggest why, in Ashley's view, 'There are a lot of crazy men out there. They haven't spoken about an emotion or feeling in their life.'

Aggression, on the other hand, is more openly expressed and socially sanctioned among young men. By adolescence, different levels of aggressive behaviour between the sexes are well established. Milder aggressive behaviour is much the same, since girls argue and swear with similar rancour to boys. But overt aggression, such as fighting and violent crime, is far more common amongst males. Exactly how nature and nurture balance out, as boys learn to be boys and girls to be girls, is unclear. Acquired gender roles clearly improvise upon biological sex differences. Yet with 'feminine' qualities stereotypically passive, dependent and expressive, and 'masculine' traits decisive, independent and stoical, social prescriptions clearly affect the freedom of the sexes to express different emotions.[9] Young women are permitted vulnerability, but encouraged to suppress their aggression. Young men are permitted more aggression, but sentenced to emotional stoicism.

These prescriptions are evident in the way the sexes manifest emotional distress. Unhappy boys more often show their feelings through 'bad conduct' such as lying, stealing, fighting or playing truant.[10] Yet the cathartic benefits of releasing hurt and frustration through aggression also bring alienation and social ostracism as boys go 'off the rails'. Disguised in belligerence, male vulnerability is easy to miss. As Janice recalled, her brother Mark never appeared depressed:

> He was the gang leader – the funniest. Everyone liked him. That's what's so difficult to understand. He was always in fights, beating people up. He was a really, really good fighter. That got his anger out. That's how he dealt with his emotions. If he was depressed you could understand. It was I all front – all an act, I think.

In contrast, young women are more likely to suppress their anger to the point where it atrophies into depression, a process recalled by Claudette:

> My parents were really strict. I wasn't allowed to express anger towards them. It just all built up – that repression of anger that you weren't allowed to show. A lot of the time that's how I feel depression. A real knot of anger – anger against the unfairness of things. I feel it so physically. I feel it in my stomach. It feels so heavy.

This stifling of anger may be one reason why depression – often regarded as the product of aggression turned inwards – is reported to be twice as common among women as men.[11]

Another may be that women present themselves for diagnosis more willingly. Research suggests that men are reluctant to define their problems as emotional ones, whilst 'women are socialised to a greater extent than men to view themselves as being in need of psychological help – as "helpless".'[12] Women visit their doctors more than men, are more often diagnosed as mentally ill and receive two-thirds of all prescriptions for psychotropic (mind-altering) drugs.[13] Young women therefore receive the therapeutic benefits doctors and others can offer, but also find their personal lives becoming more medicalised.[14] Young men preserve their independence, admit fewer problems

41

and receive less help. They also rely more heavily on alcohol and other non-medical drugs to cope with anxiety and depression (see Chapter 3). Masculine coping strategies may leave vulnerable young men more isolated as their unresolved emotional problems grow less containable. Mark took his life aged 21, cornered by problems with which he could no longer cope. For her brother to have sought help with emotional problems, Janice felt, would have been totally out of character: 'Mark would never have gone to talk to someone. He was a very secretive person – a bit of a loner. He could be really, really hurting inside but he'd still be wearing a smile.'

Sex differences in the suicide rate in part reflect male and female choices of suicide method (see Chapter 1). The complex phenomenon of self-poisoning illuminates the paradox that, while attempted suicide is far more common among young women, 80 per cent of youth suicides are currently male. The overdose, the predominant female suicide method in Britain, has a relatively high survival rate. Of the thousands who take overdoses annually, many are seeking to change, or escape from, an intolerable situation rather than to die (see Chapter 5). Associated with the 'cry for help', the overdose often provides a form of emotional surrender to temporary oblivion, medical care and the responses of others. Arguably, men's socialisation makes such 'surrender' more difficult. 'Crying for help' defies male prescriptions. For young men like Mark, the thought of surviving a suicide attempt might be anathema, making a decisive, lethal action more compelling.

A young man or woman's choice of a more or less dangerous suicide method ought not, however, to be treated as an automatic gauge of their suicidal desperation. The choice of a more deadly method may mean that a young man is more intent on dying and has chosen a method for its lethal potential. But it may also reflect cultural norms which make particular suicide methods more acceptable and/or accessible to one sex or the other. Traditionally, male and female spheres have provided different opportunities for self-destruction. Among pre-war suicide attempters men poisoned themselves with industrial toxins; women used household cleaning materials.[15] The preponderance of female casualties during the self-poisoning epidemic of the 1970s suggested the hazards of women's easy access to psychotropic drugs.[16] And the most modern 'male' suicide method of car exhausts presumably reflects, in part, women's lesser access to vehicles. More subtle aspects of socialisation are also likely to permeate suicidal choices. The prevalence of hanging among boys was attributed by the author of a 1950s study of youth suicide to the mechanical competence they picked up in their early play and exploration.[17] And noting the growing number of male deaths in motor vehicles, a British psychiatrist recently attributed this gender discrepancy to female technological ineptitude:

> It rather looks as if women, with their traditional distaste for violent methods of suicide and their equally traditional (if declining) distaste for mechanical activities, are committing suicide less often because they are less likely than men to have the sort of DIY skills necessary.

The current tendency among young women to use traditionally 'masculine' methods presumably reflects, and will go on reflecting, gradual changes in the socialisation of girls. Women's aversion to violent methods is by no means universal. Among young Asian women in Britain, self-immolation has contributed to a high suicide rate in recent years. Young American women more commonly shoot themselves in Southern states where a higher proportion of girls are taught to handle guns.

Chosen suicide methods vary with social conditions and cultural traditions. Dangerously high rates of attempted suicide among young women suggest that female immunity to self-destruction ought not to be overstated. What is clear is that current British norms governing 'masculine' and 'feminine' suicide methods load the dice in favour of young women surviving their suicide attempts. As the deadly barbiturates so readily prescribed in previous decades were replaced with less toxic tranquillisers, women began to survive their overdoses as much by chance as design.

Race and culture

> *She had a few problems with name-calling because she was mixed race – 'Black something-or-other' or 'wog'. I just used to tell her to call names back. She wouldn't go to school for a couple of days. She wouldn't go on the bus. It obviously hurt Simone more than she said – it must have done. Once she started this thing about her colour she wouldn't go out in the sun. It's quite a white area. There was one other [black child in her school] and they all said: 'Is she your sister?' She felt it.*
>
> (ANDREA, SIMONE'S MOTHER)

Patterns of suicide and attempted suicide among young Black and Asian people in Britain do not simply reflect those in the wider community. One study found that the suicide rate among 16–24-year-old women of Asian origin has been three times higher, over the last decade, than among young women of British origin.[18] In the early 1990s, The Samaritans reported growing numbers of calls from suicidal Asian girls. Yet young Asian men have proved less vulnerable than their white counterparts, a striking reversal of general sex differences.[19] Little information has been recorded about suicide and attempted suicide among young Black (Afro-Caribbean) people. A Birmingham study of attempted suicides found that young Black women appeared particularly vulnerable and that suicide attempts increased more rapidly among Blacks than whites during the late 1970s.[20] Yet it is not actually known how many victims of youth suicide are black. Whilst the statutory monitoring of race is long established in the USA's system for gathering death data – highlighting different suicide rates among young whites, Blacks and North American Indians, for example – British death certificates record no details of racial and cultural identity.

This is unfortunate. The racism she experienced growing up in a predominantly white area clearly caused Simone considerable anguish, damaging her self-esteem early on and exacerbating later difficulties. Fear of a hostile social environment creates isolation and alienation. As one Asian women's counsellor commented: 'The fact that there are more Asian women committing suicide suggests these are not just acts of despair, but statements of how they feel about their own circumstances and the way they feel about British society'. For many young Asian and Black people, growing up in British society involves the threat of racist attack and the prospect that discrimination in general may restrict their access to the crucial resources – homes, jobs, educational opportunities – on which personal security and a positive view of the future are built. Racism exaggerates the effects of widespread social problems. Male unemployment in some parts of London had reached 40 per cent among the under-25s by the 1990s. Among young Black men the figure was 60 per cent. Although, as Suman Fernando notes, 'oppression may uplift as well as depress self-worth and may promote as well as destroy communal cohesion', it may also profoundly alienate young people and destroy their hopes.[21]

Cultural pressures and preferences also permeate suicidal behaviour. Asian women's groups have linked the high suicide rate among young Asian women in Britain with family conflict and conservative parental values. Traditional aspirations – such as the hopes for a daughter's arranged marriage – may clash with the wishes and expectations of young women themselves. Studies of young Asian suicide attempters confirm prevalence of such tensions.[22] Highly dangerous suicide methods may also have more persuasive cultural connotations for young Asian women. Self-burning is a more common suicide method than in other groups.[23] In India this is similarly a common female method, with origins in the Hindu tradition of suttee or self-immolation by the widow on her husband's funeral pyre. In Hindi, 'suttee' literally means virtue.

Young gays and lesbians

I knew I was 'different' from a very early age. When I was

45

very young I remember feeling an affinity with male friends of mine, and how they reacted strangely. I picked up from their reactions that this was something alien to them. Yet it felt very natural to me. I picked up on attitudes. Kids are quite astute and I detected the hostility at a very early age. I knew what a queer was. My brother was in the army. I remember him saying, 'Two men were caught shagging in the field,' and then that phrase: 'I hate fucking queers.'

(BARRY)

Suicide is the leading cause of death among gay, lesbian and bisexual youth in the United States and suicide attempts are more common than among heterosexuals.[24] Between 20 and 35 per cent of gay youth report suicide attempts.[25] In one American study gay males were six times more likely, and lesbians twice as likely as their heterosexual counterparts to have attempted suicide.[26] The majority of these attempts occurred before the age of 21, a third before 17. In the UK, an unknown proportion of youth suicides are among gays and lesbians. Coroners are likely to use their discretion to protect the bereaved from media sensationalism. As Patricia recalled of the inquest into her daughter Elaine's death, 'It was kept quiet. We couldn't face the local press splashing lesbianism all over the place.' Nevertheless, young gays and lesbians are likely to be at high risk. The London Gay Teenage Project reported that one in five of the (mainly male) teenagers who participated in their study had attempted suicide because of their sexuality.[27]

Absorbing cultural messages about homosexuality can be a wounding experience for the self-esteem of young gays and lesbians. Social isolation and fears for the future are often compounded by lack of accurate information about homosexuality. As one young woman remembered: 'When you're sixteen you think you're the only teenager that's gay.'[28] Anticipated rejection haunts many adolescents. For Barry, disguising his sexuality was a prerequisite of survival: 'I didn't know anyone else that was gay but I knew you couldn't live in that area and be gay. I remember the fear I had of anybody finding out.'

'Coming out' – the process of admitting gay or lesbian identity to oneself, and to others – is the period during which suicide risk peaks.[29] In one group of gay teenagers, negative reactions to their sexuality had been experienced by 43 per cent from parents and 41 per cent from friends. Many had been verbally abused (55 per cent) and physically assaulted (30 per cent).[30] Barry made his first suicide attempt at 14, overwhelmed by panic and humiliation, after his peers confronted and ridiculed his sexuality:

> When you conceal something for so long you spend all your time and energy in not confronting it. When they found out it was unbelievable. I felt like a drowning man. Having hidden it all my life my first thought was suicide. I thought : 'I can't go to school on Monday. Everyone will know.'

The risk of rejection by family, friends and peer group is a fearsome one for many young people. On discovering his son was gay, Barry's father baptised him a 'fucking dirty homo'. Overrepresented amongst the young homeless, many gays and lesbians are forced to leave home because their families will not accept their sexuality.[31] A young person's self-confidence at school and work may also be undermined. Simon, now a trainee surgeon, was victimised by fellow medical students: 'a lot of them found out I was gay. They were throwing urine at me in the toilets and things like that.' In the late 1980s the US government's Task Force on Youth Suicide drew attention to suicide risk among young gays and lesbians. Of the psychological damage they sustain in growing up, it commented: 'We do not, as a society, want to continue to hold the untenable position of senselessly hurting others – especially the young.'[32]

The unemployed

> Tommy had been doing a job for British Rail, but he got made redundant. He was trying for a job, but there wasn't anything. That was a real blow for him.
>
> (PHYLLIS, TOMMY'S MOTHER)

*She started going for job interviews and of course then she had
to say: 'I've been in [psychiatric] hospital.' They were jobs she
should have got with her typing speeds – she was an excellent
worker. She had two refusals and she was really upset. She
thought the reason was that she'd been in hospital.*

(ANDREA, SIMONE'S MOTHER)

Rates of depression and suicide are high amongst the unemployed.[33] In most European countries, rising male suicide has been associated, in recent decades, with growing unemployment.[34] In the UK youth unemployment and male suicide have both increased dramatically since the 1970s.[35] Among both men and women the unemployed are far more vulnerable to suicide attempts than others, with the risk greatest just after losing a job, or after long periods of unemployment.[36] In Edinburgh, suicide attempts among the unemployed in recent decades outnumbered those amongst the employed by roughly 10:1.[37]

Employment aspirations are profoundly important to a young person's developing identity. Characterised as 'bored, lonely, depressed and watching a lot of daytime TV', the young unemployed may suffer not only the loss of social contact and financial independence, but an erosion of self-esteem.[38] The poverty of unemployment curtails social activity and creates stress and tensions in existing relationships. Competing for work, especially in a recessionary job market, becomes harder with time.

Suicidal ideas are more common among the young unemployed than those in work, and the risks to mental health of joblessness and poverty are evident.[39] Clearly implicated in the stories of many who take their lives or attempt suicide, unemployment nevertheless has a complex link with suicide. Unemployment is high among young people with mental health problems, whose vulnerability and distress may make it difficult for them to work. For these young people the problems that contribute to despair and suicidal urges may precede unemployment. But for others it is unemployment itself which

48

appears to have made life intolerable, introducing sources of stress such as poverty, isolation, loss of status and identity, with damaging impact on self-esteem and future plans. For both Simone and Tommy (above), unemployment intensified hopelessness in the months before their suicides. Whether unemployment leads to suicidal despair or exacerbates existing problems, the link between the two is undeniable.

Class and occupation

It has often been said that suicide does not discriminate between the rich and poor.[40] Certainly those who take their lives come from a variety of backgrounds, but research evidence does not support the egalitarian assumption that suicide is a classless phenomenon. A national study of suicides in Finland recently found that 70 per cent of adolescents who killed themselves in the late 1980s were from working-class families.[41] Not enough is known about UK youth suicide victims to ascertain whether this grim class difference is evident in Britain. However, suicides among adults in general do vary with socio-economic status. Those with least economic power and social status – workers in manual occupations – are at higher risk.[42] But so too are professionals. The occupational groups at highest risk of suicide are currently vets, pharmacists, dentists, farmers and doctor.[43]

Class differences in suicide are likely in some cases to reflect the stresses of poor finances, housing and employment conditions. Poverty in general is known to heighten depression and anxiety.[44] It also appears to affect suicidal behaviour. Expressing distress through taking an overdose consistently follows a class pattern: self-poisoning has been a predominantly female working-class phenomenon in western societies. Women – who earn less, experience more poverty, and often struggle to combine motherhood and employment – may experience more acute social hardship than men. Whilst women are particularly vulnerable, working-class men are also at risk.[45] Yet in young people there is some evidence that suicidal behaviour occurs more evenly across the social spectrum. Adolescents who took overdoses in an Oxfordshire study were representative of local social make-up.[46]

Easy access to lethal drugs, and occupational stresses, may contribute to professional suicides. Similarly, academic pressure is associated in the public imagination with suicide among students. Rates of suicide among students at Oxford and Cambridge Universities traditionally appeared high, but a recent study at Oxford concluded that rates of suicide and undetermined death among students were only a little higher than those among youth in general.[47] Little information is available about the death rates of students in general although a recent Dutch study found that regions with high proportions of students in higher education suffered a higher youth suicide rate.[48] Moving away to study, leaving family and friends, and being subjected to new social and academic pressures, may well make certain young people more vulnerable.

Young people in prison

My Brief thinks I'll do a lot of time on remand so you can visit anytime so long as it's only three and a baby. So don't get too happy coz I'm back in, but don't forget me please. I just hope you understand. Don't forget me. If the rest do I'll fuckin do myself in . . . So long as you care I'll try. (Letter from a 20 year old remand prisoner to his sister, found when he was discovered hanging in his cell, March 1992)

Young people in prison and remand centres are at unusually high risk of suicide. Prisoners in general are four times more likely than people outside to die through suicide, and within the prison population young inmates are most vulnerable.[49] News of cell deaths has become increasingly familiar, as rates of suicide in prisons doubled during the 1980s alone.[50] Since less than 4 per cent of the prison population are women, nearly all suicide victims have been male. Remand prisoners are particularly vulnerable. In England and Wales between 1972 and 1987, half of the prisoners who took their lives were on remand, yet remand prisoners accounted for only 11 per cent of the prison population.[51] Remand prisoners are three times more likely to kill themselves than others in prison, and the remand population is growing.[52] Currently, over 20 per cent of all prisoners are on remand. In prison, unlike outside, suicide and attempted suicide conform to similar patterns – being young, on remand or recently sentenced increases the risk of both.[53] In one prison study, 80 per cent of suicide attempts were by inmates aged 25 or younger.[54]

The most common sources of stress among prisoners who kill themselves are isolation, intimidation and the length of their sentence.[55] Overcrowding and staff shortages mean that prisoners, particularly those on remand, may be locked up for as many as 23 hours a day, with little opportunity for human contact.[56] Emotional isolation is common in the highly mobile remand population. As prisoners go for trial or are relocated to other prisons, relationships are fleeting. With less time to get to know each other, communication and trust between prisoners and prison staff suffers. Since the feelings and needs of relative strangers are more easily overlooked, the detection of suicide risk becomes less likely.[57] Staff shortages also allow bullying and intimidation to flourish. Accounts of prison life have suggested a paranoiac existence for the most vulnerable adolescents, preyed upon by other inmates and with scant protection from prison staff.[58] Difficulties in adjusting to the prison environment make the weeks and months after arrival at prison a high-risk time for suicide. Uncertainty about the future adds to this stress for remand prisoners awaiting trial or sentence.

The prison environment withholds the means of self-harm. Notably, access to pharmaceutical products is restricted, so overdosing is not possible. In the outside world the overdose commonly signals a crisis, but spares its victim. In prison, desperate individuals may try to 'cry for help' with more violent and irreversible suicide methods. The results can be calamitous. In September 1991, a 15-year-old boy was found dead in Feltham Young Offenders Institution, Middlesex, hanging by his shirt from his cell window. Would he, he had asked a fellow prisoner hours earlier, be transferred to the hospital wing if he was caught trying to hang himself? If this boy's hope was to win a modicum of care and attention through transfer to the prison medical wing, his desperate strategy backfired. The only available suicide method proved to be too deadly.[59]

Loss

> *All I could think was: I want my dad back. I'd just assumed he was always going to be there. All I wanted was to be with my dad and I got quite overwhelmed by that feeling. I was really suicidal. It was not – 'I want to die,' but, 'I want to be with my dad.'*
>
> (KAREN)

At 13, Karen longed for her father so desperately following his death that the idea of suicide offered the fantasy of reunion. A young person's mourning for what is lost can be an intensely isolating and disturbing experience. The loss of a parent in childhood has been linked to depression later on in life; and among young people who kill themselves, the loss of a parent – through death, abandonment, or a child's going into 'care' – is more common than for other young people.[60]

Loss may take many forms. Maxine first thought about suicide aged 11. Her mother's loneliness and depression and the repeated upheaval of moving house and school had left her an isolated child:

> *We moved around a lot because of my dad's work. I've been to seven schools. No one would speak to me because I was different. With moving a lot I didn't really have any friends until I was 14. I was really weird when I was young. I used to talk to myself and have imaginary friends. I had a lot of problems with people at school thinking I was a loony and things like that. I used to be really bullied by the boys. I was always try-*

ing to fit in, but when I began to make friends and fit in, then
we'd move again. My mum used to get really sad and
depressed. She'd sit outside and cry. I think me and my brother
used to get on her nerves.

The absence of emotional warmth and security in a young person's life represents a very fundamental form of loss. To this loss may be added the ongoing stress created by the kinds of problem that erode stability. Research suggests that suicidal children are more likely to have a parent who suffers from mental and physical health problems, alcohol dependence or domestic violence.[61]

Accumulated losses may make life appear unpredictable, frightening and difficult to cope with. Suicidal children and adolescents have often suffered more of them. What seems to raise the stakes for suicidal children and adolescents is when a number of things go wrong in quick succession. Adolescence is a time of life when loss is naturally and keenly felt. Loss or separation is also a common trigger for youth suicide.[62] Breaking up with a boyfriend/girlfriend, a death in the family, or even just an argument, may be more likely to trigger such a reaction if a young person has had to cope with more stress and disruption during his or her short life.[63]

Abuse

There were seven kids in his family. His step-dad had abused
him and he couldn't live in their house. They'd taken him
straight into care when he was a baby, so he'd been in care all
his life. He was just so desperate for his family. He desperately
craved his mother all his life.

(LISA, MATTHEW'S FOSTER SISTER)

Matthew was taken into care as a baby and never knew his natural mother or siblings. Knowing only that they lived somewhere in Wales, he would run away to search for them whenever his London foster family took him on holiday near the Welsh border. Nor did Matthew's rage towards the man who had injured him as a baby, leaving him with disabilities and depriving him of his family, ever subside. In fact throughout adolescence Matthew openly expressed the desire to track down his stepfather and murder him. Although many victims of youth suicide have certainly not been abused by those close to them, young people who kill themselves have, as a group, experienced more parental abuse or rejection than their peers.[64] Abusive treatment from a parent may clearly do long-term damage to a child's self-esteem. Abuse of a child can be emotional, physical or sexual, perpetrated by adults or by other children.

The devastating impact of sexual abuse on young people's mental health was suggested by a British study which found that 50 per cent of women who see a psychiatrist have been sexually abused as children. Nearly 60 per cent of victims in one British study were abused by family members.[65] Among suicidal adolescents the experience of abuse and incest is more common than for others.[66] Many young people who have been sexually abused struggle to survive emotionally through self-harm and depression, and suicidal behaviour is more common among them.[67]

Abuse and harassment can, of course, come from sources outside a young person's family. One in five children are either bullied at school or are bullies themselves. Regular bullying causes considerable fear and suffering, yet half of victims tell no one, at school or home.[68] Those bullied in childhood are more likely to experience depression as they grow older, and a number of suicides among schoolchildren in recent years have been linked to victimisation at school.[69] Kaye, a young lesbian, became depressed after being attacked at a party: 'We were "queer bashed". Three men got in with baseball bats and started beating the shit out of us. I was in quite a state after. I was having real problems sleeping. I got antidepressants.' At 13, Ashley felt deeply humiliated by the 'rough justice' bestowed on him in his local police station: 'I left the cell with bruises and I was crying, but it was shock more than anything. I wasn't used to being treated in that way.' Humiliating situations, which shake a young person's self-respect, are common precipitants of suicide attempts.

Depression

> *I just didn't have any emotions at all. I didn't used to do anything. I didn't used to talk or smile or cry. I had no ability to show any emotions. I felt like I wanted to sleep all the time, but I couldn't sleep. I didn't have any sense of a future. I couldn't even think of the next day. I just used to pray that I wouldn't wake up in the morning.*

(CARRIE)

Around one in ten children and one in five adolescents may suffer relatively serious problems with their emotional well-being and mental health.[70] Deep unhappiness tends to show itself through emotional problems such as depression, anxiety and phobias as well as through difficult behaviour such as aggression, truancy and stealing.[71] Indicative of considerable unease and suffering, young people's mental health problems increase their vulnerability to suicidal thoughts and actions. For some the common experience of depression may intensify into a life-threatening condition.

'Depression' describes a range of states, from the mildest bad mood to intractable mental suffering. Their common denominator is feeling 'negative'. The common cold of psychiatry, depression intrudes into most lives in one form or another. Yet at its most serious, depression becomes a state close to despair, causing intense emotional pain. The signs and symptoms of serious depression are described in Chapter 5 (see page 125). Amongst children and adolescents who are depressed, thoughts that they would be better off dead are common.[72] At least four out of ten young people who kill themselves appear to have been suffering severe depression at the time.[73] Carrie tried twice to kill herself during her sixteenth year, while caught in the grip of a relentless depression. At that time, she did not merely regard her future with pessimism – it had become inconceivable. Death appeared to her to be the only way 'forward'.

The debate about the origins of mental suffering is long-running and emotive and points to a complex mix of social, psychological and physical causes. The balance of causes varies from person to person. For some young people, depression may be triggered by trauma or rooted in early relationships. Cheryl traced her depression to a childhood dominated by the unpredictable rages of an alcoholic and authoritarian father:

> It was hell living in that house with him. His moods were so volatile you could never monitor him. You'd never know when he'd turn on you. He'd rage around the house and his language was so violent – all apocalyptic stuff. He was so Victorian – I couldn't express any anger. I couldn't answer back. There'd always be negatives thrown at me. He'd call me an 'ugly little sod'. There was never any praise at all. Even now I have an easy time accepting the bad things about myself and a hard time accepting the good things.

Others attribute their emotional pain to internal, biochemical causes. One young man observed in his suicide note that there were no 'reasons' for the depression which had made his life intolerable over recent years:

> If love alone could have made me better I would be the most well-adjusted man on earth . . . It's not like I killed myself because I didn't get an 'A' on an exam, or I broke up with my girlfriend. Those are the kind of depressions that have a reason to happen. My depression comes without help from outside. Nothing bad has happened to make me depressed except my depression. (Extract from a suicide note from a 22-year-old man to his parents)

It is only in recent years that mental health professionals have begun to acknowledge severe depression in children and adolescents.[74] In all, up to 2 per cent of children and 10 per cent of adolescents are now thought to suffer depression in its more extreme forms.[75]

Schizophrenia and manic depression

He'd had this voice that told him he was the disciple of God and that he was being told to do these tests. He ended up going up an air ventilator to do the 'air test'. He got himself through by taking off all his clothes. He spent about 24 hours up in this ventilator. Then some workmen came and he fell out when they opened it.

In hospital he'd tried to commit suicide in the bath doing one of his tests. He was going to drown, but someone came in. So he'd achieved his 'air' and he'd achieved his 'water'. And then he started setting fire to his hair. He burnt his hair so he had to have it absolutely shorn. So he'd done the air, fire and water – the elements. I knew that he still hadn't done the earth test.

Nobody actually saw him fall or jump. The train driver didn't see. We don't really know whether he jumped thinking this was another test, with a voice in his head saying, 'Jump, you'll survive. This is a test.' One is inclined to think he was carrying out an order.

(HILARY, SIMEON'S MOTHER)

Major mental health problems are suffered by only a small minority of young people. The symptoms associated with the condition known as schizophrenia usually appear between about 17 and 25 years of age, interfering with a young person's thought processes and feelings. There is considerable controversy about what causes this to happen, but schizophrenia is frequently experienced as a process of disintegration. Hijacking the mental functions which allow a basic sense of separateness, identity and self-direction, it may lead people to believe that their thoughts and feelings are known to others, and that others

57

control them.[76] Hearing voices is common, as are hallucinations, delusions and feelings of persecution.[77] Simeon, an 18-year-old diagnosed as schizophrenic, died under a train on the London Underground. Whether he intended to die, or whether he acted under the influence of the voices that he had recently been hearing, remains uncertain.

Young people with schizophrenia are an extremely vulnerable group. The arrival of frightening and distressing symptoms during late adolescence or early adulthood disrupts the natural search for an adult identity and intimate relationships. Although some do adapt and learn to live positively with 'hearing voices', others have great difficulty coping with both the symptoms and stigma of schizophrenia. The risk of suicide appears to increase with more severe hallucinations and feelings of persecution. Being regarded as crazy leaves a young person dangerously isolated. One in seven of the callers to Saneline – the helpline for schizophrenics and their families – wants to discuss how to deal with suicidal feelings. Suicide is the leading cause of early death amongst those suffering from schizophrenia, commonly within ten years of problems commencing.[78] Simeon may have acted under orders, but other young people with schizophrenia who take their lives are motivated by hopelessness about their condition and its implications for their future.

Another source of considerable anguish is manic depression, in which moods may undergo extreme swings between elation and depression. Again, this increases a young person's vulnerability to suicide. Both schizophrenia and manic depression, in their severest form, may distort perceptions to such an extent that a young person is said to be 'psychotic', or out of touch with reality. Julian was diagnosed as suffering from manic depression at 19, when for weeks he was driven by tremendous energy and believed he had unusual powers. When Jake's 'manic' phase subsided, he not only entered a deep depression, but regained insight and recognised his own delusions. He was, his sister recalled, abject and frightened prior to his suicide:

You're in such a position of vulnerability after psychosis –
when you're coming down. You're realising that you lost your
mind completely. Perhaps you believe you can no longer exist.
You've lost your self. At that stage he probably thought he had
very little to lose.

(CAROL, JAKE'S SISTER)

Drug and alcohol abuse

One of the reasons I drank was just to feel reasonable. It was-
n't to get pissed. It was just to keep the lid on. I couldn't
handle being sober.

(ASHLEY)

In her flat we found bottles and bottles of wine and vodka
under her bed. She'd been drinking and drinking, presumably
after her boyfriend left. She hid so much, you don't know how
long it had been going on for.

(LISA, EMMA'S SISTER)

An adolescent alcoholic, Ashley's first reason for drinking was
to alleviate the intolerable tension he felt when sober. He used
alcohol as a medication, in order to cope and defend himself
against depression. Emma first went into hospital for help with
depression when she was 22. Unknown to her family she had
been relying heavily on alcohol in the months beforehand.
Despairing young people may use alcohol to relieve emotional
pain. Alcohol abuse in general is associated with depression,
anxiety and other mental health problems.[79] It also shows a
clear link with suicide and this is evident in its youngest victims.[80] Two-thirds of 17–19-year-old boys who killed themselves
in New York had a drink problem.

Dependence on drugs is also common among young peo-
ple who take their own lives.[81] Clifford recalled that his friend
Earl entered adolescence relying on drugs: 'He started smoking
drugs at 12. He was smoking pot every day and a lot. He was
heavily into it – desperate for it.' At 18, Earl began to develop

bizarre behaviour and beliefs. His friend attributed these to his years of heavy drug consumption.

Both alcohol and other drugs may be used as a strategy for maintaining control when a young person fears disintegration. Both may mask underlying problems and sustain vulnerable young people at a high cost. Long-term drug use interferes with emotional and social development. And although their physiological and psychological effects may be different, alcohol and drugs present a young person with new problems. Ashley's physical and mental state deteriorated as the combined effects of alcohol and drug dependence stoked his existing anxiety: 'I was paranoid. I was hallucinating all the time. I was having panic attacks. If I sat in the road hitch-hiking the road would move about. I wasn't very well.' Different studies of youth suicide report that between 26 and 62 per cent of those who die had problems with alcohol or drugs.[82]

Personality, ways of coping and sensitivity

> *I remember when Terry smashed the radio, thinking he was being like his father. And when he put his fist through the bedroom door. His father used to go really over the top when he was angry. He used to smash things. They used to have a lot of arguments. His father would say to him – 'Come outside and we'll sort this out man to man.' His father used to hit him around the head a lot.*
>
> (ANGELA, TERRY'S MOTHER)

Young people deal with the anxieties and pains of life in very different ways, often emulating their parents' means of coping. Terry was prone to explosive anger, which reminded his mother of her ex-husband's violence. A tendency to act impulsively or aggressively increases the susceptibility of young people to suicide. Overwhelming feelings of rage and hostility may nurture suicidal behaviour as an expression of revenge. Lilian felt that her son Steven took his life in anger at his girlfriend, with whom he had recently had a row: 'It sounds an awful thing to say, but

I think he wanted to get back at her. I think it was anger. His head was in a muddle. He must have taken leave of himself for a few hours.' Steven died in his car surrounded by photographs of his girlfriend.

Perfectionism may also be a dangerous trait.[83] Some children internalise the high expectations of those around them and maintain a sense of control by rigidly adhering to them. Achieving these standards becomes integral to their self-esteem and fear of failure is a threatening prospect. Children who fear that approval and love will diminish with school marks will experience greater pressure to pass an exam and exaggerated horror at failing it. Perfectionism is a survival strategy which inadvertently increases pressure and anxiety. As bright but fragile children achieve academic success, they raise expectations and find they have further to fall:

> *I wonder if it's just my personality. When I look back I can't remember a lot of times when I was a child being really happy. I've no idea why I was unhappy at first. I used to put myself under a lot of pressure at school. I was very much a perfectionist. If I couldn't get things perfect then it was better not to do them at all.*
>
> (CARRIE)

Certain personality traits – perfectionism or impulsiveness – appear to put some young people in greater danger of suicide than others, and coincide ominously with the uncertainties of adolescence.[84] In addition, parents bereaved by suicide often observe that their child possessed a special sensitivity which, in retrospect, appeared to have made them more vulnerable. The impression is of young people with their emotional pores wide open: 'Tommy was very intense. He'd take everything so serious. Sometimes you'd feel as if you'd want to breathe for him. He had a very special feeling – a deep feeling' (Phyllis, Tommy's mother).

Young people who have been exposed to suicide

I did have three brothers, but one killed himself. I was so much like him, I had a fear of going like him. I wondered if I was schizophrenic at all. I wondered if it was hereditary – does it run in family lines? I used to think of what he must have been going through to do those things.

(BARRY)

Maybe it introduced him to the idea of suicide. They went the same way, so there must be a link. He was really upset by [his sister's suicide]. I remember him disappearing off to his room and playing a song that she'd been playing over and over again before she died. And then he kept playing it.

(LISA, MATTHEW'S FOSTER SISTER)

Young people who kill themselves are more likely than others to have a relative who has previously attempted or died through suicide.[85] Clearly, suicidal behaviour has powerful effects on those close to it and posits an extreme response to crisis. After a self-inflicted death, the usual bereavement themes of loss and adaptation have an explosive subtext. For Lisa, the suicides of both her sister and her foster brother made it difficult to envisage mental health crises as anything other than life-threatening: 'I find it hard to believe now that there are people who have breakdowns and come out of them and carry on living.' Barry was 15 when his older brother, a diagnosed schizophrenic, killed himself. Vulnerable already, Barry identified with his brother and felt tremendous fears for his own safety. The idea that suicide 'runs in families' added a dangerously fatalistic fuel to his fire.

In fact, the modelling of suicidal behaviour extends beyond family boundaries. Young suicide victims are more likely than their peers to have friends, as well as relatives, who have attempted or died through suicide.[86] The aftermath of a suicide appears to be a dangerous time for those in close proximity, who identify with the victim and are already vulnerable. The emotional furore that follows a death may loosen internal restraints against self-destruction. History is littered with evidence of suicide epidemics. In 1908, 70 children killed themselves in a Moscow school district within two and a half years.[87] Suicide appeared to be catching. A similiar effect is suggested by the clusters of suicides that sometimes occur within psychiatric wards, prisons and small communities.[88] Sending shock-waves through social and institutional networks, one suicide can apparently trigger another. The shock-waves are greater where the suicide is close to home. Researchers have concluded that 'exposure to suicide or suicidal behaviour of relatives and friends appears to be a significant factor influencing a vulnerable young person to commit suicide'.[89]

Accumulated Causes and 'Last Straws'

Having read Ashley's story in the Prologue it would be facile to conclude that he slashed his wrists early one morning because he had had an argument with his girlfriend. The argument was, in Ashley's words, just the 'last straw'. The hopelessness, alienation and fear that culminated in his suicide attempt at 20 had been brewing for years. Ashley emerged from a childhood disturbed by his father's alcoholism, with high levels of anxiety. Life at home was tense and dominated by his father's emotions. Sensitive and unhappy, he rebelled rapidly against the ethos of his school – a large boys' comprehensive in a northern town – which he felt to be authoritarian and unimaginative. Feeling his teachers had classed him as 'a loser' early on, he soon gave up on school. His first concern at school was to emulate his favoured role models, the 'harder kids', by becoming 'one of the loonies', by 'misbehaving and hanging about with idiots and druggies and pissheads'. Coinciding with a growing need to soothe his own anxiety and hurt – at 13 he was sexually abused by an older woman – his own alcohol and drug use became progressively heavier. As a vicious cycle of anger, frustration and further alienation set in, he began to get in trouble with the local police, courting a string of juvenile convictions: 'I wanted to fit in with some criminal underclass – that's who I identified with.' At the earliest opportunity Ashley left behind an education system which he felt offered him nothing, and found himself on a Youth Training Scheme. Passing it over as a 'big con', he remained unemployed and disenchanted, lived in a squat and involved himself in a militant politics. He left his home town at 18 in flight from the police, and settled in a new city. Squatting on a large estate where unemployment was the norm, drugs rife and his alcoholism unremarkable, the only future Ashley could picture for himself involved prison or death. His friends were those who tolerated his constant intoxication and sex was something he did when drunk, with anybody and not much joy. When he did finally meet a girlfriend who meant something to him, the relationship proved unsustainable. Thoughts of suicide had flashed through Ashley's mind for years. But now, as drug and alcohol dependence took their toll, he began to lose control physically and mentally. Finally, after a confrontation with his girlfriend, Ashley decided to act.

Every youth suicide has its last straw – an event or shift in perception that makes going on seem impossible and triggers a self-destructive act. After suicide attempts young people often refer to these 'last straws' as the reason for, or cause of, their action. Since they often appear too trivial to have caused such an extreme response, these 'reasons why' may often be more mystifying than illuminating, to those who take them at face value. In fact, these final precipitants are generally preceded by far longer-term causes. The origins of hopelessness lie much further back in time. Vulnerable children tend to become vulnerable adolescents. Although a major trauma may, in some cases disorientate a young person so suddenly that he or she can no longer cope, hindsight more often illuminates how a young victim of suicide was struggling with a combination of the stresses and problems already discussed. The social, psychological and biological causes of a single youth suicide are multiple. As the number and intensity of their effects grow, the accumulated stress may eventually overwhelm. The mounting pressure and fallout from long-standing difficulties becomes the 'Everything' that has finally become 'too much'. In the presence of one problem too many, suicidal desperation may escalate towards an irrevocable action.

CHAPTER 3

Why Has Youth Suicide Increased?

It is predominantly young men who are currently suffering lonely and self-inflicted deaths. To ask why their numbers are increasing raises the attendant question of why young women have been protected from this fatal trend, even though they attempt suicide more often. The role of gender in mediating both the causes, and the fatal and non-fatal outcomes, of young people's suicidal acts is an impressive one. The explanation lies in a constellation of factors – from the economic pressures and social changes now moulding young lives, to modern ways of coping with alcohol and drugs, through to changing attitudes towards suicide and the evolution of British suicide methods. Whilst suicidal feelings ferment in unique personal conditions, a number of ingredients appear repeatedly in the mix and suggest why it has become more explosive in recent years.

Changing Roles and Modern Pressures

Modern adolescence

The Western adolescent is presented with a 'find yourself' culture, in which the stress on personal freedom has become emphatic. In post-war Britain greater educational and work opportunities, for both sexes, increased young people's choices of social destinations. Personal choice grew with the acceptability of divorce, extramarital sex and contraception, while the moral certainties of formal religion subsided with church attendance. The modern mass media thrived and chronicled the diverse ways in which people lived their lives. Inevitably, greater freedom of information and opportunity has introduced new questions and uncertainties into young lives. The choices required for adulthood – careers, aspirations, values – have become daunting as well as liberating: 'groping through a limitless thicket of possible career choices and possible ethics and life-styles leaves many adolescents feeling lost at sea'.[1]

Paradoxically the abundant choice of modern adolescence is kept in check by increased dependence on the adult world. Two major steps towards autonomy – leaving education and gaining work – are now delayed. The school-leaving age has risen throughout the century. In 1900 the median school-leaving age in Britain was 14 and children took up working roles early.[2] Now, in contrast, the educational process of many young people extends into their early twenties and adolescents wait years to acquire the status and identity of the wage-earner. Between 1945 and 1970 the British higher education system quadrupled in size.[3] With the largesse of relative affluence, modern Western cultures have designated adolescence a time of preparation for the challenges of an opportunistic society.

Such contemplative liberty may easily become the stuff of existential angst. Speaking on radio, in 1993, the head of a university counselling service described how students often express the feeling that they are parasites.[4] A spirit of indebtedness, of not belonging to the 'real world' and having no recognisable value in it, promises little for young self-esteem. The young unemployed face an even cruder sense of their own superfluity. For those who have never worked, the prospect of perpetual dependence on relatives and state benefits provides meagre cause for hope.

Meanwhile, the pressure to succeed is keenly felt. As post-war social policy championed equal opportunities and meritocratic rewards, working one's way to the top has been perceived as ever more possible. Real levels of mobility between classes have, in fact, been low compared to these ideals.[5] Yet doused with the lubricant of social mobility, the British class system has become less rigid and personal expectations have changed. So too, within an aggressive consumer culture, have material measures of personal worth. Reared on advertising, young people are highly attuned to its sophisticated codes of glamour and status. From children's trainers to young men's cars, emblems of kudos abound. With its own niche in the marketing imagination, youth culture peddles a heady blend of street credibility, sexual sophistication, intellectual ease, material comfort and bodily perfection.

Heightened expectations may reinforce young people's sense of inadequacy, when 'success' proves elusive. Lisa watched her sensitive and perfectionist sister struggle with the burden of self-definition more than most, before Emma took her life at 24:

> *Emma had this idea you had to do all the things the magazines told you to do. She set such impossible standards for herself they were never achievable. She felt she didn't measure up. I think she felt the stress of living in modern society. It's to do with having so much choice in life and having to choose what you want to do. It's a trauma having so much open to you. And failing is so much more unacceptable. I think as there's more chance to succeed the average sense of failure goes up.*

Economic decline, recession and unemployment

Economic conditions have imposed increasing strains on the young in recent decades. Many have grown up in families under financial pressure. A generation back the so-called 'baby-boomers' – that unusually large batch of post-war babies who reached young adulthood between 1960 and 1975 – faced novel financial stresses as they matured and competed for resources and jobs.[6] Tough competition for work and higher costs of living made financial survival harder, as did raised living standards and expectations. Most families now relied on two incomes. As women moved into the labour force stresses on working parents, particularly mothers, grew. These pressures seemed to show, as mental health surveys reported that the baby boom generation suffered more depression and emotional problems than previous generations.[7]

As their children matured economic pressures continued unabated. In fact, during the recession-ridden late 1980s the prospects of many young people appeared increasingly blighted. By 1993 the British unemployed numbered 3 million: a third of them were under 25.[8] As in many industrialised countries, unemployment rose dramatically in Britain from the 1960s. It peaked at 3 million in 1982, fell briefly in the late 1980s, and rose again thereafter. The young have been hit hard by recession. Youth unemployment (15–24) has usually been double the general adult rate.[9] In 1993 the rate of joblessness among 16–19-year-olds was 19 per cent, and 17 per cent among 20–24-year-olds.[10]

The appearance of an 'army' of jobless in the UK might reasonably be traced to the combined forces of domestic and world recession, the monetarist economic policy of 1980s Thatcherism, as well as to Britain's longer-term economic decline within the post-war international economy. Yet surveys of British attitudes show widespread suspicion of those who live on 'handouts', with many believing that those on welfare could find work if they wanted to.[11] Despite the existence of a sizeable underclass of long-term unemployed, being out of work in the 1990s retains its stigma.

Alongside unemployment, relative inequalities have increased. The proportion of the British population living on or below the poverty line climbed from 12 per cent in 1979 to 19 per cent in 1987.[12] A substantial proportion of this new poverty has been amongst the young unemployed. The 1988 Social Security Act disqualified thousands of young people from claiming benefit, notably students and the youngest school-leavers.[13] In theory, every school-leaver was to be offered a Youth Training Scheme place, but by 1992 over a million

16- and 17-year-olds not in full-time education were without a job or YTS place.[14] Of these, according to independent research, 80,000 had no income at all due to their ineligibility for state benefits.[15] The introduction of student loans schemes in the 1980s combined with cuts in grants has made hardship and debts among students a common story.[16] And as recession choked job opportunities during the 1980s, earnings among the young fell relative to other workers.[17] Unemployment and low incomes have made it difficult for the young to gain access to a diminishing housing stock. Shelter estimates that there are now 156,000 homeless under-26-year-olds in Britain and the plight of young people sleeping rough has become more visible in the major cities.[18]

The rapid increase in youth suicide among young men during the 1980s seems likely to reflect a number of these pressures. To many, the spoils of a consumer culture have become unattainable yet, as one mother observed, 'The pressure nowadays is materialistic. They have to be able to provide a house and a car to impress a girl, or their family or mates. The pressure is tremendous.' As youth unemployment and low pay become more prevalent, a crisis of expectations is likely among the economically vulnerable. Those without work lack not only a wage packet, but a sense of control over their own lives and a reason to feel positive about the future. Youth unemployment, poverty and homelessness pose a substantial threat to young people still in the process of working out who they are in the world. In some communities prospects are unacceptably bleak. By the 1990s, unemployment rates among young men in some areas of London stood at 40 per cent.[19] A sense of having little stake or worth in the society to which one belongs has become more common among the young. The rising rate of juvenile crime may be just one of the symptoms.

Suicide statistics suggest that men may be paying a high price for economic adversity. The status of the wage-earner remains central to male identity, and the impact of unemployment on the self-esteem of young men may be correspondingly high. Despite many adjustments to modern sex roles, boys are still socialised to rely more exclusively than girls on a work identity. Women's paid work has become essential for the welfare of most families, yet children still associate men with higher-status occupations and heftier pay.[20] Male prerogatives, including the responsibilities of fatherhood, tend to be orientated towards earning: 'They're the breadwinners, the wage-earners, the achievers' (Joan, Jason's mother). Ironically, the inherently sexist attitudes which attach less importance to women's working lives may also attach less stigma to their unemployment.

Research suggests that adolescent girls experience considerable confusion and conflict about a future which prescribes a dual identity as worker and mother.[21] But they enjoy the psychological 'safety net' of a status which is independent of the workplace. Becoming a mother is less dependent on economic prospects than the breadwinning function of traditional fatherhood. Lillian's son Steven became depressed after two years in a dead-end factory job, which was poorly paid, utilised few of his skills and offered no chances of promotion. He became pessimistic about his future and, aged 20, killed himself: 'I think Steven felt a failure. There's a choice for us [women]. We either have a career or have a family and in some cases are clever enough to combine the two. But men in most cases are there to achieve and the job is so important.' The isolation of unemployment may be a greater liability for young males. Unemployment and financial hardship put pressure on relationships. Young women have less to gain from sharing their lives with men who are out of work, demoralised and frustrated: 'Many women, caring for children on benefits, prefer to manage alone rather than share their homes with a man who adds nothing to the family income, but still seeks to control it.'[25]

Lost parents

He hadn't seen his father. His father had not got in touch with him. A lot of fathers wouldn't have just not got in touch, would they? He used to send him a birthday card and a

Christmas card and that was all. I thought maybe it would help Terry to speak to his father. He had all these angry feelings toward him, but there were lots of bits of Terry that were like his father.

(ANGELA, TERRY'S MOTHER)

During the 1960s and 1970s the social cement of marriage began to crumble. British marriages broke up at an unprecedented rate as social attitudes changed, the Divorce Reform Act was passed and working women gained more financial independence. Since then parental divorce and separation have become increasingly common. One in five young people in Britain now experiences an irreparable parental split before the age of 16.[22] Family instability is often cited as an explanation for various social problems experienced by contemporary youth – including their suicidal behaviour. Yet in some ways families have become more stable entities in the late twentieth century.[23] As health and social conditions have improved, mortality and morbidity have declined. A child is now far less likely than its forebears to experience the death or serious illness of a parent early on in life. Nevertheless the effects of parental break-up and single parenting on children have, in recent decades, aroused concern and been the subject of extensive research, speculation and polemic.

Although parental separation appears likely to be a painful and disruptive experience for children, most appear to adapt to their new circumstances. Studies consistently suggest that children are better off in divorced families than in intact families riven with conflict.[24] Obviously enough, the effect on a child of parental separation depends on a number of factors – the child's contact with the absent parent, how the parents manage financially and emotionally after the split, whether or not the child is exposed to recriminations and torn loyalties and the amount of support they receive from other adults.

Unfortunately the textbook separation or divorce is rarer than it might be. Fathers without custody of their children tend to become less active in their child's life following divorce:

'Some manage to share parental responsibility successfully, but most do not. The prevailing pattern is that fathers decrease their involvement in child-rearing over time. A large proportion have little or no contact with their adolescent children, and those who do rarely take an active role in supervising them.'[25] The 'lost' parent is invariably male and it is now more likely that the most abiding and involved relationship in a child's life will be with his or her mother. This shift in the parenting structure has been called, by the sociologically inclined, a 'matrilineal tilt'.[26] It is a tilt which may well have different implications for sons and daughters, since studies have suggested that boys may be more negatively affected than girls when contact with their father stops.[27]

Although young people who have lost a parent through separation, divorce or death seem to be more likely to attempt suicide than others (see Chapter 2), studies have found less conclusive evidence regarding youth suicide.[28] Nevertheless, rates of divorce appear to be associated with rates of suicide at the national level. Between 1960 and 1985 the divorce rates of European countries were among the most accurate predictors of changes in youth suicide.[29]

Sex and relationships

At a time of growing insecurity in other areas of their lives, young people may invest higher hopes and deeper needs in their personal relationships. However, the rules of personal involvement have become far from certain. Young people's sexual freedom, expectations of relationships and practical living arrangements have changed profoundly within a few decades, with marriage appearing increasingly outmoded.

As convention has become less binding, marriage has ceased to be a necessary prerequisite for sex, living together or having children. To many, its reputation has been compromised by the unremitting divorce rate. Between 1971 and 1991 the number of first marriages in Britain fell by 40 per cent, one in five couples now cohabit and those who do marry, marry later. Yet the demise of marriage, it has been argued, may have contributed to men's growing susceptibility to suicide.[30] Whilst the companionship, status and domestic support of marriage traditionally appeared to protect men against isolation and stress, nuptial order has had less obvious benefits for women. Married men suffer fewer mental health problems than their single counterparts, married women more.[31] Suicide is rarer among married men than among single, divorced or widowed men, but such differences are far less evident in women.[32] And notably, during the 1980s the suicide rate climbed most steeply among single men.

Earlier sexual activity has exposed young people to the emotional and physical risks of sex, as well as its pleasures. The 'sexual revolution' of the 1960s, brought about by more permissive social mores and the arrival of the contraceptive pill, separated sex from the necessity of marriage and the fear of conception. Premarital sex became more common and young people began sexual relationships at an earlier age. The average age for loss of virginity is now 16.[33] Dan recalled that 'Around 14 or 15, there was all this emphasis on fucking. It was expected that you really wanted to.' Although casual sex in adolescence is not the norm, neither are long-term involvements: 'Much more often, teenagers have intense, short-term relationships which may cause pain when they end.' Relationship difficulties are often implicated in young suicide attempts – over half (52 per cent) of the adolescent overdosers in one study reported having problems with a boyfriend or girlfriend.[34] The underlying causes of unhappiness are likely to be more profound than this, but vulnerable young people clearly experience acute stress when their relationships go wrong. Sexual intimacy raises the emotional stakes, and lends potency to rejection.

Tommy's fiancée left him a few months after he was made redundant from his job as a delivery driver. Not long ago a young man like Tommy would have had more emotional security. Marriage, for better or for worse, to his girlfriend would have been more likely, cohabitation unlikely and social pressures binding. But for Tommy the dream of marriage gave way, shortly before his suicide, to deep depression:

74

They were going to get married. They were living together. He
was so happy – exceptionally happy. And it looked as though
she really loved him from the Valentine card she sent him in
February. But she was acting a bit funny with him. Next
thing she went. When she was gone he was in a terrible state.
He was all sad. I don't think boys can take it. They're not sup-
posed to show it. You're a wimp if you do. Boys don't show
their feelings, but he was in such a state.

(PHYLLIS, TOMMY'S MOTHER)

As marriage has declined, social isolation has increased. Since
1961 single-person households in the UK have doubled. A proportion are elderly citizens, or those who choose to live
independently. But these bedsits, flats and houses also accommodate those young people left out in the cold by changing
patterns of kinship. In areas of south London, where the rate of
female suicide is double the national average, the most vulnerable group in the early 1990s has been single mothers – often
trapped in poor housing and high-rise flats.[35]

In earlier generations most young people lived with their
parents until they left home to marry and start a family. Many
now leave home independently, setting up their own living
units. An 'on your bike' job market and expanding student population has provided new reasons to move long distances from
home, leaving behind the support of family and friends. The
stresses of leaving home must now often be coped with alone,
and in unfamiliar surroundings.

'New Man' and the changing status of women

A lot of women's stuff is dead good, but I think some of the
anti-sexist stuff is a load of shite. A lot of people are getting
damaged. I took it on board. Women don't abuse; women are
really good to each other; women are supportive; we men
should be ashamed of our sexuality. I was new, young, vulner-
able. I could agree with most of it. I can't ignore how men are.

(ASHLEY)

Women's lives changed radically during the 1960s and 1970s. More women moved into the workforce, acquiring the status of the wage-earner and the freedom of the pay packet. As their educational opportunities grew, girls began to catch up with boys academically. Better-qualified young women entered the labour market to compete with men, as they gained more control over their personal lives. No longer solely wives and mothers, women eased free of biological imperatives and became less dependent on men.

The ideas of feminism accompanied them. By the late 1960s, a strong women's movement demanded such rights as economic equality and abortion, while providing the impetus for an intellectual reappraisal of the forces that subordinated women. As the 'personal' became 'political', the feminist analysis of power extended into the home, uncovering the frequency of violence in domestic relationships, and the grim facts of child abuse and rape. These were emotive times for sexual politics. As masculine abuse was exposed, women gained the moral ascendancy. With time the assumptions of feminism permeated mainstream culture. The orgasm usurped recipes and knitting patterns on the front covers of women's magazines and as the media strove to rehabilitate masculinity, the prototype 'New Man' emerged.

Commenting on the relentless rise of suicide in young men, Simon Armson, Chief Executive of The Samaritans, observed in 1993: 'We have this concept of the "new man", but it seems that he is a confused young man and he is not quite sure how he is supposed to behave, respond or relate in different relationships.'[36] For many he is a cosmetic creation, adapting to his changing social order by doing his share of the washing up. Real changes in male status and identity have had more tortuous effects. For 'new', but also 'young and vulnerable', adolescent males like Ashley, empathy with women was no defence against the confusion, anxiety and guilt associated with male culpability.

New Man is hardly thriving. He is committing crimes, filling the prisons, killing himself, abusing drugs in ever increasing numbers. New Man appears, in many ways, a more alienated creature than his predecessors. As Angela Phillips describes in *The Trouble with Boys*, more boys appear to give up on their schooling, embrace their perceived 'failure' angrily and adopt alternative sources of identity – bullying, petty crime, drug use:

> Boys labelled as behaviourally and emotionally disturbed out-number girls by four to one. In British inner cities, where toughness in men is prized above academic success, the all-male comprehensive schools lag behind the comprehensive schools for girls in exam results and, across the country, there are nearly 26 per cent more boys than girls who fail to obtain any exam results at all.[37]

Ashley left school frustrated and angry, with more juvenile convictions than exam qualifications. His sisters conformed at school, achieved academic success and eventually went on to university, but Ashley's energies were invested in a far more destructive search for status: 'We were the hard kids – the kids you wouldn't mess with. We ended up being quite respected. But we were all very insecure. We all feared being the next one to be ridiculed.'

Crime and punishment

Prison suicides account for approximately 5 per cent of the increase in suicide among men under 45 since the early 1970s.[38] Around 15 suicides a year occurred in prisons throughout England and Wales in the early 1960s, but by 1990 the annual total was around 40. Young people in prison and remand centres have proved to be at unusually high risk of suicide.

The official UK crime rate has increased dramatically in the post-war years, pushing up the prison population. Despite their innocence in law, remand prisoners – who now account for 20 per cent of all prisoners – endure some of the worst prison conditions. A rapidly changing group of fellow prisoners makes friendships difficult and remand prisoners face the additional stress of uncertainty about the outcome of their impending trial or sentence.[39] They are three times more likely to kill themselves than are others in prison.[40] A burgeoning system of pre-trial detention appears to have brought increasing numbers of suicides while in custody.[41]

The British prison system is marred by overcrowding and staff shortages, and the effects of these deficiencies inevitably filter down to vulnerable prisoners. Despite the needs of suicidal prisoners for special care and supervision, overcrowding too often means they are placed in the next cell that becomes vacant. Many prisoners are locked up for 23 hours a day, with little opportunity for human contact.[42] Not only do staff shortages increase lock-up time, they increase the freedom of dominant prisoners to bully and extort. Lee Waite was subjected, by fellow prisoners, to a sexual assault with a snooker cue hours before his suicide in Feltham Young Offenders Institution. The report of the inquest into his death concluded that 'The evidence points clearly to the conclusion that the immediate cause of taking his own life was fear caused by bullying and acts of violence committed upon him.'[43] At Lee's inquest the Governor of Feltham commented, of the prison regime, 'If there is no activity you get bullying . . . If the inmates are not occupied, they create terror.'

Unfortunately the grim realities of prison are experienced by large numbers of highly vulnerable prisoners. A third of those in prisons suffer mental health problems, some so serious that they have lost touch with reality.[44] In 1989 eight men died in Brixton Prison in south London within a year. Six of them were from the notorious 'F Wing', where, prison officers es45mate, 85 per cent of prisoners are 'mentally disturbed'.[45] As large psychiatric institutions were closed in the 1980s, many former in-patients were discharged into 'community care' with inadequate provision for their shelter, welfare and support. More people with mental health problems may now be drifting into a prison system with a pitifully understaffed Prison Medical Service.

Taking the Strain: Young People's Mental Health Problems

Deteriorating mental health

Using information gathered from successive generations this century, researchers have observed that more children, adolescents and young adults now suffer from serious mental health problems and that these are developing earlier.[46] Caution is clearly essential when comparing one generation with another. A multitude of changes affecting social attitudes and medical practice seem likely to have affected the reporting of depression in recent decades. Psychiatric diagnosis may be given out more readily by modern medicine. Media discussion of emotions and mental health have made us more psychologically minded. We more readily seek help for problems which earlier generations might put down to slights of fortune. Yet increases in depression and mental health problems in general among the young *do* appear to be real. Dramatic rises in young people's suicidal behaviour would seem to offer an irrefutable piece of corroborative evidence.

It seems likely that environmental pressures have much to do with these recent developments. Vulnerable young people might be shielded, in more favourable circumstances, but must struggle harder to survive in periods of emotional, social and economic stress. Traditionally, depression has been associated with the dejection of growing older and iller, with retirement, loss and loneliness. High suicide rates amongst the old seemed to bear this out. Yet in recent decades suicide in the elderly has declined, as youth suicide has increased. As old age has become more bearable, this suggests, the quality of life for the young has deteriorated. This deterioration may have been compounded by modern ways of coping.

Chemical culture I – pills for problems

My mum was on tranquillisers. I used to take them and steal them off her and she used to give them me. I just couldn't

79

handle it at school. All she was trying to do was keep me afloat – keep me going.

(ASHLEY)

The overdosing epidemic of the 1970s was helped on its way by certain cultural conditions. One was the easy availability of drugs. Post-war medical expansion brought with it an abundant drug harvest, as a powerful pharmaceutical industry tirelessly developed and promoted new and lucrative products. At the same time doctors became more familiar figures in people's lives. The proud arrival of the National Health Service in 1948 opened up free access to general practitioners and hospital care, and since doctors did not send patients away empty handed, the market for pharmaceutical products expanded. By 1991 the average patient took home eight prescriptions a year compared to only five in 1949.[47]

As the domestic medicine cabinet filled up, its contents were changing. These changes reflected new medical ambitions. A major new item on the post-war medical agenda was mental health. Psychological well-being became a legitimate goal of general medicine and new chemical remedies for mental distress were resourcefully promoted by the pharmaceutical industry. Existing sedatives were joined in the 1950s and 1960s by the major and minor tranquillisers, antidepressants and lithium. Modern psychiatry now had the means to extend beyond the psychiatric hospitals, out into general practice and the community.[48]

Psychotropic (mood-altering) medications were soon offered routinely by GPs in response to the cacophony of anxious states and bad feelings that patients brought to surgery. For overworked doctors the new drugs bestowed the Midas touch. A chat about a patient's difficulties could now be optimistically curtailed with the prescription pad. By 1970 nearly 30 per cent of all prescriptions were for mood-altering drugs.[6][49] Anti-anxiety drugs accounted for a large proportion of these – barbiturate prescriptions had shot up after 1947, giving way to benzodiazepine tranquillisers in the late 1960s.[50] Armed with repeat prescriptions, many took these drugs year after year.[51] Tranquilliser use became so prolific that by 1977 a brand known as Valium was reported to be the most widely prescribed drug in the world.[52]

Mass use of 'tranxs' for stress relief turned out to be a predominantly female phenomenon, twice as common in women as men.[53] This fitted a general pattern. Throughout the postwar years psychological medicine distributed its remedies unevenly. Studies of psychotropic drug use consistently show that women receive twice as many prescriptions for these medications as men.[54] Unsurprisingly, they have also been more likely to use them in overdose.

The paradox that therapeutic drugs were used for self-destruction began to contaminate the pharmacological elixir early on. From 1947 prescribing of barbiturates rose rapidly. So too did self-poisoning with these drugs. When they fell out of medical favour in the late 1960s, fewer prescriptions meant fewer barbiturate overdoses, but self-poisoning continued to climb inexorably, now in line with prescriptions for the new tranquillisers. By the 1970s, when hospital casualty departments were receiving overdosers – most of them women – in unprecedented numbers, 60–80 per cent of casualties were swallowing psychotropic drugs.[55] In regions where more psychotropics were prescribed, rates of self-poisoning were higher.[56]

Young suicide attempters confirmed the link. In the mid-1970s young women (aged 15–29) in Oxfordshire were prescribed psychotropic drugs three times more often than young men.[57] Among suicide attempters in Oxford, more adolescent girls than boys overdosed on psychotropics and as they grew older, and presumably got themselves down to the doctor's surgery, girls became *more* likely to use psychotropics in overdose.[58] Evidence like this alarmed the medical profession, which naturally did not like to regard itself as a purveyor of poisons. GPs became more cautious in prescribing drugs commonly used in overdose. Prescriptions for minor tranquillisers fell from 30 million in 1979 to under 18 million in 1990,[59] and tranquilliser and sedative overdoses have decreased.[60] However, overdosing remains a massive problem, not least because drugs are ubiquitous and available over the counter at any chemist's or supermarket.

To understand the meteoric rise of the overdose since the 1950s it is necessary to look beyond a plenitude of tablets – prescribed or not – to an underlying shift in coping strategies. History suggests that the availability of a poison only goes part of the way to explaining its abuse. Cleaning fluids, disinfectants and medicines, part of the domestic paraphernalia of every pre-war household, were not associated with large outbreaks of self-poisoning; nor was there an 'epidemic' of opiate poisoning when, at the beginning of this century, it was possible to buy opiates from any pharmacy. The modern tendency to overdose may have much to do with the expectation, encouraged by post-war medical practice, that drugs can medically protect the individual against unhappiness.

When at 15, Ashley had difficulties coping at school, his mother's solution (see p. 79) mirrored the medical response to her own problems. With too little money, four children to keep and a depressed and alcoholic husband, she fended off crisis with chemicals. Her strategy was common, and one that caused growing consternation.[61] Chemical palliatives ignored the real causes of stress in people's lives, critics suggested, and tinkered only with the symptoms. As one put it: 'For many people taking tranquillisers is akin to sitting on a fire and taking pain-killers'.[62] Medicine appeared to be making promises it could not keep. The notion that pills could magic away psychological distress – often caused by tangible disadvantage or trauma – encouraged unrealistic expectations and nurtured chemical dependency.

Post-war medicine provided a legal source of mind-altering drugs on a scale unknown before. These chemicals owed their 'respectability' to the concept of illness. Medical pathology identified mental distress with internal rather than external causes. In assuming more responsibility for lives blighted by distress, medicine, with its lexicon of mental illnesses, subtly reinterpreted them. As distress was medicalised, patients who could not cope were more readily seen as suffering personal disorders than social pressures. This tendency, it has been argued, has taught and legitimised 'helplessness' – that sinking sense of having no control over one's own life.[63] As the health service landed a disproportionate quota of female misery this particular lesson was learned by women more often than men. Meanwhile, as with any chemical dependency, sustained use seemed likely to deplete what natural resources an individual started out with.

Chemical culture II – Drowning sorrows

I'd get up in the morning and drink Special Brew. I'd go to bed at night and drink Special Brew. I'd be pissed all day.

(ASHLEY)

As a nation's drinking habits grow more voracious, its young become more vulnerable to suicide. In Europe, increases in youth suicide between 1960 and 1985 were clearly associated with the growth in a country's alcohol consumption.[64] At an individual level alcohol abuse leaves people at high suicide risk. Yet alcohol is Western culture's most popular mood-altering drug and in the post-war period the UK has become determinedly 'wetter'.[65] Copious enough at the turn of the century, alcohol consumption fell here during the First World War and the Depression, and stayed low until its resurgence after the Second World War. Since 1945, per capita consumption has doubled following steep rises in the 1960s and 1970s. The UK steadied itself in the 1980s, but more recently alcohol use has crept up again.[66] Glamorised by advertising, increasingly affordable in relation to post-war incomes and easy to buy from ubiquitous pubs and off-licences, alcohol has vastly increased its role in British social life.

The growth of a drinking culture clearly involves risks for the young. The first is the increased likelihood of growing up with a parent who drinks heavily. Between four and five million people in England and Wales now live in families seriously disrupted by alcohol abuse.[67] For a growing number of children and adolescents, home life is dominated by parental drinking. At the very least this introduces tension and unpredictability into their immediate environment. At worst, as the NSPCC confirms, alcohol use is often implicated in the abuse of children.[68] The families of alcoholics have been called the 'forgotten and ignored victims of problem drinking'.[69] They are forgotten and ignored in growing numbers.

The alcohol boom has had another damaging effect: 'alcohol misuse amongst young people has become established as a chronic problem in the United Kingdom'.[70] Youth has traditionally been a time for relatively heavy drinking, giving way to more moderate habits in adulthood. But excessive drinking is now more often sustained into later life. Major alcohol use among young adults has increased in recent decades and the casualties of long-term alcoholism have become younger. Deaths from cirrhosis of the liver (the divining-rod of alcohol-related diseases and a chronic illness which takes years to develop and kill) have increased in line with alcohol consumption. A growing proportion of victims have not reached middle age.[71] Problems with alcohol are starting earlier in life.

As alcohol has become more accessible and affordable to adolescents, its role in their social life has grown. Drinking typically starts early, and increases through late adolescence.[72] Heavy-drinking 14–16-year-olds report that alcohol makes it easier to mix at parties, talk to the opposite sex, calm nerves and relax.[73] The social lubricant may rapidly prove indispensable. Among 15-year-olds, 5–10 per cent exceed drinking limits deemed 'sensible' for adults (14 units for women, 21 units for men per week). By 18–24, around 10 per cent of women and 33 per cent of men may do so.[74] Sex differences widen among the heaviest drinkers, with young men more likely to drink dangerously. Around 10 per cent of 18–24-year-old males consume in excess of 50 units weekly – the equivalent of 25 pints of beer.[75] Clearly our drinking culture anoints young men more ritualistically than it does women.

Sex differences are traditional in alcohol use, and evident in contemporary habits. Men of all ages still consistently drink more, outnumber women among high-risk drinkers by as much as 6:1, and die more often of alcohol-related diseases.[76] Early socialisation establishes rules relating to alcohol use. Studies of childhood drinking show that boys are encouraged by their elders to drink more than girls, and experience their first drink at an earlier age.[77] The male role models in a child's life are more likely to be seen drinking than the female. Whilst the stigma attached to women's drinking has undoubtedly relaxed, alcohol still has less positive connotations for female than male identity. Excessive consumption and uninhibited drunken behaviour are just not 'feminine' traits. During adolescence, the formation of drinking habits coincides with intensified concern over issues of gender and sexual identity. Cultural prescriptions about what is appropriate masculine and feminine behaviour inevitably influence how the sexes use alcohol.

Heavy drinking often masks deeper underlying problems. Alcohol provides a means of coping with anxiety and depression, but the rules governing the social acceptability of alcohol inevitably influence who uses it to cope.[78] Drinking is a classic 'masculine' strategy for drowning out sorrows and numbing anxiety. The habits of vulnerable young men, as well as drinking patterns in general, appear to reflect this. In one study, adolescent boys who had attempted suicide were eight times more likely to report that they took drugs 'when feeling very upset, sad or unable to cope', than boys who had not attempted suicide. Such an admission was rarer amongst girls, and spread equally between female attempters and non-attempters. Vulnerable boys therefore appear more distinguishable for their tendency to resort to alcohol and other drugs for stress relief.[79]

Chemical culture III – Getting high

Whatever drug you wanted you could get. You could smoke dope in all the pubs there. Flats in the block were like shops where you could buy the drugs from. Everybody was into

drinking and drugs, so you weren't really any different. It was
just a way of escaping, really, because life wasn't anything.
There was nothing stimulating, nothing enjoyable. Everything
was boring. I needed kicks. Drugs gave me a buzz.

(ASHLEY)

Many young people use illegal 'street drugs' and solvents, some
in early adolescence. Access to illegal substances is evidently
more restricted than to alcohol, but increasing proportions of
young people are exposed to them. Around 10 per cent of
English schoolchildren have tried illegal drugs or glue-sniffing,
most frequently cannabis.[80] There is less exposure to harder
drugs. A Gallup poll in 1992 found that one in a hundred 15–24-
year-olds have used 'hard' drugs, such as heroin and cocaine.[81]
One, two and three per cent of 13–20-year-olds in England,
Wales and Scotland respectively, report they have been offered
a syringe to inject.[82] Contrary to patterns in psychotropic drugs,
but reflecting patterns of alcohol use, street drugs are more commonly used by young men. Cannabis, the 'softest' drug, has
been used by about 20 per cent of young men and 10 per cent of
young women.[83]

Unlike alcohol and pharmaceutical products, the strength
of street drugs is impossible to regulate. Their illicit status
and source means their content and strength are unknown.
Fatal accidents happen all too often. Seven were killed by a
rogue batch of heroin in King's Cross, London in 1993. Four
died in 1994 in Bristol. Drug use of this kind courts unpredictable dangers: 'There was all this fear attached to drugs –
getting out of it on a bad trip or taking too much' (Ashley).
The underground status of street drugs also contributes to a
lack of information about their likely side-effects. Cheryl
found, to her cost, that the compounded effect of repeated
amphetamine use exacerbated the original feelings from
which she had sought to escape: 'I'd been taking quite a lot of
speed. I was very naive about drugs. I didn't realise the basic
depressive nature of them. I'd been taking sulphate and I kept
topping it up. I got into a terrible depression.' Drug use offers

a temporary release, but no resolution of existing problems.

In the 1990s the most striking development in the drugs scene has been the integration of the 'dance drugs' LSD and Ecstasy into mass youth culture, within a 'rave' dance scene now estimated to be a £2 billion a year industry involving one million young people a week.[84] This has occasioned an upturn in drug use among British youth: 'the relatively stable youth drug-use patterns of the mid '80s were disturbed in the late '80s, and . . . by the '90s there was increased use of established drugs like cannabis, solvents, amphetamines and magic mushrooms and an upsurge in the use of ecstasy and LSD'.[85] Between 1989 and 1992, admission of drug use doubled from 15 to 29 per cent.[86] Given the clear evidence that substance abuse increases suicide risk, the entrenchment of drugs within youth culture has proved dangerous.

Chemicals for coping

I was heavy into drugs at 14. I graduated from gas to cannabis, eventually leading to mushrooms, acid, speed and even snorting smack. I was in a constant drug haze from about 16 to 19. It was an escape for me. I needed something to sustain me. If I hadn't had that I would possibly have had a complete nervous breakdown.

(BARRY)

Drugs now play a prominent role in many young lives, used not only for recreation, but also for reducing anxiety and providing a temporary escape from depression. Abuse of alcohol and other drugs is frequently likened to a slow form of suicide. Their self-destructive element is evident in the vocabulary used by the young to celebrate their effects: 'Some favourites include "smashed", "wasted", "obliterated", "stoned", "wrecked", "shit-faced" . . . For some adolescents the goal is obliteration, to act upon oneself in such a way as to blot out one's conscious existence, at least temporarily to become insensate, unthinking, unfeeling.'[87] Barry felt he could not have survived, as an isolated gay adolescent, without anaesthetising himself with drugs. Serving a similar purpose for many young people, the overdose is the ultimate route to oblivion.

Young people who rely routinely on chemicals – whether alcohol, pharmaceutical or street drugs – develop resistance. A common response is to increase the dose. This dangerous strategy leads many, inevitably, towards the risk of overdosing. Different drugs may become, as Ashley found, interchangeable: 'I'd have took anything. I used to take tablets, mushrooms, glue, a little bit of butane, tranquillisers and alcohol.' The 'relief' of a chemical fix is increasingly short-lived and chemical dependence undermines young people's natural resources. Drug misuse now poses a considerable threat to the psychological well-being and physical safety of the young and there is compelling evidence of its association with youth suicide.

The Suicide 'Solution': Changing Attitudes, Images and Means

Changing attitudes towards suicide

At one time self-destruction carried with it some powerful disincentives – if the prospect of Hell did not put the would-be suicide off, the fear of prison might. But in recent decades suicide has undergone a rapid rehabilitation. The crime of the 1950s has become, in the euthanasia debate of the 1990s, an action affiliated to personal dignity. Suicide has become more acceptable. A benign concept of death, a loosening of moral prohibitions and an emphasis on personal freedom have combined to create relatively liberal attitudes. It seems likely that greater tolerance has reduced the number of psychological obstacles standing between young people and suicide.

Sin

> My mum always told me that if you killed yourself it was a
> really bad sin. But my parents also told me once you were

Born Again you were saved and you wouldn't go to Hell. But there was always this nagging doubt in the back of my head. If I hadn't had the religious dilemma I might have thought – get on with it.

(SUSIE)

As a Born Again Christian, Susie was unclear whether suicide would qualify her for eternal damnation. The fear that it might helped, for some time, to curb her self-destructive impulses. Religion may act as a buffer against suicide in various ways. The social life of the church, the belief that suicide is a sin or the fear of a punitive God might all keep suicidal feelings in check.

Active involvement in religion does appear to insulate some individuals against suicide but participation in religion has been waning in the United Kingdom for several generations. For centuries, the church's refusal to bury suicide victims on consecrated ground within its cemetery walls provided a mark of religious disapprobation. Now, for most, religious values and institutions no longer shape attitudes to suicide. A generation gap accounts for the recent shift in thinking. Parents are more likely to judge suicide in religious and moral terms, whilst their children regard it in terms of individual rights.[88] Liberal norms, of a secular bent, encourage acceptance of suicide. The exact influence of a more permissive cultural milieu is hard to fathom, but the European countries which experienced the sharpest drop in church membership, between the 1960s and mid-1980s, suffered sharper increases in youth suicide.[89]

Crime

They sat heavily but rather sympathetically by my bed and asked me questions they clearly didn't want me to answer. When I tried to explain, they shushed me politely. 'It was an accident, wasn't it, sir?' Dimly, I agreed. They went away.

(A. ALVAREZ, *The Savage God*)

Before 1961 suicide and attempted suicide were crimes in English law. Telling the tale of his own suicide attempt in the 1950s, Alvarez offers a glimpse of a procedure nearing obsolescence. In hospital, depleted by the effects of a large overdose, he received a visit from the police. Whilst his inquisitors were eager to be lenient, the presence of policemen at the hospital bedside reflected the criminality of his offence.

By the 1950s the suicide law was increasingly out of kilter with public opinion, and a medically led campaign for its reform proved influential. Nevertheless, those who attempted suicide were, from time to time, subjected to the ignominy of a public shaming in the magistrates' court. An unlucky few were sent to prison. 'You have been here before,' declared a magistrate in 1950 on sentencing a second-time suicide attempter to six months' detention, 'and we gave you every opportunity to go straight.'

In 1961 England and Wales became the last countries in Europe to decriminalise suicide. The term 'committed suicide' still hinted at felony, but suicide now passed into the hands of the medical profession. Medical status promised cures and prevention, and suicide became an object of pity more often than recrimination.

Self-deliverance

He was creating a space that was agony free and he had every right to do that.

(JANICE, MARK'S SISTER)

The 'right to die' is a peculiarly modern entitlement. It has gained ground in recent years through growing public support for euthanasia. Euthanasia – the bringing about of a gentle and easy death, usually in face of a terminal and painful illness – has been dubbed 'the issue of conscience for parliament in the 1990s'.[90] Essentially it challenges us to decide at what point, if any, someone is entitled to choose what Janice called the 'agony free' space of death.

Active euthanasia or 'mercy killing' remains illegal in the United Kingdom, but public opinion has shifted in its favour. Nearly 80 per cent of the public now believe that a doctor should be allowed to end a life, if a patient with an incurable and painful disease requests it.[91] In 1992, the conviction of a tearful Dr Nigel Cox for the attempted murder of a 70-year-old patient aroused a wave of public indignation. His trial, at Winchester Crown Court, became a euthanasia test case. Dr Cox's patient had suffered acute rheumatoid arthritis. The list of excruciating ailments, recited in court, left no doubt that the dying woman had been in unrelieved agony. A nurse described her howling with pain like a dog.[92] After repeated pleas from his patient, the hospital consultant finally gave her a lethal injection. During his trial the words of one defence witness had popular resonance. 'There are,' he said, 'things worse than death.'[93]

In modern medicine the Hippocratic Oath – by which doctors are bound to preserve life at all costs – has collided head on with the need for doctors to appraise their professional and personal role in the death of patients. The principle that life is inviolable is clearly under pressure. Life can become demeaning, many now believe, and death may provide respite. In 1992 the AIDS charity the Terrence Higgins Trust introduced the 'living will' to Britain, allowing individuals to state in advance whether they want their natural dying process speeded up, in the event of incurable illness, by the withdrawal of life-sustaining medical treatment ('passive' euthanasia).[94] For Barry, who is HIV positive, this is a reassuring development: 'It's the quality of life that matters. If I became seriously ill I might consider euthanasia as an option, which I suppose is suicide in a way.'

The right to choose one's own moment and method of death is supported by the euthanasia lobby only in special circumstances. But open discussion of conditions and techniques of dying reflect an increasingly liberal relationship with death. In August 1991 a book called *Final Exit*, a do-it-yourself guide to self-deliverance, topped the American bestseller list.[95] Addressing 'a mature adult who is suffering from a terminal illness and is considering the option of rational suicide, if and when suffering becomes unbearable', the book sold out of its first edition within a week. 'Rational' suicide was clearly topical.

There are likely to be losers, as well as winners, as taboos loosen. Extending the notions of rights and autonomy into thinking about death may make suicide appear a more legitimate option. Once suicide has been accepted as a solution to physical suffering, it may more easily be regarded as a solution to psychological suffering. Young men, in particular, are likely to regard suicide as an acceptable escape from terminal illness, pain and stress.[96] Once the distinction between physical and psychological suffering gives way, the concept of rational suicide may coincide neatly with 'logic' of the young and suicidal:

> *One night when he was very suicidal we talked about euthanasia. He asked me if I believed in it. I said I did in certain circumstances. He asked me what they were. I said something like – when life becomes unbearable. He said in that case would I help him to die, because his life had become unbearable. I was panicking, so I couldn't argue. Then I remembered about terminal illness. I said I only believed in euthanasia for the terminally ill, and he was not terminally ill. He said did I really think he'd ever get better? I said, 'Of course you'll get better. You won't always feel like this.' He looked at me, with that look in his eye, like I didn't understand.*

> (HELEN, MICK'S SISTER)

Media suicides

The modern media has ensured that revised attitudes to suicide are conveyed to mass audiences. Dramatically lucrative and rich in 'human interest', the portrayal of suicide has proliferated with the news and entertainments industry. Suicide is popular with television scriptwriters. Research in America found that adolescents have witnessed about 800 TV suicides each by the time they leave school.[97] With self-destruction such common currency in the modern media, concern has arisen about the role of imitation in young people's suicidal behaviour.

Learning through imitation partially explains why suicidal behaviour in a relative or friend leaves young people more susceptible themselves (see Chapter 2). The media spreads examples of suicide far beyond a small social network. Its persuasive powers are the *raison d'être* of the advertising industry and controversy has long centred on the suggestiveness of screen violence. The 1970s alone saw 2,500 studies of its impact on off-screen behaviour.[98] More often than not, studies reported an association between TV violence and children's aggression.[99] The power of the media to spread information about suicide, and loosen internal restraints against self-destructive behaviour, has created parallel concerns. Vulnerable individuals, anecdotes suggest, may be swayed towards action. As Maxine recalled: 'I'd seen this bit on *Romeo and Juliet* where Juliet stuck the knife in her, and I wanted to do it.'

The influence of one well-known suicide on others has been called the 'The Werther Effect'.[100] Werther, the romantic hero of a novel by Goethe, made his literary appearance in 1774, consummating his sorrows, sensibilities and unrequited love at gunpoint. Werther made despair distinctly fashionable.[101] He so moved the eighteenth-century reading public that Werther clones appeared, dressing as he had dressed and – as a spate of self-shooting by young men throughout Europe was attributed to Werther's example – dying as he had died. The clergy denounced Goethe's novel and the authorities in Italy, Denmark and Leipzig banned it.[102]

Modern Werthers are everywhere. Research over the last 20 years has suggested that news stories about suicide may well influence suicidal behaviour, particularly those reporting celebrity suicides.[103] In the month after Marilyn Monroe's fatal overdose in 1962, the American suicide rate increased by 12 per cent.[104] Janis Joplin and Freddy Prinze also proved influential.[105] Teenagers and young adults in particular appear vulnerable to imitative influences. An American study found that teenage suicide rates rose by 7 per cent following TV news stories on suicide, compared to only half a per cent among adults.[106] In

1986 the suicide of an 18-year-old Japanese pop singer, Yukiko Okada, was followed by a spate of suicides among Japanese adolescents, many jumping off buildings as the singer had done. Identification with a dead star – on grounds of age, sex or race – makes it more likely that someone will be swayed by their death.[107] The suicides of a young, Black, male singer and a middle-aged, white, female actress might be expected to encourage imitative behaviour in different groups.

As Werther first suggested, suicides do not have to be real to wield influence. In Britain, suicide attempts in soap operas and other popular dramas have kept debate about copy-cat behaviour lively. The BBC was criticised, in 1986, for encouraging suicidal behaviour after Angie overdosed in *EastEnders*. Drunk and distressed over husband 'Dirty Den's' philandering, a weeping Angie downed gin and pills in front of 14 million viewers. By the next episode she was back on Albert Square. Real-life medics were unimpressed. Casualty doctors in one hospital, fractious after pumping the stomachs of more overdosers than usual, complained:

> *Angie appeared to be in hospital for less than 12 hours; presumably she underwent gastric lavage (not shown) and when she was allowed home later that day she looked only slightly the worse for wear. Subsequently her wayward husband Den has appeared to be more in tow and Angie might rightfully consider the overdose to have had the desired effect.[109]*

Prime-time soap opera, they clearly felt, was modelling the overdose as an effective way of tackling marital breakdown. A study of 63 British hospitals found inconclusive evidence that overdosing had increased in the week after Angie's overdose, which allayed immediate fears.[110] But anecdotal feedback following other soap and celebrity suicides has kept doubts simmering since.[111]

Those investigating the media's influence on suicide have had to ask two questions. Firstly, does suicidal behaviour in the media, whether real or fictional, stimulate imitative behaviour?

There is strong evidence that it does. The second question must be whether this suicidal behaviour would have happened anyway; or does the media provoke acts that would not otherwise have occurred? There is evidence that the media may affect the real numbers, as well as the timing, of suicides. A German television serial *Death of a Student*, shown in the early 1980s, dwelt on the suicide of a 19-year-old in front of a train. Following its screening, deaths on the railways clearly increased, especially among young men of around the same age as the student.[112] Since suicide by other methods stayed at its usual level, and no slump in the suicide rate followed, the Werther effect appeared to have claimed victims who might not otherwise have died.

Young people are clearly affected by a milieu in which suicidal behaviour plays a familiar, sometimes romanticised role. Books, films, news stories and songs can provide both an emotional reference point and a source of information for those who are already feeling vulnerable. Barry was peculiarly sensitised, as a suicidal teenager, to references to suicide:

> *You keep an eye out for suicidal information – you're aware of it. The Police had a suicide anthem 'I can't stand losing you' about killing yourself. The cover of the record had an iceblock with an electric fire and a rope, so that as the fire melts the ice the rope tightens round your neck. I thought, someone else is going through what I am going through.*

The role of the media in rising suicidal behaviour among young people is undoubtedly complex. Liberal attitudes towards suicide clearly allow a more permissive approach to its portrayal in news reports and on-screen dramatisations. In turn, the young have become familiar with suicidal behaviour, picking up on its emotional subtext from an early age. Children nowadays *know* about despairing protagonists and bottles of pills. Occasionally a process of identification may be the emotional catalyst to action. The young are then likely to refer to a choice of suicide methods that the media has inadvertently helped to popularise.

Changing suicide methods

*Towards the time he died I noticed his car was getting a bit
dusty. There were even cobwebs on it. Normally he would
really clean it and shine it up.*

(CLIFFORD, EARL'S FRIEND)

The suicide rate is naturally affected by how easy it is to die.
Until domestic gas was detoxified in the 1960s the gas oven
was Britain's favourite suicide method. As poisonous coal-gas
was phased out, kitchens became safer places and the British
suicide rate fell.[132] The soporific effects of gas were not simply
exchanged for other methods. It seemed that for many the
more violent, lethal alternatives were unappealing enough to
curb suicidal urges. Technological changes introduce new suicide methods as they remove the old. If popular, available and
deadly enough, a suicide method affects the number of deaths.
The youth suicide rate seems likely to have been affected, in
recent decades, by the emergence of car-exhaust poisoning.
This method now accounts for one in four suicides among
British males under 25, and is the most common suicide
method among adult (15–44) males (see Chapter 1). Young
women use it less; it accounted for only one in ten female youth
suicides between 1988 and 1992. Carbon monoxide poisoning
is currently a 'male' suicide method and, as such, it has contributed, in recent decades, to the rising number of young male
deaths.

The casualties of change

Periods of rapid social and economic change may be costly in
human terms. At the end of the nineteenth century, Britain witnessed an epidemic of female self-poisoning, as demographic
and industrial developments brought major changes in
women's roles.[114] During the Great Depression of the 1920s and
1930s, mass unemployment and financial collapse saw suicide
climb.[115] Unprecedented rates of self-poisoning, again much of
it female, coincided with the rapid evolution of women's

domestic, social and working lives during the 1960s and 1970s. And between 1960 and 1985, throughout Europe, the social changes most strongly associated with the growth of suicide among the under-30s were rising rates of unemployment, divorce, murder, alcohol consumption, the increased number of working women and changing church affiliation.[116] These changes have had far-reaching implications for personal identity, social life and cultural expectations. Their pressures have been considerable and the victims of suicide and self-harm figure prominently among its casualties.

The changes and stresses of recent decades appear to have been hard on young people in general. Rates of suicidal behaviour among the under-25s, and their increasing vulnerability compared to older people, suggest the considerable hazards of modern adolescence. Many are losing their balance before they have found a footing: 'Teenagers often experience themselves as an entity within a darkened room attempting to discern boundaries and dimensions, confused and rather frightened by the lack of solidity, predictability, and clarity in their environment.'[117] Recent decades appear to have blurred boundaries and distorted dimensions more than ever. The decline of communal values has made the discovery of a personal creed, philosophy or status a more private process. Those things which give life some meaning and sense of purpose, which anchor us psychologically and emotionally, have become increasingly individualised.

Shifts in social and economic conditions, cultural expectations, social life and psychology may favour one social group over another. An ironic footnote to the cultural agenda of sexual equality during the 1960s and 1970s has been the rapid divergence of male and female suicide rates during the 1980s in the UK. Young women appear resilient, young men increasingly vulnerable. In part, these appearances are likely to be deceptive. Young women are certainly dying less often, but not for lack of trying. Many survive suicide attempts by chance, having chosen a suicide method that proved non-lethal. Nevertheless, the escalating suicide rate among young men suggests an appalling level of psychological distress and points to a costly male identity crisis, exacerbated by economic pressures, changing work and gender roles, uncertainty in relationships and high levels of drug use.

CHAPTER 4

Preventing Young Deaths

'We could not prevent suicide,' noted Norman Keir, 'without a total surveillance of all potential victims. Suicide reduction would be a more accurate term.'[1] Certainly the eradication of suicide would be a foolish goal for any society to set itself. Suicides will always occur, but the implicit assumption behind prevention work is that some need not.

Controversy in the suicide prevention debate rests with the 'preventability' factor. Optimists believe that at least some deaths are preventable. Sceptics are less convinced. Laudable intentions, they would argue, do not save lives and the effectiveness of suicide prevention work is unclear. Nevertheless, as suicide rates have risen, making self-destruction one of the leading causes of premature death in the UK, the debate about prevention has become more audible.

Suicide Prevention by Decree

In 1992 the Secretary of State for Health, Virginia Bottomley, launched the White Paper *The Health of the Nation*.[2] The document identified five areas of health associated with premature and preventable deaths – cancer, accidents, heart disease and strokes, AIDS, and suicide. On the assumption that clearly defined goals would focus the minds and resources of the health professions, targets have been set for reducing deaths in these areas. By the year 2000, the general suicide rate in England and Wales is to be reduced by at least 15 per cent, that of 'severely mentally ill people' by 33 per cent.[3] Youth suicide receives no special mention.

The Health of the Nation commitment to reduce British suicides represents a timely admission that suicide is a social tragedy as well as a personal catastrophe. Yet suicide prevention has not moved on to the public health agenda without signs of nervousness from policy-makers. The Scottish Health Department declined to set itself targets for suicide. In England and Wales their inclusion was touch and go, with target figures for reducing suicide penned in only after the consultative Green Paper of 1991. Such caution was not unwarranted. In the United States, youth suicide proved impervious to *Health of the Nation* style targets set for 1990. Embarrassed by its own forecast, the American Health Department set up a Task Force on Youth Suicide to investigate. In due course it reported that youth suicide is 'indeed a perplexing problem which, for health professionals and laymen alike, defies ready solutions'.[4] Target-setting reiterates the need to examine the scope and efficacy of measures to prevent youth suicide. These are considered next.

Education, Care and Prevention

Raising public awareness of suicide

He was talking about shooting himself. Or gassing himself. He kept saying about that last year. He didn't say himself, he was just talking. I think he knew he was mad. He had this thing in his head that people could hear his thoughts and feelings. He'd say to me: 'You can hear my feelings.' I'd say, 'No, I can't.' He'd say: 'You're lying.' He'd become paranoid. I thought it

was the drugs. Too much drugs. He had far too much drugs
and that was it.

(CLIFFORD, EARL'S FRIEND)

She'd just sit staring at the wall. She wouldn't see anybody,
she didn't watch TV, she wouldn't go out. I didn't know any-
thing about depression at all. I didn't know what the outcome
might be, how long it might be, did you go up and down. I
suppose I just thought she would gradually come up.

(ANDREA, SIMONE'S MOTHER)

So-called psychological autopsy studies, based on interviews
with the relatives and friends of young suicide victims, reveal
that suicide is often mentioned in advance. In addition many
young people clearly suffer serious mental health and substance
abuse problems in the time leading up to their death.[5] With the
tortuous benefit of hindsight, the bereaved recall having missed
the clues, threats and signs of vulnerability that might have
warned of suicide risk (see Chapter 5). Enabling the general
public to recognise this risk is vital to suicide prevention.[6] Only
30–50 per cent of young people who kill themselves have consulted mental health care professionals.[7] Young men – currently
at highest risk of suicide – are least likely to seek help from a
doctor or other professional.[8, 9] Since so many victims of youth
suicide do not reach the arms of professional helpers, opportunities for suicide prevention must be created closer to home.

In the USA in 1993, the Secretary of State for Health's
plans to spend $1 million on a 'public information campaign' to
discourage suicide attracted derision from some quarters, with
statements such as: 'It defies imagination how any intelligent
person can seriously believe that . . . exhortatory methods can
reverse the steady rise in suicides amongst young men.'
Leaflets and adverts alone cannot save lives, yet greater public
awareness of suicide risk could well avert some tragedies.
Where suicidal feelings and behaviour are poorly understood
many crises escalate unchecked as vital danger signals are
missed:

I would have been able to help Mark if I'd known more about suicide. He said to me once or twice he was going to commit suicide. One time he said he was going to blow his head off. What do you say when somebody says that to you? I didn't understand.

(JANICE, MARK'S SISTER)

Essential information about suicide risk and suicidal crises, as well as guidelines on how to respond to suicidal talk and how to seek further help, might help the general public to recognise and respond to the needs of vulnerable individuals close to them.

In 1992 a survey of public attitudes towards depression found a prevailing stigma attached to mental health problems/psychiatric disorders, with a presumption of their implying weakness, abnormality and instability'.[10] Such stigma discourages those who are troubled from seeking help and makes it more likely that mental health problems will be denied, or coped with in defensive ways:

Matthew certainly could have done with psychiatric help. But he would never have turned to a doctor in his depression. I don't think he saw himself as having a problem. He wasn't 'ill', but alcohol abuse and drug abuse were both things with him.

(LISA, FOSTER SISTER OF MATTHEW)

Lessening the stigma associated with depression and other psychological difficulties is important for suicide prevention. As long as mental health problems carry negative connotations, those who need help will be reluctant to admit their difficulties and seek support. Gareth avoided people for months in order to conceal the arm wounds he had inflicted during a suicide attempt: 'I just had to make sure that no one found out about it. To tell people was like admitting you were weak.' One of the aims of the Defeat Depression campaign, launched in 1992 by the Royal College of Psychiatrists, is to de-stigmatise depression through public education. Likewise The Samaritans' 1992 campaign, Tell It Like It Is, aimed to encourage young people to talk about their feelings. In conjunction with BBC Radio 1, a series of programmes were targeted at a younger radio audience and included discussions of depression and suicide.

Too general an approach to public education about suicide and mental health may be ineffectual. The Samaritans' Youth Outreach campaign has targeted the young with specially designed advertising campaigns. Over a quarter of first-time callers to The Samaritans are now under 25.[11] Recent education campaigns about HIV and AIDS have addressed the specific needs of vulnerable groups, such as young gay men and intravenous drug users. Education about suicide and mental health must also be adapted to various needs. The reluctance of young men with personal problems to seek help, or the vulnerability of young Asian women to suicide, stresses the need for educational initiatives which are sensitive to different social and cultural groups.

Schools and suicide prevention

I thought one of the things I had to do before I killed myself was to try and get help. I remember going to see Mrs Rothsmere. I would tell her how awful I felt. I got the feeling she never believed I'd actually do it. She would tell me there were all these things to live for. It used to reassure me for a while, but then I'd go down again and I couldn't understand why they wanted me to live. I thought if I was an animal they'd put me down.

(DEBBIE)

The Director of a suicide prevention centre in California developed an educational programme for teachers after visiting schools which had experienced the suicide of a pupil: 'On several occasions we were struck by how often teachers recounted information that could have provided clues to the suicidal act – if they had been aware of its significance.'[12] Teachers were often anxious about their ability to assess the danger posed by a child's professed suicidal feelings and unclear to whom they should report them. Basic training in how to assess the lethality of a child's suicidal intentions, and clarification of their individual responsibility, substantially boosted teachers' confidence in helping suicidal pupils. A school's first step towards suicide prevention might be to prepare teachers to cope with suicidal communications from pupils and to recognise other signs of suicide risk and depression.

Suicide prevention work in schools also involves pupils. Perceptions of its appropriate form have evolved with experience. In the USA, where the teenage suicide rate rose by nearly 300 per cent between 1960 and 1980, suicide prevention programmes in schools became increasingly common.[13] California and Florida passed laws making them statutory.[14] The general aim of school programmes has been to raise awareness of suicide and encourage vulnerable adolescents to seek help. Details of suicidal 'warning signs' are disseminated along with information about sources of treatment. School students, it is hoped, will then be equipped to recognise their own suicidal feelings or those of their peers.

These programmes are not without critics. There is a danger, they contend, in creating too sympathetic a milieu around suicide.[15] The stance of school programmes has tended to be that all teenagers are potentially vulnerable to suicide, given sufficient stress. Videotapes showing attractive, articulate adolescents talking about past suicide attempts neglect a more unphotogenic reality of emotional disturbance, depression and substance abuse. Given the suggestive powers of filmed materials, the mass exposure of schoolchildren to videos showing – for example – re-enacted suicide attempts, may be counterproductive. In one assessment study, adolescents did *not* seek help for emotional problems following a school programme, but a small proportion *did* move towards the view that suicide was a reasonable solution to problems.[16] There is a delicate balance to be struck between de-stigmatising suicidal feelings – in order to encourage young people to share them with others – and eroding the inhibitions that restrain suicidal impulses. It may well be that too specific, or indulgent, a focus on suicide is not conducive to suicide prevention.

A more general mental health education may be of greater value. Lacking the emotional insight that life experience brings, children and adolescents can have little perspective on their own moods and emotions. Depression may seem incomprehensible, fear inexplicable and frustration nameless and volatile. Education can go some way to compensate. It may be reassuring for children and adolescents to learn that 'depression has a beginning, a middle and an end. Coming out of depression can take just as long as entering it. What has taken months to build will take weeks, maybe even months, to heal.'[17] Basic skills for emotional survival might be promoted in schools – strengthening children's ability to cope constructively with disappointment, failure and rejection, *as well as* to court success and popularity. New programmes are now being developed which aim to increase the self-esteem of schoolchildren.[18] The teaching of problem-solving skills can help children and adolescents to evaluate the difficulties they face, communicate them effectively and find solutions to stressful problems.[19] Programmes of this kind can address the different styles of coping acquired by boys and girls early on in life, so relevant to their diverging rates of suicide.[20]

Those charged with the care of vulnerable children and adolescents cannot afford to wait simply for actively disturbed adolescents to surface with their problems. By taking steps to identify young people at risk of suicide, and securing help for them, schools might play a more direct role in preventing youth suicides. As school-leaving age approaches, time is of the essence. If suicide among young men, in particular, is to be prevented, schools must capitalise on opportunities to identify and help the vulnerable before they leave the education system and slip away from potential sources of help. In American schools, questionnaires have been used to identify adolescents in risk groups for suicide. Completed in class by 14–18-year-olds, the questionnaires mixed questions about depression, suicidal feelings, past attempts and levels of alcohol and drug use with more general health questions. Young people appeared willing to answer questions and those who appeared vulnerable were subsequently offered the chance to talk in confidence to a counsellor.[21]

This approach identified not only children who teachers already suspected were troubled, but others whose feelings had gone unrecognised. The Samaritans, who have consistently promoted school-based suicide prevention work in the UK, confirm that children report suicidal feelings in situations where teachers see no problem. Of 2,000 children who answered questionnaires in London schools, 10 per cent reported a previous suicide attempt, yet often the adults who knew them were totally unaware of the attempts.[22]

The extent to which individual schools promote the emotional welfare of their pupils will vary according to their ethos and policies. Positive anti-bullying measures help protect vulnerable children. Efforts to investigate truancy and encourage poor attenders back to class avert permanent 'school failure' with lasting consequences. Similarly, the long-term impact of traumas such as abuse and bereavement may be influenced by the support a school provides for pupils under emotional duress. The attitudes of schools to behaviourally difficult pupils are also vital. Disruptive behaviour often masks emotional vulnerability and the alienation of a child from the education system may prove costly. Suspensions and exclusions from school are a common experience among youth suicide victims.

Inevitably, school responses to the emotional needs of pupils are also affected by resources, staff workload and the level of local liaison a school commands with other professionals and voluntary groups. Teachers must be able to refer pupils who are at risk to appropriate help and support. The availability and quality of a range of local social and mental health services will therefore affect the prospects for effective suicide prevention work in schools.

Improved mental health care for young people

I went in and said to the doctor I was feeling depressed. She said, 'Oh, right.' She gave me the antidepressant tablets and that was it. I suppose it was really busy. There were queues of people outside waiting with real problems.

(MAXINE)

Identifying and helping young people who are depressed, suicidal, abusing drugs or suffering other serious mental health and emotional problems is clearly vital to suicide prevention.[23] So too is the quality of help available to vulnerable young people. One very commonly used source of help is the general practitioner (or family doctor). His or her skill in recognising and responding to depression and suicide risk is vital to suicide prevention, since it is usually GPs who treat mental health problems, including 95 per cent of reported depression.[24] Yet experience in mental health care (or psychiatry) is not, at present, a compulsory part of the GP's training.[25]

By the time Maxine, aged 17, visited her GP for help with depression, she was drinking heavily, neglecting food and taking frequent showers. Maxine's GP prescribed antidepressants with few questions asked. Neither the reasons for her depression, nor the possibility that she felt suicidal, was explored. Maxine had in fact recently been raped, following a childhood marred by loneliness, relentless bullying at school and sexual abuse by an older male cousin. Now she started taking antidepressants. With no other outlet for her feelings, Maxine grew increasingly frustrated and prone to aggressive outbursts. For the first time in her life she cut her arms and wrists, which seemed to numb her emotional pain and leave her feeling – briefly – calm. After one such incident she returned to her GP, who tended to her injuries tersely: 'She said that it was a stupid thing to do and asked me if I got on with my mum and dad. That was that.' Again Maxine was not asked whether she felt suicidal, and no appointment with a psychiatrist or counsellor was offered. The same night Maxine injured herself again. In the weeks that followed she felt increasingly alone and desperate. It was only when she began to fear that she might 'do something stupid' that she rang The Samaritans, who supported her regularly after that (see chapter 9).

Improving GPs' understanding of mental health problems and suicide risk is vital to suicide prevention. The Defeat Depression campaign is currently aiming to increase professional understanding of depression.[26] Training in the assessment of suicide risk is also needed if GPs and mental health workers are to be confident enough to broach, rather than evade, their patient's suicidal feelings. Suicidal behaviour arouses anxiety in doctors, as it does in others.[27] Half of adolescents who saw their GP in the month following an overdose reported that their suicide attempt was not discussed during the consultation.[28] Educational programmes about depression and suicide risk aimed at GPs have had positive effects on treatment elsewhere.[29] Sensitive treatment from a GP can provide vital support during a crisis, as Carrie found: 'Last year I went through a really bad patch. There were times when I could have tried killing myself again. I went to see my GP every week. I used to tell her how I felt. It was a relief that somebody else knew.'

Of course GPs' skills will make little difference to suicidal youth who steer clear of their surgeries. Young people do not seek their doctors' help for depression as readily as adults. Younger people (aged 15–34) are *less* likely than older people to ask their GP for help if they are depressed and *more* likely to ask a family member or friend.[30] Forty per cent think GPs are too busy to deal with depression.[31] Sadly, those who avoid doctors include some young people struggling alone with very serious difficulties. Recent British studies show that, amongst suicide victims, young men are *least* likely to have visited their GP in the month before their death.[32]

Walk-in services for those who want face-to-face help, and improved child and adolescent mental health services, have been identified as two areas of need in the prevention of youth suicide.[33] Also vital is close work between mental health workers and services helping young people who are dependent on alcohol and drugs. The flexibility of support for young people in crisis is crucial, as one bereaved mother emphasised:

> There's got to be more help available – there's got to be. And not the kind of help where they have to wait for an appointment in x amount of weeks. It won't wait at times, if you're mentally upset, will it?

(JOAN, JASON'S MOTHER)

Unfortunately, services supporting emotionally distressed young people *are* often besieged by long waiting lists. And these may be getting longer. In 1993 the National Association for Child and Family Mental Health, Young Minds, reported that 'a wide range of well-established, well-functioning and essential services are being cut or seriously threatened with closure'. If existing services are being undermined, the ideal of preventative work to promote mental health and avert youth suicides begins to appear a little fanciful.

Training of non-medical professionals

The need to help teachers recognise suicide risk has already been discussed. Beyond the education system are many other areas in which professionals have regular contact with people in crisis. Counsellors, social workers, prison officers, police, sheltered housing staff, women's aid workers, staff in unemployment offices and Citizens' Advice Bureaux are all employed in areas where they will encounter a relatively high proportion of vulnerable individuals. Training programmes in suicide awareness are needed for these professional and voluntary groups.

It seems likely that knowledge of groups which are unusually vulnerable to suicide should be used to target professionals and volunteers in special need of training. Workers in services helping young people with alcohol and drug problems are prime candidates for training. So too are those counselling and supporting vulnerable minority groups – such as young Asian women or young gays and lesbians. Following the rapid rise of prison suicides in recent decades it became apparent to the Home

Office that prison officers required training to improve communication within the prison system and to identify vulnerable prisoners. Much of the groundwork for general suicide awareness training has already been done. Thousands of Samaritan volunteers have already received comprehensive training, in preparation for answering the phone to suicidal callers.

Reducing opportunities for 'copy-cat' behaviour

In 1948 the British Medical Association proposed a ban on press reporting of suicide inquests, making public its suspicion that such coverage might encourage other suicides. Caution has been vindicated by the research evidence of recent decades, which suggests that young people may be highly susceptible to media portrayals of suicide and suicidal behaviour (see Chapter 3). A general code of practice relating to media portrayals and reporting of suicide has recently been called for:

> *It is highly desirable that the dramatic reporting of suicides be replaced with simple factual reporting, that television producers should seek help from experts before including suicidal behaviour in programmes, and that such programmes should be followed by adverts for helplines and other means of obtaining assistance.*[34]

In its *Producer's Guidelines*, the BBC already warns television and radio producers that reported suicides may encourage others.[35] The guidelines urge moderate reporting and stress that details of suicide methods should be omitted.

Crisis Intervention to Save Lives

Improved help for young people who attempt suicide

> *My dad got the doctor. I remember going really woozy and drowsy and slurry and my lips were purple. I said: 'I've just*

*had a couple', and that was that. The doctor left. I was not
taken to hospital or pumped out. I had to take quite a long time
off school because it was decided I'd had a nervous breakdown.*

(CHERYL)

*I was taken to hospital. They cleaned me up and gave me a
talking to. They said: 'It's not really serious, but don't do it
again, because we'll get in touch with the police if it happens
again.' I don't know if they were trying to frighten me.*

(GARETH)

Much research has been devoted to discovering which groups
are at highest risk of suicide. The *raison d'être* for such enterprise
has been suicide prevention. The suicidal must be identified
before they can be helped, and knowledge of high-risk groups
can help to do this. One highly vulnerable group of people are
those who have made suicide attempts in the past (see Chapter
1). The quality of care and support given to young people who
attempt suicide will therefore play an essential role in the prevention of future youth suicides.

Cheryl took an overdose when she was 13. The family doctor visited her at home and asked her how many pills she had
swallowed. Ashamed and frightened, she told him she had
taken only a couple. In fact, she had taken considerably more.
The GP left, asking no more questions. Cheryl was neither
referred to hospital nor asked about her suicidal feelings and
intentions. Neither the physical nor psychological risks implicit
in her overdose were adequately assessed.

The treatment meted out in hospital casualty departments
may also be poor. Each year thousands of young people end up
in hospitals having taken overdoses or harmed themselves, as
Gareth did. They arrive in busy and crowded accident and
emergency departments, staffed largely by nurses and junior
doctors who may have no mental health training. Patients do
not automatically see a psychiatrist, and in many hospitals there
is not even a private room available to talk with patients about
their suicide attempt. Despite the indubitable evidence that they

111

will be at high risk of future suicide, they are often dispatched from hospital with inadequate plans for their care.[36] Many receive little more than physical first aid.

At its worst, the 'care' given in casualty may, in itself, be emotionally damaging. A brusque reception at such a time can alienate a young person from the very services responsible for their follow-up care. In a recent television interview a doctor recalled the attitudes he imbibed as a medical student. The person who attempted suicide was generally regarded as 'a complete waste of time', and 'taking a bed that a real sick person should be in'. Training in the care of the suicidal – and this doctor was young enough to typify the current generation of hospital consultants – appeared to be based on a crude notion of deterrence:

> *When I was a student in casualty I was taught to give people who'd tried to commit suicide a hard time – 'If you're washing them out, or giving them a stomach pump, you give them a hard time because then they won't do it again.'*

Unlike many young people who are at risk, those who attempt suicide and seek medical help make themselves known to professionals. They come within reach of help, but many are let down. Neither Cheryl nor Gareth received adequate care after their first suicide attempts. Their problems remained unresolved and they both went on to make more dangerous attempts later on in adolescence. The only evident effect of their contact with medical professionals was decreased faith in them. The academic understanding that young people who attempt suicide and harm themselves are at high risk of suicide in the future is now well established. It can only help to save lives when it is put into day-to-day practice in hospital casualty departments and general practice.

The Samaritans and crisis services

> *I went out in the afternoon and got drunk. When I came back I rang The Samaritans. I said: 'I can't handle it' and spurted out*

112

*all this rubbish. They were really good. They put me in touch
with Alcoholics Anonymous.*

(ASHLEY)

In the UK, 24-hour telephone support for the suicidal, and face-
to-face befriending, is provided by The Samaritans. Over the last
40 years the organisation has developed a national policy and a
uniform procedure for the selection and training of its volunteers, who now number 22,400. Each local Samaritans' branch, of
which the UK has 200, is advised by a consultant psychiatrist.
Yet independence from formal services is carefully preserved,
and respect for callers' anonymity upheld, in order to encourage
contact: 'Many of those at the highest risk of suicide never come
into contact with any of the services designed to help them:
through a combination of fear and mistrust they seek support
from those who are perceived to be different from professionals.'[37] Nevertheless The Samaritans will, as in Ashley's case,
encourage callers to seek further help where this is needed.

The Samaritans' respond to around 2.5 million contacts a
year in their 200 centres – one contact every 12 seconds. About
half of these come from men and, from a sample of branches, 22
per cent of first-time callers are under 25, 7 per cent under 15.
The Samaritans are very concerned about the growth in youth
suicide and undertake to reach people in this and other vulnerable groups. The figures suggest that the offer of confidentiality,
anonymity and time to talk may encourage young people over
their reticence about seeking help. Youth-orientated advertising,
as well as visits to schools, has heightened the Samaritans' profile among the young (see Chapter 9).

Developing support for groups at high risk of suicide, but
ill-served by existing services, is also crucial to suicide prevention. The Samaritans' Prison Outreach policy provides an
innovative example. Volunteers visit prisons to talk to vulnerable inmates and, in conjunction with the Home Office, help in
the training of prison staff. A Listeners Scheme is currently
being developed which selects, trains and supports prisoners
who will befriend emotionally distressed inmates. Other crisis

services for vulnerable groups, who might not otherwise receive support, are needed.

The impact of suicide prevention centres and crisis phone-lines on the suicide rate has not always been clear. One American study found that suicide prevention centres reduced the suicide rates of young, white females only.[38] Another found that the presence of a suicide prevention centre in a city did *not* reduce its suicide rate.[39] American services do, however, vary in their principles and practice, providing an assortment of tele-phone hotlines and drop-in centres for those in crisis. In contrast, The Samaritans have developed a national service and strategy. Between 1963 and 1975 their branches increased from 41 to 165 and the suicide rate in England and Wales fell by a third.[40] It is certainly plausible that the arrival of The Samaritans *helped* to prevent suicides, especially among women, although detoxification of domestic gas must be held largely responsible (see p. 120).[41] Nevertheless a study of British towns with and without Samaritans'[41] branches found, in the 1960s, that the sui-cide rate dropped in towns with a local service.[42]

Controlling access to suicide methods

On the Tuesday he got another big bunch of drugs. They shouldn't give them so many antidepressants. They should give them four days at a time or something – not big boxes of them.

(PHYLLIS, TOMMY'S MOTHER)

Sceptics would argue that if you remove one means of suicide from someone who wants to die, they will simply find another. Yet the commonsense intuition that people will substitute one method for another is not borne out by the evidence. In 1962, 2,469 suicides in England and Wales were caused by domestic gas poisoning. By 1974, when coal gas in British homes had been replaced by non-toxic fuel, this figure fell to 50.[43] There was no simultaneous increase in suicides by other means. The British did not substitute other methods and the UK suicide rate consequently dropped at a time when rates were rising elsewhere in Europe.[44] Restricting access to popular suicide methods, this story suggests, may well save lives.

Just *why* different methods are preferred is not fully understood, but choices are likely to be influenced by fear of pain and disfigurement, as well as easy access and effectiveness. Some people will undeniably be so determined to die that they will use any means possible. But many more are ambivalent about dying and act relatively impulsively.[45] An accessible and dangerous suicide method rapidly turns impulses into fatalities. Young people's suicidal behaviour is more impulsive than most. In the United States, where access to guns is widespread, half of teenage suicide victims shoot themselves.[46] Many young deaths could be prevented, it has been argued, if gun-control laws were introduced.[47]

In the UK it is the control of drugs that is more relevant to averting youth suicides. Those who take overdoses often do so relatively impulsively, using whatever drugs are at hand.[48] The more toxic drugs around, the more fatal overdoses are likely. During the 1960s, barbiturate drugs were widely prescribed for anxiety and sleeplessness, but proved to be highly dangerous in overdose.[49] The suicide rate among young women has been associated with the availability of these drugs.[50] As GPs reassessed their prescribing habits and safer tranquillisers became available, fatal overdoses became less frequent.[51] Prescribed drugs now account for far fewer suicides. Nevertheless, careless dispensing may still cost lives. Tommy (above) died from an overdose of antidepressants; his mother wondered at the quantities her son received on a single prescription. Research suggests that limits on the number of tablets permitted per prescription may decrease the suicide rate, a finding which corroborates her concern.

The supply of prescribed drugs is obviously easier to control than drugs which can be freely bought in supermarkets and chemists. Over-the-counter drugs are now being used more often in overdoses, claiming growing numbers of young lives. Of greatest concern is paracetamol. Widely sold in non-prescription medicines, this drug, in relatively small overdoses, can cause a slow and harrowing death from liver failure. Many young people, reaching for the 'headache pills' during a crisis, will be unaware of their deadly potential. However, it seems that the danger posed by over-the-counter drugs *can* be limited. In France, deaths from paracetamol overdoses fell after sale of the drug was restricted to packets containing a maximum of 16 tablets.[52] Calls for similar controls have been made in Britain, where paracetamol is still sold in large quantities.

The substitution of less dangerous drugs is also important in preventing fatal overdoses. Safer antidepressant drugs are, for example, now available to replace the old tricyclic variety that killed Tommy. Yet many GPs continue to prescribe the older, cheaper and potentially lethal drugs from a combination of thrift and habit. 'Our advice has consistently been that doctors should prescribe the anti-depressants which are less lethal in overdose,' one specialist commented in 1992, 'but the impact of this advice in this country has been minimal.'[53] Safer substitutes for aspirin and paracetamol are also available, but they are considerably more expensive. Price also obstructs another solution – the possibility of manufacturing toxic drugs with antidotes or emetics.[54] More simply, the public might be encouraged not to hoard unwanted drugs.[55]

Another UK suicide method with potential for change is car-exhaust poisoning. In 1993 catalytic converters became a requirement for all new British cars, drastically cutting carbon monoxide emissions. Few young men drive brand new cars. But with time, this technological development will obstruct youth suicide. The introduction of similar controls on car exhausts in the United States coincided with a reduction in suicides by asphyxiation.[56]

Restricting access to suicide methods does nothing to address the underlying causes of suicidal crises. In effect it only plays for time and inhibits self-destructive impulses. But since so many suicidal crises are short-lived, ambivalent and impulsive – especially among the young – time and inhibitions can save lives.

Constraint and sanctuary

I suppose they could have hospitalised me before I did it, if they wanted to prevent it. I see why they do stop people. Society doesn't let you just kill yourself. The nurses used to say to me: 'It's just because you're ill, you won't feel like this for ever.' I don't know, really. I have mixed feelings about it. I couldn't get away. There was somebody with me all the time. I don't know how I coped. In fact, I didn't have any choice.

(CARRIE)

Carrie was prevented from killing herself at 16, when she was legally detained for six months in a psychiatric ward. Her suicidal feelings were intransigent and coincided with debilitating depression. For much of her time in hospital she wanted to die, yet she had no choice but to stay alive. She was under constant surveillance on the ward and had no access to suicide methods.

The assumption that people ought to be stopped from killing themselves, by any means necessary, begs certain ethical questions. Suicide prevention may be biased towards preserving life at a cost to liberty. To deprive someone of autonomy certainly erodes personal freedom and dignity, yet it may also provide safety and reassurance. Autonomy can be deeply threatening to someone in the grip of suicidal feelings and fantasies. Whilst Carrie felt extremely ambivalent about her involuntary stay in hospital – resenting its coerciveness – she recognised the protection it provided. 'Although I hated somebody being with me all the time,' she recalled, 'it was very safe. I was very scared of myself and of my feelings when I didn't have anybody with me.' Many young people's enduring suicidal feelings are fear, confusion and ambivalence. Their crises are often short-lived. Even though Carrie was more determined to kill herself than most, her desire to die abated with time. Constraint and a place of safety ensured her survival in the mean time.

117

Suicide prevention in the community

Current government community care policy aims to transfer the provision of care for people with mental health problems from large institutions into the community. During the 1980s many of Britain's Victorian psychiatric hospitals were gradually closed. Since these monolithic institutions had come to be associated with stigma and incarceration as well as care and sanctuary, this process was welcomed by many. The vision of community care offered promising alternatives. Mental health problems were to be disassociated from the stigma and alien territory described in Kate Millett's *The Loony Bin Trip*.[57] Hospital care was now to be reserved only for the most acutely distressed, vulnerable and disturbed. In future, most of those suffering mental health problems were to remain at home, receiving help from community-based mental health teams. These included thousands of former long-stay psychiatric patients returning to live in local communities, supported by local services.

Yet the enlightened philosophy of community care has been dimmed by the reality of massive underfunding. Hospital closures have been poorly synchronised with the development of alternative care programmes and provision of housing for former patients has been dismally inadequate. Between 1980 and 1990 the average number of beds available daily in long-stay hospitals in England fell by 27,000. The number of places in local authority, private and voluntary hostels and homes increased by only 5,840.[58] A London survey found that one in eight former psychiatric patients was discharged to a homeless persons' unit or 'no fixed abode,' and Shelter reports that a growing proportion of the homeless are mentally ill.[59] The swelling prison population has been linked to the loss of psychiatric beds, suggesting that some are swapping the streets for the prison cell.[60] In 1990 the House of Commons Social Services Committee found the government's community care policy to be underfunded and poorly planned.[61]

Suicide risk is now one of the most common reasons for admission to psychiatric in-patient care, but finding one's way

118

on to a hospital ward has become more difficult. Patients are discharged speedily due to drastic reductions in the numbers of hospital beds.[62] Yet it is known that in the weeks after leaving hospital, ex-psychiatric patients are at particularly high risk of suicide.[63] Clearly, community care has major implications for suicide prevention. It has moved many people at risk of suicide from hospitals into the community. Only high-quality, accessible services will ensure their safety.[64]

Ideally, community-based support for the suicidal could have many benefits for individuals in crisis. Support in a familiar home environment reduces the fear and stigma associated with hospital treatment: 'I thought they'd cart me off to a mental institution. I thought I'd be sedated and strapped down or something. I was really frightened' (Gareth). Autonomy can be preserved at home, and personal resources and social support encouraged.[65] Yet there are also risks involved in community care for the suicidal. Nine-to-five, Monday to Friday services make it more difficult to ensure the safety of individuals whose suicidal feelings may fluctuate rapidly.[66] As the 'asylum' of a hospital stay becomes rarer, families and friends will more often be involved in protecting the actively suicidal from their own impulses:

I heard the back door go. I was half asleep. I was so tired, because I work nights and you get really shattered, but I got up to investigate because I knew he was really depressed. I put my dressing gown on and went out there. He was just coming in. I said, 'Where do you think you're going?' He said, 'Never mind, mum, just go back inside', and he picked up the car keys. I said, 'Jason, you're not going anywhere.' Luckily I realised what he was going to do. I tried to stop him and he was pushing past me. He was going down the path towards his car and I knew he was determined. I was screaming at my husband – 'Get out here and stop him!' I ran out in my dressing gown and slippers. Jason was in his car starting it up. My husband overtook me, stood in front of the car, yanked up the bonnet and ripped off one of the plug leads, which stopped the

car. Jason jumped out of the car and ran up the road crying . . .
(JOAN, JASON'S MOTHER)

Such desperate scenarios become more likely with an under-resourced and patchy mental health service. Currently, a substantial proportion of people with serious mental health difficulties are experiencing inadequate community care. Young people diagnosed as schizophrenic, known to be at very high risk of suicide, are a prominent example: up to 80 per cent may not currently have a community psychiatric nurse.[67] Between 1991 and 1993 the National Schizophrenia Fellowship identified 164 suicides among people diagnosed as schizophrenic. Of these, 13 per cent had died within a week of leaving hospital and 7 per cent were not found for up to five days after dying. Many extremely vulnerable individuals are currently falling through the community care net *and* losing contact with the mental health professions. Through major underfunding of community care, the government may have shot its own suicide prevention strategy in the foot.

The question of scope
The Health of the Nation has deposited suicide prevention in the 'Health' tray of government, yet suicide rates reflect a host of pressures, many of them beyond the orbit of health policy. Substantial changes in the British suicide rate have been driven, this century, by major social upheavals and flukes of technology. During both world wars suicides dropped notably, as the grim cohesion of the war effort distracted despair. In between, the economic and social disintegration of the Great Depression saw suicide climb.[68] Developments in technology – the arrival of natural North Sea gas in the 1960s, the growth of a modern car culture – have massaged the suicide rate in one direction or another by removing or providing popular suicide methods, as have changes in pharmacology.

Evidently the vicious spirals of despondency that lead young people towards suicide will feed on pressures which health professionals are helpless to alleviate. To reduce youth suicide substantially, underlying societal pressures must be eased. Psychological suffering is intensified by unemployment and homelessness. Economic pressures strain relationships. As sexual politics and power bases shift, social support networks are changing. And some young people face additional stresses. Racism and homophobia contaminate the quality of some young lives, as do negative social attitudes towards people with disabilities or mental health problems. Improvements in health care alone are unlikely to halt increases in youth suicide. Ideally, policies to prevent suicide should address the social causes of hopelessness, alienation and depression alongside the symptoms.

The success of suicide prevention work is hard to prove. Suicides that do not happen generate no data. However, there is some positive evidence in support of suicide prevention. Between 1980 and 1987 American states which launched preventative policies – such as inquiries, task forces, advisory groups, manuals and leaflets – in general experienced a slower increase in youth suicide rates than other states.[69] The remedies for suicidal despair among the young are likely to be as complex as its causes. Nevertheless, it appears that whilst prevention initiatives will not procure U-turns in youth suicide, they can save some young lives.

—— Part II ——

Responding to the
Young and Suicidal

CHAPTER 5

On the Suicide Threshold

The Suicide Spectrum

Somewhere in the region of 44,000 young people under the age of 25 turn up each year in the casualty departments of general hospitals throughout the UK, having injured or poisoned themselves. These self-destructive actions arise from a range of motives and emotional states. A desire to die motivates some, but by no means all of them. The diversity of behaviour that gestures towards suicide is disorientating, yet its interpretation is essential if young people in crisis are to be understood and helped.

News of a suicide poses ominous questions. A common reflex is the need to know whether a young person really *meant* to do it. This element of choice gives suicide its peculiar potency and draws us, moth-like, to the dead person's state of mind. What were they thinking when they made this final, deadly choice? Did they realise that their actions would end in death? Did they really wish to die or had they hopes of rescue? Intentions are crucial to the psychological meaning of the act. We have an intuitive need to understand them in order to make some sense of what has happened.

Naturally enough, the paradigm of the 'genuine' suicide attempt is often used to interpret the behaviour of young people who, in moments of desperation, take overdoses or injure themselves. Was this a *real* suicide attempt, onlookers may ask, or was it just a cry for help? Unfortunately the logical assumptions behind this question – firstly that young people who 'attempt suicide' *know* what they want, and secondly that what they want is *either* life *or* death – are often inappropriate to the confusion of young people who behave self-destructively. Those who overdose or injure themselves are often afraid and desperate, states which do not encourage clear thinking. After a 'suicide attempt' young people may find their actions difficult to explain or even comprehend and a desire to die may seem to have had little to do with it. Those who *have*, at times, longed for death or contemplated suicide, may be uncertain that they really wanted to die as a result of a 'suicide attempt'. The constant play of conflicting desires, trivial or momentous, that seasons our emotional life, extends to suicidal ambivalence when crises deepen. The desire to die is a mercurial element. Varying between individuals, fluctuating over time and intensifying during a crisis, it frequently conflicts with a desire to go on living.

The tenuous link between self-destructiveness and death may make it difficult for some young people to fathom their own behaviour. Actions not intended to be lethal and not, therefore, strictly suicidal may still convey connotations of suicide and death:

> *I tried to commit suicide four times. I slashed my hands,*
> *wrists and arms. I just felt so much mental pain inside. When*
> *the blood came out it felt like all the pain coming out. I felt*
> *calm. I still don't know whether I was trying to kill myself or*
> *just hurt myself. Later someone told me it was impossible to*
> *kill yourself that way. I think maybe I just really, really*
> *wanted to hurt myself.*
>
> (MAXINE)

Maxine associated self-mutilation with suicidal behaviour, and since suicidal behaviour invokes death, felt that she had tried to 'commit suicide'. Despite her assertion she was confused –

aware that her injuries had not been life-threatening and uncertain whether or not she had wanted to die. She had, she recognised, wanted release from intolerable anger and tension, and cutting herself provided it. With hindsight she felt it may have been this release, and not death, she was after.

As Maxine's experience suggests, self-harm is often preceded, not by thoughts about dying, but by a build-up of intolerable tension.[1] As one survivor of sexual abuse observed: 'Self-harm is not about suicide, it is about surviving and getting through each moment.'[2] When powerful feelings of anger, frustration or despair threaten to overwhelm, this survival strategy provides a way of maintaining control. Ironically, physical self-harm can also function as a form of emotional pain relief or numbing, which offers a temporary release from the grip of threatening emotions. For Debbie, self-harm became a regular way of discharging her feelings and calming herself:

After the rape I began to cut myself. It wasn't a suicide thing at all. I kept away from my wrists because that suggests suicide, so I used to cut my arms. And it helped. It was a relief. When my brain went into overdrive it just helped concentrate all the pain on my arms. It got to be regular once I had discovered it. It was almost constant. I used to let one arm clear up before I started again. Occasionally I would give up and just do my whole body. I still do it. I still get days where I get absolutely mad and very upset and I can't show it to another person. So I cut my arms with a razor blade.

In a similar way, young people may overdose as a desperate survival strategy, swallowing pills as some people down alcohol – to temporarily escape or blot out intolerable feelings of misery and anxiety.[3] At 19, Claudette took an overdose not 'in order to die', but in a bid to obliterate depression:

I wanted to try and change that feeling. I wanted to end the depression. Depression's a pain that you don't feel with – it's kind of weird. Maybe I wanted to feel pain. Women slash and

burn themselves from the need to feel a different kind of pain.
You can express that pain. I just wanted to make something
change.

To escape the noxious ache of depression, Claudette took an overdose to gain relief from intolerable feelings. Her predominant feeling was not 'I want to die', but 'I can't cope with this any more.'

As John Eldrid of The Samaritans has said: 'It is ironic in this age of extensive technical communication . . . that so many thousands of people, especially young ones, feel they can only communicate their inner emotional distress through taking overdoses.'[4] Functioning as an SOS flare, when other forms of communication fail, such behaviour signals the inability to cope. It is in this communication that the transformative promise of overdosing or self-injury often lies. Making a young person's unhappiness and needs explicit, the actions may exert pressure on others and help to produce longed-for changes in life.

Somewhere between one-fifth and one-third of young people who take overdoses – which accounts for the vast majority of young people's suicide attempts – say their goal was death.[5] Yet in all other cases young people say that they overdosed meaning to survive or they did not care whether they lived or died.[6, 7] Like throwing the dice, the overdose often leaves things in the hands of fate, making this a risk-taking strategy that might be dubbed a gamble with death. The motives behind the acts we call suicide attempts are anything but uniform, although all involve a wish to escape or change a current state or situation. The gamble between death, and a life which is a little improved, a little changed, a little closer to happiness perhaps, may seem a risk worth taking if the present feels intolerable.

Irresolute motives may be as perplexing to young suicide attempters themselves as they are to others. Following her overdose Karen became *less* certain of her own motives:

Looking back now I don't know if I did want to die. At the time I was convinced that I did. Now I think: Did I? Or did I just want out of it for a while? I didn't know what I wanted. I knew what I didn't want.

The suicide attempts of some young people are motivated by a clear wish to be dead. Lorraine wanted to die for some months before she finally took an overdose, aged 20. After a childhood marred by her father's alcoholism and violent behaviour, Lorraine's older sister was killed in a traffic accident. Whilst she was living away at college Lorraine coped, but two years later unemployment forced her to move back to her family's home. There, surrounded by memories, she was finally overwhelmed by the fact of her sister's death and slipped gradually into a depression from which there seemed to be no relief. When she attempted suicide, Lorraine's only concern was to escape relentless emotional pain:

It's a terrible thing when you wake up in the morning and you don't want to be alive. I genuinely wanted to die. It's just something you can't get away from. Life seems so pointless. You can't ever see things getting better. You cannot think about the pain you might cause anybody else. That's not even a consideration, because you feel so unimportant in yourself you don't think it will affect anyone else. I didn't want to be here. I was sure I'd die.

The motives of young people who overdose or injure themselves are wide-ranging. The *suicide spectrum* comprises the range of actions which carry connotations of suicide. At the near end of this spectrum is self-harm, often regarded as suicidal gesturing. At the far end is that unambiguously suicidal behaviour motivated by a desire for death. In between lie actions spurred by the highly ambivalent, volatile and confused motives of most young people who poison or injure themselves. The strength of a young person's desire to be dead – what doctors call their *suicidality* – increases across this spectrum. It is a desire which may be subject to peculiar distortions among the young. The suicidal motives of children and adolescents are closely involved with their developing understanding of death.

Young People's Ideas about Death and Dying

I had an image of little demons dressed in black. I used to lie awake all night thinking about it. I had nightmares when I was a kid – monsters and fires and things. I used to think a lot about this hell business. As I got a bit older I thought: it can't be this fiery pit. That's too childish. I thought Hell must be like a grave; like lying awake all day in a grave. Heaven was a big green field with pink cherry blossoms, with lots of people singing.

(SUSIE)

Gleaning an understanding of death and dying is one of life's more pensive necessities. All children and adolescents think and fantasise about death as part of their natural development. Young children regard it as a temporary state, like sleep, and have difficulty comprehending its causes and finality.[8] Whilst death brings separation, this is not always understood to be lasting. Children invariably visualise death as similar to life.[9] The dead mimic the living – eating, drinking and playing with toys, perhaps – but they do so in a new location. The question, 'where do people go when they die?' reflects a need to clear up the logistics. The somewhere else of death may be associated with Heaven, Hell, the sky or underground places.[10] Cheryl recalled trying to make a telephone call, as a child, to her dead grandmother: 'She had died and the phone was disconnected, but I thought I could get through.'

Between the ages of about five and ten children begin to recognise the possibility of their own death, and the death of people around them, but they have yet to grasp its finality.[11] Death is not understood to arrest consciousness and children

130

define death through concrete associations. Having relinquished a picture of Hell peopled by demons, Susie (above) visualised death as 'lying awake all day in a grave'. Death also tends to be personified as a hostile external force – the monster, bogeyman or witch that comes to get you – rather than an internal biological process which brings about physical cessation and the interruption of experience.

The permanence of death is not usually fully understood until early adolescence. Half of children aged 6–11 in one study believed death was reversible.[12] Yet as the capacity to think more logically and grasp abstract concepts develops, adolescents come to understand that death lasts for ever. The end-point in an internal biological process that ends in the arrest of bodily functions and conscious experience, death is understood to be irreversible and universal.[13] The average adolescent comes to understand the finality and biological causes of death by the age of 13.[14]

Conceptions of death are naturally subject to cultural influences and religious dictates. In the absence of spiritual consensus or prescriptive teachings, today's children and adolescents must develop a personal understanding of death with relatively little guidance. The raw material from which they must derive this understanding is often perplexing. Contemporary taboos taint the subject of death with morbidity, and contact with the real thing is relatively limited. Yet the abundant screen deaths of modern entertainment appear as rewindable as the video machine: 'Television and the movies regularly depict reversible, clean deaths as characters are killed in one show and reappear on another.'[15] Despite these decoys, the scientific consensus of Western culture proposes that death brings physical and psychological cessation.

Yet for many adolescents more contentious death lore offers the prospect of immortality. Only 20 per cent of 13–16-year-olds, in one study, saw death as total cessation and the same proportion thought they would still be cognizant when dead.[16] In another study, one in five 15–16-year-olds retained an element of fantasy, most commonly reincarnation, in their thinking about death.[17] One in three British adolescents (aged 12–18) believes in life after death and one in three believes in Heaven and Hell.[18] The ideas a young person holds about death will clearly influence its allure. Where Heaven is a big, green field with cherry blossoms there may be every reason to go there.

Desiring Death

I knew I wouldn't go to heaven, but I imagined I'd be alone – not with other people tormenting me. Because I used to be really bullied at school by the boys.

(MAXINE)

Death was a state where there was no tension, where everything was fine. It was just the end of trauma, the end of being upset and of crying and having to live with these horrible people. It would stop this racing round in my head and it would have just been sleep and I'd be going to Heaven.

(CHERYL)

Death may appear desirable because of what it is *not*. As a child, the thought of death was comforting to Cheryl because it offered a negation of life's pain and conflict. Similar in her mind to the restfulness of sleep, sweetened with vague afterthoughts of Heaven, death offered an escape. But it was largely her feeling that life was intolerable that made her consider the alternative enticing. The desirability of death has a symbiotic relationship with the undesirability of living.

A child's attraction to death may be expressed in statements which are not explicitly suicidal – 'I'd be better off dead' or 'I wish I would die in my sleep.' Susie desired death long before she began to consider the possibility that she might take her own life:

My mum had had two miscarriages and I thought, I wish I'd been one of those miscarriages. I was going round all day

*wishing I was dead. I really wanted to die. I prayed to God
every day: 'Why don't you give me an illness and just let me
die?' I'd wake up and think – 'I'm still here.' I was really disappointed to wake up alive.*

(SUSIE)

Susie's desire for death expressed itself passively at first. Active
suicidal fantasies came later.

As one might expect, suicidal children are more preoccupied with death than others. Thoughts and dreams linger on
their own imagined death, the deaths of family members and
how people die in general.[19] Not only is death a greater concern
to such young people but it is perceived to be more benign:
'Many suicidal children believe that death is a temporary, pleas-
ant state that will relieve all tensions.'[20] A study of
13–16-year-olds in the USA found that those with frequent
thoughts of suicide were more likely than other children to
believe in the reversibility of death and/or to believe that they
would remain cognizant after they had died.[21] By contrast, non-
suicidal children are more likely to understand that death is
final.[22]

It is not merely immature thinking or intellectual confusion
that causes suicidal children to idealise death while others hold
a cooler view of it. Psychological functioning changes under
emotional pressure, changes which are reflected in perceptions
and reasoning. Prior to her first suicide attempt at 13, Cheryl's
misery and fear about the deed she was contemplating brought
about an uncharacteristic interest in a compassionate God. This
allowed her to reason away some of her worst anxieties about
suicide:

*I started to think about Christianity, missing out the big
chunk about not taking your life. I thought God will understand, because he's seen how this family operates. He'll know
that I can't survive this, and the world is too frightening and
people are too cruel.*

Associating it with understanding and concern, Cheryl was able to cushion herself against her natural fear of death.[23]

Under pressure, young people's perceptions of death may fluctuate, to the extent that their basic understanding becomes distorted. A child who has understood in happier times that death lasts for ever may lose sight of its irrevocability when distressed: 'Suicidal children may understand that death is final, but when stressed they begin to believe that death is temporary.'[24] The emotional meanings associated with death – punishment, reunion, separation – change with a young person's experience and emotional needs.[25] Lorraine became deeply suicidal two years after her sister's death. She suspected death was 'nothingness', but the possibility that it might reunite her with her dead sister fed her suicidal resolve:

> *I think death is just like nothing. But I was thinking I might*
> *catch up with my sister somewhere. That wasn't why I did it,*
> *but that was in my head. I thought, 'It would be all the better*
> *if she was there.'*

Being attracted to death does not mean that a young person does not at the same time fear it. To overcome this fear as suicidal ideas are formulated, death may become idealised. Infused with new emotional meanings, death becomes more attractive.

Idealising death and dying allows suicidal fantasies more freedom. Those working with suicidal children have noticed that their suicidal impulses grow less when their idealised ideas about death are challenged by more realistic ones. The real thing may be more frightening, and fear can protect.[26] Half an hour after taking an overdose Debbie was overwhelmed by panic: 'I was almost hysterical with the actual physical fear – what is going to happen between now and death?' Her instinct was entirely appropriate. 'Humans,' noted one writer, 'are hard to kill.' If not fatal, suicide attempts can, and do, end in disasters short of death for many individuals. Permanent brain damage, a broken back, respiratory failure, coma and organ damage are some of the more appalling outcomes of non-fatal suicide attempts. Yet in preparation for a suicide attempt young people must overcome or deny their own anxiety about dying. Barry perceived overdosing as the gentlest of releases: 'It seemed a really clean way of doing it – you just go to sleep and don't wake up.' Susie betrayed little sense of the physical havoc that must be wrought on a young and healthy body to rid it of life: 'I'd heard of people dying of alcohol poisoning. I thought drinking would be a nice way because it makes your head all floaty.' A relative ignorance of biology may aid the young in their evasiveness.

Running Out of Answers: the Suicide Solution

A young person's attraction to death is nurtured by how he or she feels about life. Debbie was a deeply depressed 12-year-old when she took a large overdose. Like many young people who attempt suicide, she had been struggling to cope with her feelings and problems for some time prior to her overdose. Yet none of the strategies by which Debbie tried to improve her lot proved to have a lasting effect. Her suicide attempt represented an end-point in an unsuccessful search for other, less desperate solutions:

> *The bullying started off as being spat at and then it got to being beaten up occasionally. I didn't want to go to school ever. I remember my parents just saying, 'It's not that bad – you'll have to go.' And my brothers used to beat me up. They got bullied at school, so they bullied me in turn. I know everyone beats up little sisters, but they really used to beat me up. Nobody ever told them to stop. There was never any kind of protection. I used to lock my door and just sit in my bedroom.*
>
> *I used to get very depressed and I couldn't cope with being awake at night. I didn't feel like lying awake all night. Really, I couldn't cope with anything. I used to drink and just fall asleep. They had a wine cellar. Between the ages of 9 and 12, I*

drank the wine cellar. They must have known. You can't lose 50 bottles of wine and not wonder where it's gone.

I was pretty big. One day I was sitting there eating this big bag of crisps. I was shovelling them into my mouth. And suddenly I realised I eat like that. I don't know why – for comfort probably. At the age of 11, I put on three stone, very suddenly. You get so much abuse for that. And I was going out a lot to nightclubs. I can't believe I got away with it at that age. I was 12 but I looked older. I used to lie and say I was going to stay with my friend. We'd go out and get drunk. I remember men trying it on. People would say – 'There's that girl again . . .'

It felt like I was a mistake – that I shouldn't really have been here at all and that was why I was so unhappy. I was aware of being very ugly. I thought I was very stupid and unattractive, in every sense of the word. I just felt worthless and hated myself.

I thought one of the things I had to do before I killed myself was to try and get help. I really tried, but I couldn't find it. I remember endlessly going to see [a teacher]. I cried a lot. I would tell her how awful I felt and she would tell me there were all these things to live for. I got the feeling she didn't believe me.

But they sent me to a psychiatrist before I tried to kill myself. I told him everything. I sat down and said, 'I feel like committing suicide and I think I'm going to do it. Please help me.' I remember feeling really terrified, but I just thought I should tell him. I thought if there was something wrong with me, if I wasn't thinking straight, he would tell me. I had two sessions with him and then he said: 'Everything's fine. She's a normal, healthy little girl.'

They don't take you seriously. I thought – I've tried everything. What more can I do? I'd been building up to it for a long time. I just couldn't handle it any more. I remember one time I was at school and I just exploded and started screaming at people. I said: 'If I was a dog you'd put me down.' I used to think that it was just because I was human that they wanted me to live. The only reason they wanted me to live was because

they were so scared of death. It seemed that nobody could make
an attempt to understand.

I was trying to see if there was any reason at all that I
should live and I couldn't find one. I did feel angry and
deserted. I had that feeling that nothing's ever going to get bet-
ter. It was in February and you know how cold and dark it is
then. I had real trouble sleeping before the suicide attempt. I
used to stay awake till dawn, which is really depressing. It was
really logical the way I thought about it. I remember writing
lists with the pros and cons of each one – slit your wrists,
jump off a bridge . . .

By the time of her overdose Debbie had exhausted her ability to
cope and felt powerless to defend herself against the anxieties
and hurts of living. She attempted suicide when she had 'tried
everything' and run out of alternatives. Hiding in her bedroom,
pleading with her parents, drinking alcohol to sleep at night,
bingeing on comfort food, getting drunk and going out to clubs,
confiding suicidal feelings to a teacher and eventually a psychiatrist – all failed to stop the bullying, rescue her self-esteem
or offset the depression which eventually became unbearable.
Suicide now appeared to Debbie to be her only remaining
option. Withdrawn and depressed, she planned a suicide
attempt.

The sense of powerlessness described by Debbie is common among young people who are suicidal. Struggling to cope
with problems and feelings that will not go away, often in isolation, a young person will feel increasingly helpless. Those
who attempt suicide, in general, appear to experience the events
and feelings in their life as less under their control than others.[27]
As the struggle to cope becomes increasingly uphill, strategies
for maintaining control become more desperate.

Usually adolescents develop coping skills – or ways of handling stress – between the ages of about 11 and 15 and these
often stay with them long into adult life.[28] Some of these soothe
anxiety, express pain and release tension in ways that ultimately
prove destructive. Alcohol and drug use, fighting or crime,

daredevil risk-taking, social withdrawal, self-starvation or bingeing may generate a new set of problems – chemical dependency, personal rejection, isolation, punishment. Amongst the most dangerous ways in which young people may strive to cope will be thought and behaviour which is explicitly self-destructive. The coping strategies developed during adolescence may come to *include* self-harm, suicidal fantasies, talking of suicide and, finally, acting. Suicidal behaviour may represent a desperate 'solution' to all problems, but a solution nevertheless. In *Suicide: The Forever Decision*, Paul Quinnet observes:

> *Suicide is a solution. No matter what anyone tells you, suicide does solve problems, at least your problems. And if you succeed it solves them once and for all . . . Once you are dead nothing can hurt you anymore. Once you are dead you are beyond feeling bad . . . Whatever pain you are in, it will end just as soon as you stop breathing.*[29]

As young people grow more despairing, and as their self-esteem slips with their sense of control, suicidal 'solutions' become more comforting and attractive.

Suicidal Thinking: Fantasies and Motives

> *I see myself lying in the casket. I am in my blue dress and my hands are folded over my chest. I can see my parents and friends around me. They are crying.*[30]

The punitive childish fantasy – 'You'll be sorry when I'm dead' – reflects a child's growing awareness that death has an impact on others. It exerts extraordinary influence and commands full attention.[31, 32] It may be used aggressively to punish others and to demonstrate power. In a distressed child, the growing awareness of death may cultivate suicidal motives. Anticipating a leading role at her own funeral allowed the young girl above regular gratification.

The idea of his or her own d̶... son for a number of reasons. It may o̶... with someone loved. It may seem to be a̶n̶... quillity. Dying may offer a rare chance to wi̶... anger, retaliate for abandonment. It can be a punish̶... oneself or others. And undeniably, death makes a stu̶... statement. Others are forced to look in its direction and copiou̶s̶ amounts of love and attention may be visited on the dead. As children become more aware of death and suicide they natu-rally incorporate new perceptions into their thinking. Although some younger children *may* be deeply suicidal, suicidal thoughts, fantasies and desires become far more common from around 12 years of age. As the capacity to appreciate despair develops during adolescence, the insight that death may end suffering and intercept the unbearable flow of consciousness, becomes more pertinent.

Fantasising about suicide may become a way of compen-sating for reality, overcoming, in the imagination, threats and circumstances which are unyielding in real life. Cheryl gained comfort from her suicidal fantasies because they were an expression of a power that eluded her in reality. Defying help-lessness, she preserved a tenuous grip by reminding herself that it was *she* who controlled whether she lived or died: 'I have the power to terminate it if I want. I know I can take control and it's the last thing I have to take control of.' Barry felt his regular fan-tasising about suicide, during early adolescence, provided both an exemption clause for failure and retribution against those who had left him feeling neglected and isolated:

> *I just saw it as a way out; a cop-out from everything. If I couldn't do my schoolwork I'd think, 'Well it doesn't matter, because I'm going to commit suicide next week.' And I felt angry as well, because no one could see. How on earth could I be going through the most profound, acute torment that I'd ever experienced and they were all blind? It seemed like they didn't want to see it. I used to sit there in class and think of ways to do it. It was like the words of that song: 'You'll be*

...ay diminish painful states.
...al behaviour and may be the
...tain a sense of control over their
...is far more common than suicidal
...ent of adolescents are reported to
...consideration at least once, suggest-
...cide are common enough at times of
... American schoolchildren 8.9 per cent
rep... ...ation, compared to 2 per cent who had
either tr... ...icide or made attempts.[34]

Young pe... ...e who cope through suicidal ideation are extremely vulnerable. Suicidal fantasies may be comforting but since they nourish suicidal motives and foster active impulses, this is a highly dangerous source of consolation. Savouring death or imagining the effects of suicidal behaviour on others may provide temporary reassurance. Yet suicidal fantasies may grow less potent with use and, if a young person's circumstances do not improve, the temptation to enact fantasy will grow.

Suicidal Talk

Once he said he was going to kill himself. And one time he said he was going to blow his head off. He didn't really mean it at the time. But in the back of my mind I thought – why is he saying that? It played on my mind, but I knew that he wasn't going to get up that moment and kill himself.

A lot of people say they're going to commit suicide because they want someone to help them. It's their way of saying 'Help me.' They don't really want to commit suicide, but if no one's going to help they'll have to, because that's the only way they can cope with their problem. Because Mark was such a deep person he couldn't turn round to me and say, 'Janice, please

*help me.' So he did it in a way which I didn't understand. He
said he was going to commit suicide, but I knew he wasn't
going to do it.*

*This time I could tell in his eyes. He had a frightened look.
A very frightening look. It was frightening me and he was also
very frightened. That was why I knew he was going to do it,
because of his fear of what he was going to do. He was petrified
I think. He was petrified that he was going to do it. He kept on
repeating himself, saying: 'I'm going to commit suicide, I'm
going to commit suicide.'*

(JANICE, MARK'S SISTER)

As Janice suggests, young people may verbalise their suicidal
desires and preoccupations in the hope of eliciting care, attention and help from others. As the suicidal process intensifies,
those with explicit plans may threaten suicide. Six months
before he shot himself Mark talked about doing so to his sister.
At this point, the suicide threat lacked urgency and seemed so
improbable that Janice, aged 17, was left feeling uneasy but certain that it would not be carried out. In the short term it was not.
But on the day of Mark's death he again spoke of suicide. This
time Janice, alone in the house with her brother and a gun, was
left in no doubt that he meant it. His fear of what he was about
to do was palpable and spilt over in his words and manner.
Mark took his life soon after. In the months following her
brother's death Janice felt, with the torturous benefit of hindsight, that Mark's earlier talk of suicide had been a plea for
help.

Clues, warnings, threats are commonly given by those who
are suicidal to people close to them. Talk of suicide may be indi-
rectly expressed, since shame, guilt and fear of rejection forge
strong prohibitions on such communications. Comments which
express the view that a situation is hopeless, that there is no way
of solving one's problems and that life has no meaning may
indicate suicidal thinking. Unfortunately oblique warnings are
often overlooked. 'I can't take any more', 'What's the point?'
'You wouldn't miss me', are not the remarks of happy children,

141

but they do not immediately suggest suicide. Warnings may be similarly obscure, only recognised as such after a death. On the day of his death 20-year-old Steven turned down an invitation from his sister to come to dinner saying, 'I shan't be coming Viv. I shan't be here.' As his mother Lillian recalled, they assumed he had already arranged to go out, 'because we had no idea he had thoughts like that. No idea at all.' Yet many young people make quite explicit references to their self-destructive feelings and intentions. Feelings – 'I want to die' – and plans – 'I am going to kill myself' – can be expressed very directly.

Suicidal talk may often be a sign that the suicidal process is escalating. Reaching out to others, through hints, warnings or threats, is common before a suicide attempt. It may only be as a young person becomes more frightened and unable to cope that desperation drives them to offend the taboos which forbid talk of suicide (see Chapter 7). Yet it is also vital to recognise that many young people will be extremely wary of sharing suicidal feelings. Some young people anticipating suicide will *not* talk about it, because secrecy allows them to maintain a vital sense of control. For Cheryl: 'It was a comfort to have a private solution. It was my little box of tricks. It was the last thing I had to take control of and I never discussed it with anyone.' For Carrie suicide was a similarly private consolation. The drugs she secretly kept in her bedroom made her feel safe: 'I know that I've got enough tablets to kill myself if I wanted to. I have these tablets in my room.' And for some, silence may reflect determination to go through with it. The wish to die may be so strong that they simply will not risk the intervention of others. The majority of young people who take their lives however *do* express their suicidal feelings and intentions beforehand (see Chapter 6).

Suicidal Plans

He was talking about suicide, kind of jokingly. Me and a friend were in his car and he was saying: 'The best way to kill

142

*yourself is gassing.' I said: 'No it ain't. The best way to kill
yourself is pills.' I thought he was just talking. It's unbeliev-
able – only 19 – a good friend of mine. Then he actually said he
was going to kill himself. He said he was going to jump off a
tall building.*

(CLIFFORD, EARL'S FRIEND)

As suicidal feelings intensify they may give way to concrete
plans. Suicidal talk may escalate into suicide threats, driven by
despair and depression, anxiety or anger. This planning stage,
revealed in Earl's preoccupation with the different suicide methods available to him, marks the final, highly dangerous stage of
the process. Nevertheless, many youth suicides do not appear to
be the product of such advance planning. A suicide attempt
can be a carefully planned action, or one that occurs with a sud-
denness that takes even the attempter by surprise.

Acting on Impulse

*I don't think it was planned, but it wasn't an accident. He did-
n't fall off. He might have gone up on the balcony to see what
it felt like, but when he got there I think he knew what he was
doing. I think certainly in another situation he wouldn't have
done it. It was definitely something he needn't have done that
night. That night was certainly arbitrary.*

(LISA, MATTHEW'S SISTER)

*Something came to a head very quickly that day. It was a very
spontaneous thing she did. I think she did it in a fit of anger.*

(PATRICIA, ELAINE'S MOTHER)

A suicidal urge may culminate in death with terrible rapidity.
Studies of youth suicide confirm the impression that these
deaths can be highly impulsive. Young people leave less evidence than older men and women that their death was
planned and premeditated. Suicide notes are rare, methods

143

chosen are usually those close at hand, and precautions against being caught in the suicidal act are not generally taken. Particularly among the youngest victims, suicides may appear to have been rapidly conceived, often carried out in anger shortly after a 'last straw' event.[35] These events themselves are rarely very different from those experienced by adolescents in general.[36] An argument with a parent, separation from a girl-friend or boyfriend, a disciplinary incident at school or a failed school exam might all be considered relatively normal occurrences. It is the reaction of the young person which is extraordinary.

Research suggests just how quickly a crisis may escalate towards suicidal behaviour. The time spent planning a suicide attempt is often a matter of minutes, rather than hours or days. In one study of young people who had taken an overdose, fewer than half of those recovering in hospital said they considered the overdose for more than 15 minutes beforehand.[37] Only 8 per cent thought about it for over 24 hours.[38] In another study, few children's overdoses (5–7 per cent) showed evidence of premeditation, and these tended to be amongst the most depressed and suicidal.[39] Precariously balanced emotions can tip very quickly towards wanting to die or harm oneself, just as they can tip very quickly back again. Grabbing a razor blade or a bottle of pills may even be spontaneous. Explosive reactions to stress occur when a young person is already in an emotional danger zone, feeling out of control and unable to cope. In this context, a final blow to self-esteem may take a young person to breaking point and precipitate a tragedy.

Yet suicides are not *so* impulsive as to have left no time for self-destructive feelings to have spilt over into threats and warnings. Young people who try suicide are likely to have gone over the idea in the past, a thought process that has been called a 'cognitive rehearsal' for suicidal behaviour.[40] They may have fantasised about suicide, imagined its effects on others, wondered which method they would choose and the circumstances in which they might use it. A suicide threat or warning suggests that such a 'rehearsal' is going on. Although interest in suicide may subsequently wane, as life temporarily improves, it can quickly re-ignite during a fresh crisis. A suicide attempt may then occur with little apparent planning. Six months before his death, Lillian's 20-year-old son Steven said of his girlfriend: 'You know, mum, if I lost Jacky, I'd kill myself.' He was never to refer to suicide again, but when he perceived his relationship with Jacky to be in jeopardy, he took his life without further warning. Similarly Elaine confided suicidal feelings to a teacher in the weeks before her death, although her final decision to act appeared very rapid.

Suicidal Danger Signs

That last Saturday he said to me, 'I want to be free. I want to be free.' He had tears in his eyes. When he said he wanted to be free I thought he meant free of college, of work. I put my arms round him and gave him a hug. And he suddenly said to me: 'I'm just having a last go on my computer. I don't want it any more. And d'you think you can get rid of my leather jacket?' I said, 'Why me? You can sell it. It'll give you a bit of money.' He said to me, 'I've written it all down.' And he did leave a letter. But when he said these things I never thought he was going to take his own life.

(ANGELA, TERRY'S MUM)

Suicidal young people do *not* fit an identikit list of warning signs, since their depression and despair has many guises. One adolescent's vulnerability may be masked by angry and defiant behaviour, another's may resonate with the subdued hopelessness more commonly associated with despair. The contrast between impulsive and premeditated youth suicides suggests the difficulties of generalising about suicidal crises. Nevertheless a number of warning signs may help identify young people who are moving towards a life-threatening crisis. **Talk of suicide** is a common one. More rarely a young person may **give away possessions**, as Terry tried to do before his

145

death. This putting in order of personal affairs suggests a very imminent danger. So too may a sudden **lift in mood**, following a long depression. On the night of his death Nicole went to the pub with her brother Jason. After months of depression, his mood was noticeably lighter than usual: 'I didn't think it was particularly unusual. I was just relieved. There hadn't been any [good moods] for so long.' Sadly, after prolonged emotional pain and struggle, deciding to kill oneself may bring a sense of relief, lifting the spirits of someone who has been intractably depressed for months.

The link between youth suicide, depression and other mental health problems (see Chapter 2) suggests how vital it is to identify young people who are becoming increasingly distressed and isolated by emotional problems with which they cannot cope. **Signs of depression** therefore double as danger signals for suicide. Yet the testimonies of bereaved relatives provide constant reminders that the vulnerable are easily camouflaged at this time of life. Changes in mood and behaviour are expected in adolescence and few young people move from childhood to adulthood without bouts of 'teenage blues' and attacks of self-doubt. The depressed adolescent may not immediately stand out from his or her peers: 'We didn't think he was that depressed. We thought – typical young person – up and down'; 'There was probably just a sense of withdrawal. But as a mother I know that that's part of the growing-up process. You've got to give them their space'; 'Now with hindsight I would say he was depressed, but before I just thought he was becoming a moody young man.'

Common signs of more serious depression may help to distinguish a young person who is becoming dangerously vulnerable. By the time she took an overdose, aged 12, Debbie had stopped sleeping at night and was struggling to function socially. She became increasingly isolated at school and her appearance changed.

I'd got very withdrawn. I almost stopped talking. I mean, they must have known something was going to happen. There was

*a change in my behaviour. I just got really quiet and talking
was such an effort. If someone talked to me it was almost like a
physical assault. I couldn't really handle it. And everything I
wore was black. I just didn't wash my hair. I had greasy hair
and my clothes got black.*

**Social withdrawal, changing sleep patterns, lethargy, loss of
interest and concentration problems, changes in appetite or
weight, neglected appearance** are common signs of depression.

Debbie's depression was a self-blaming spiral, which
sapped her energy and gave way to hopelessness. At the same
age, Karen was expressing her misery very differently, directing
her anger outwards, at those who had hurt her. Karen's father
died when she was 13, shortly after she was sexually abused by
an uncle. In the aftermath of his death she was suicidal. Her
subsequent rebellion was, she felt, a reaction to the acute sense
of loss and abandonment these events left her with:

*I just changed. I became this totally outrageous person. I felt
one of the crowd and secure in that feeling. I felt really big,
proving to myself that I could take care of myself. We were a
crowd that were smoking at school and going out and getting
pissed. I just didn't care. The number of pubs I got thrown out
of for being under age. And I was sleeping around. I think it
was a response. I think if my dad had been around I wouldn't
have dared do it. But everything I'd been brought up to
believe, honour and value had just gone to pot. Like my dad
being around to protect me. With him, if I did anything wrong
I was going to get in trouble for it, whereas with my mum I
just didn't care. I think I felt – people have really hurt me and
they're not going to hurt me again. I'll do what I want, thank
you very much.*

Certain signs of depression and suicidal depression may
unfortunately be regarded by others as symptomatic of adolescent rebellion or bad conduct rather than deep

unhappiness. **Excessive drinking or drug-taking** may reflect an adolescent's need to escape overwhelming feelings and relieve depression, yet this may not be recognised. When a young person gets conspicuously drunk, plays truant from school, fights and bullies, steals, gambles or generally 'acts up', his or her vulnerability may be masked whilst others become increasingly disapproving and alienated. The vulnerable 'troublemaker' may receive short shrift. Expressed aggressively, depression may appear to be something else entirely. Research suggests that mental health professionals may often overlook the despair of suicidal adolescents whose behaviour is aggressive and defiant, whilst recognising the kind of internalised, resigned depression described by Debbie above.[41] Yet anger and defiance do not exclude vulnerability to suicide. They merely reduce the likelihood that a young person will be helped.

Finally, suicide may occur just as a young person appears to have been 'getting better' following a severe mental health crisis. Young people suffering with severe depression for example, experience not only an intensification of suicidal thoughts and intentions but loss of energy and listlessness which makes it hard to act upon them. As depression lifts, a return of energy makes it possible to put self-destructive feelings into action. Another young person – perhaps suffering with schizophrenia or manic depression – may have lost touch with reality during a crisis (psychosis). Improvement may make him or her aware of what has happened. Restored insight may bring with it fear and a cruel sense of hopelessness about the future. The months after discharge from psychiatric hospital are known to be a high-risk time for suicide.[42] A young person emerging from a mental health crisis will remain extremely vulnerable for some time to come. Carol imagined how her brother Jake felt as he emerged from psychosis: 'You're realising you've gone right over the edge. You've temporarily lost your sense of self ... And it all gets reinforced – that you're sick, you're ill.' The complexity of the recovery process should not be underestimated.

Suicide Attempts:
Meaning to Die and Knowing How

*I did act, it was just in a very naive way. I didn't have the
information. I remember being in my room crying and trying
to suffocate myself with my pillow. I was eight or nine. I
remember on a number of occasions trying to force myself to
stop breathing.*

(BARRY)

I took some seeds because I'd heard they were poisonous.

(DEBBIE)

*I have often thought of a variety of ways of killing myself such
as the guillotine. I would go to France and have it done. (A 12-
year-old, quoted by Cynthia Pfeffer in* The Suicidal Child)

Meaning to die and knowing how are distinct, and the need to
draw this distinction is nowhere more vital than in responding
to suicidal behaviour among the young. Children and adolescents are unlikely to have a sophisticated understanding of how
to kill themselves. There may be a wide gulf in young minds
between deadly intentions and lethal know-how. Yet it is only a
matter of time before comprehension of death and dying
matures and a vulnerable young person gains a better technical
understanding of death. If the wish to die remains intact, a
lethal suicide attempt becomes more probable as their know-
how increases. Debbie and Barry experienced suicidal feelings,
at times very intensely, from childhood onwards, but their
'naivety' about suicide methods precluded serious damage. Yet
their suicidal desires left them at increasing risk as they grew
older. Both went on to attempt suicide during adolescence, having had time to acquire more knowledge.

Some young suicide attempters mean to die but survive.
Others mean to survive but end up dead. The severity of the
physical damage sustained during a suicide attempt does *not*
necessarily reflect the strength of a young person's commitment

to dying. In her study of young people who took an overdose Sally O'Brien observed: 'Whether people actually died or survived did not depend on how determined they were to die.'[43] Among the young, suicidal gestures not intended to be fatal may backfire with devastating results. Children and adolescents are unlikely to choose drugs with any knowledge of their pharmacological properties. Most younger children who overdose use tablets found at home. The chosen drug is the one within arm's reach, as in Barry's case: 'There were always pills in the house, left over from when my mother died. No one had ever got round to throwing them out.' Given the huge variation in the toxicity of drugs, taking an overdose is, for most young people, a chemical Russian roulette. In hospital receiving treatment for liver damage, the survivors of paracetamol overdoses, many of them adolescents, were asked by researchers what they knew about the drug. Few had known that it was dangerous to the liver and most said they would not have taken the drug if they had realised what its consequences would be.[44] In circumstances like these, the young are particularly liable to lethal 'accidents'. *Any* act of self-harm or attempted suicide in the young must be regarded as extremely serious.

CHAPTER 6

Perceptions of the Suicidal: Unthinkable Fears, Comforting Myths

'Adults,' observed one counsellor of suicidal adolescents, 'harbour an almost pathological aversion toward recognising that young people intentionally end their lives.'[1] Subsisting on taboo, denial and understandable fear, this aversion cultivates a number of myths and misconceptions. Some of these are straightforward fallacies, perpetuated by our natural fear of self-destruction. Others have a footing in truth, but one that slips easily away into misconception. The danger, if these myths prevail, is that self-destructive feelings become impossible to communicate. Faced with the incomprehension of others, the young and suicidal find themselves dangerously isolated. Left alone they are more likely to resort to the last form of expression available to them.

Taboo

People would avoid the subject of his death. They passed on a sense of fear. I felt like I carried an infection they were frightened of. It was perhaps their own fear too, of that element of self-destruction in themselves. Or maybe that his death seemed like a defeat. Someone I was very close to and loved very much was a defeatist. He'd done the ultimate human crime of leaving life. Their shivering away hurt – their inability to say anything – not even to say 'I'm sorry.'

(CAROL, JAKE'S SISTER)

Bereavement provides harsh insights into the taboo that surrounds suicide. Carol was 18, and a student, when her 20-year-old brother killed himself. Returning to college after his death, she sensed fear, embarrassment and judgement amongst her peers and tutors. All knew of Jake's suicide, yet almost without exception his death went unmentioned.

Death is often said to have superseded sex, in contemporary Western culture, as *the* late twentieth-century taboo. People now live longer. Premature death is a rarity. Confined to hospital beds, the dying are often unseen, and when death does come, our repertoire of mourning rituals is limited. A century ago high mortality rates made the death of a child a relatively common event. In many parts of the world it still is. But in Western industrialised nations, enjoying relative affluence and advanced health care, most parents now find the prospect of losing a child unthinkable. As health and longevity have reduced contact with death and the dying, they have also established an imaginative impasse between death and youth. Long life is now an expectation, dying young a rare tragedy. The barrier of disbelief erected by such modern certainties is the first obstacle facing the young and suicidal.

The second is the formidable taboo surrounding self-destruction. Suicide has always inspired fear. Down the centuries, and across cultures, a grim catalogue of punishments has been devised to degrade the corpses of suicides, outwit their ghosts and disinherit their families.[2] The brutal treatment of 'self-murderers' in previous eras says something of the fear and hostility aroused by suicide – a crime against God and State.[3] Nowadays self-destruction evokes pity as often as outrage. Widespread sympathy for euthanasia suggests that suicide may now be acceptable in certain circumstances, if only for the terminally ill. Taboos against 'playing God' with human life have been significantly eroded by a concern to alleviate suffering. But despite changing attitudes, suicide in the broader sense remains at least unacceptable, at worst a transgression.

Judgements of suicide tend now to be relative to its circumstances and consequences. Suicide may be disliked for the damage it inflicts on others. It leaves the bereaved with a cruel kind of grief, often marked by stigma, guilt and torturous self-questioning. Suicide ends one person's suffering, but at a price. As Lisa put it, in a hypothetical question to her dead sister, 'Couldn't you have stood it a bit longer? Because the effect of what you did was so completely devastating. It *might* have got better. Why didn't you look beyond that?'

Suicide defies our most fundamental social rules and emotional bonds. It shows the obligation to go on living to be only as binding as individuals allow. In retaliation it may be reviled as an 'easy way out', resented for cheating fate and evading responsibility. Yet the suicidal person's last action shakes us, by rejecting so much. Its message, an implicit condemnation of the world left behind, is a potent one. This particular life, it suggests, had no value; lacked meaning; was too painful to sustain. Both the lonely desperation of the decision to die, and the action which extinguishes life from a healthy body, leaves behind a profound sense of shock.

Two powerful taboos, death and self-destruction, find their most unacceptable incarnation in the suicide of someone young.

Fear and Hostility

Suicidal feelings and actions in someone close to us are deeply threatening. We fear for their safety and we fear for ourselves. The real possibility of serious injury, or death, can create psychological panic. Andrea's daughter Simone first tried to kill herself by driving into a wall. Visiting her daughter in hospital afterwards, Andrea lost control:

> *I was really angry with her. I went and shouted and screamed*
> *at her. I said: 'Simone how could you do that? How could you*
> *do it?' I handled it all wrong.*

This outburst proved a source of guilt and considerable anguish for Anne, following Simone's subsequent suicide. It was only after talking to a counsellor that she was able to recognise the protectiveness and dread implicit in it: 'If a child runs into the road, you shout at them, because they're in danger. It was that kind of thing.'

The fear created by a child's brush with death is explosive. On learning she had slashed her wrists, Maxine's father lashed out at his daughter, physically and psychologically: 'My dad started going mad at me and shouting. He punched me in the face. He said – "You must be really stupid to slash your wrists. It proves how stupid you really are."' Unfortunately this reflex is not unusual. Interpreting suicidal talk or behaviour as attention-seeking or manipulative, or assuming the suicidal is 'playing dirty', may be more subtle expressions of the same hostility. They imply that such speech and behaviour is futile and senseless. This denies its psychological meaning and vindicates a punitive response, all of which is likely to reinforce a vulnerable young person's feelings of worthlessness and alienation.

Yet the possibility of a hostile response is part of what makes suicidal behaviour a high-risk strategy emotionally, as well as physically. It *may* backfire, introducing further conflict into already fraught relationships. Suicidal behaviour attracts censure for its effect on others. After a death, the punishing aftermath of suicide descends on relatives and friends. A non-fatal suicide attempt makes the threat of such a shattering loss explicit and may alter existing relationships. Lisa recalled that her sister's suicidal behaviour introduced a distance between them. Emma had made her first suicide attempt on the day that Lisa, then aged 18, had left their home and gone to travel abroad for three months. Lisa was stunned by the implications of her sister's overdose:

It happened on the day I went away. For me that was the turn-
ing point in my relationship with her. She didn't do it because
I went away but if she'd died I would never have known. I
could never become so closely involved with her again. I
became wary. I suppose it sounds selfish but I thought: 'My
God, if she died I would have blamed myself.'

It is not only the threat of loss that evokes guarded reactions.
Suicidal behaviour reveals the extent of another person's psychic
pain and ambivalence about life, and this deeply unsettling
prospect touches many defences. An unbearable burden of
responsibility seems to hover just beyond acceptance of another
person's suicidal feelings. New imperatives to protect and support, for which most are totally unprepared, wait in the wings. To
acknowledge the quality of suicidal misery is often to feel helpless. The stronger the emotional ties between us, the more painful
this revelation can be and the more threatening its implications.

Denial

I knew when I went in that he'd killed himself. I could see him
lying down on the floor in an arch. I could see the gun between
his legs going up towards his head – he was in a pool of
blood – but I didn't want to believe it. I stood there saying,
'Mark are you all right? Are you all right?' I knew he was
dead, but I blanked it out of my mind. I ran into the bedroom
to grab the gun, before he shot himself.

(JANICE, MARK'S SISTER)

When reality becomes too painful, denial can provide vital protection. Janice's 'blanking out', on finding her brother's body,
demonstrates graphically how the mind can push away that
which threatens to overwhelm it. Threatening thoughts are forbidden to rise to a conscious level or, once conscious, are
banished. When reality literally does not bear thinking about,
denial shields us.

Denial is a common response to the threat of suicide.[4] Relatives may experience an indistinct sense of foreboding or semi-conscious anxiety rather than a conscious recognition that suicide is possible.[5] Young people's suicidal wishes are intensely painful and frightening for close relatives and friends. Joan's son Jason killed himself at his third attempt. Whilst the possibility that he might die remained inconceivable to her, her fear for her son's safety transmuted into physical tension:

> *It's difficult to see it. You don't want to. It's hitting you in the face. You'd see it, because he made several attempts, but every time I would think, 'He's all right now.' I used to be so relieved. I didn't think it might happen again, although I knew he was desperately unhappy. In my mind the episode was over. But I had this terrible pain in my chest for a few months. Now when I think about it, it was a worry, a pain, a fear.*

Denial reflects a natural dread and a disinclination to hear, and believe, that someone close to us feels like dying. Inevitably this has far-reaching implications for those in suicidal crisis. Their feelings may arouse such acute anxiety in others that potential sources of help are immobilised.

Myths

A number of common beliefs about suicide are inaccurate. By reducing thinking about suicide to unhelpful norms, these beliefs encourage inappropriate responses to the young and suicidal, marooning them from potential sources of help.

One: Children don't think about suicide

> *I had suicidal thoughts as early as about nine. I thought about it a lot of the time. My parents lived by a big river. I often walked by the river and thought about throwing myself in. I*

knew that I couldn't swim, so I thought that would be the ideal thing to do.

(SIMON)

I'd always viewed it as an option, as a way out. I thought about it in a very naive way from maybe eight or nine. Later on I used to get really black moods. If I couldn't do my school-work I'd think: 'Well it doesn't matter really, because I'm going to commit suicide next week.' I used to sit there in class and think about ways to do it.

(BARRY)

Adult reluctance to concede that children entertain ideas about suicide has been compared to earlier generations' reluctance to acknowledge children's sexuality.[6] Adults cling with tenacity to a notion of childish 'innocence' when suicidal expressions in the very young arouse their confusion and anxiety.

Suicidal thinking *is* relatively rare in childhood and becomes more common in adolescence, but children can and do feel suicidal. The Samaritans and Childline receive thousands of calls annually in the UK from children in sufficient distress to be thinking or talking about harming themselves. Up to 2 per cent of children suffer major depression before puberty, during which, 'feelings of guilt and thoughts that they would be better off dead are commonly reported'.[7] Children as young as three have been known to suffer from severe depression.[8]

A professional handbook on young people's suicidal behaviour, published in the late 1980s, includes the observation that, 'a few years ago, suicide among children as young as six years old was considered an impossible phenomenon'.[9] If child psychologists and psychiatrists have found it difficult to recognise suicidal potential in distressed children, the rest of us can expect to experience resistance to the idea. On the other hand few would deny that some children's lives verge on the intolerable. Parental death or abandonment, sexual, physical and emotional abuse, severe physical or mental illness in family members are among the experiences that make it so. Suicidal children tend to have suffered more loss, abuse and disturbance in their short lives than others their age.[10] In addition, some experience very serious depression, even before puberty, with less obvious causes.

Children may, as Barry did, begin to think of death as a 'way out'. Although suicide attempts are very rare prior to adolescence, depression and stressful conditions may foster an attraction towards death in some children. They will be at increasing risk of acting on their suicidal thoughts as they reach adolescence. The belief that children are immune to self-destructive thought must be relinquished if this vulnerable minority are to be recognised and helped.

Two: Young people who threaten suicide do not kill themselves

He said, 'Can you get some sleeping pills?'

I said, 'What d'you mean?'

He said, 'So that I can just take them and go. I don't want to be here any more.'

'Look Tommy,' I said, 'I'm not going to the doctor's to get pills for you to kill yourself. Mums don't do that sort of thing.'

I tried to make light of it. You don't think a young kid's going to kill himself. I was worried, but not really worried. I didn't believe him.

(PHYLLIS, TOMMY'S MOTHER)

Perhaps the most common fallacy about suicide is that people who talk about it will not go ahead and do it.[11] This belief is unfounded. About three-quarters of the people who kill themselves give clear warnings of their intentions beforehand.[12] The young are no exception. Among adolescents in one American study, half who took their lives had actually threatened suicide beforehand, and nearly all (85 per cent) had expressed a wish to die to someone close to them.[13]

Happily, many young people *do* stop short of acting on suicidal feelings. But to conclude from this that talk of suicide is inconsequential is a strange leap of logic, with obvious risks. Suicide threats are vital alarm signals. At the very least they show that someone is in serious psychological distress; at worst they warn of self-destructive behaviour to come. Unfortunately their significance is often denied. Studies of young suicides show that families and therapists alike tend to ignore or misunderstand suicidal warnings.[14] For many the possibility of a suicide is either too horrifying or improbable to recognise.[15] Suicide threats also produce feelings of helplessness. Janice, whose brother Mark shot himself after making a number of suicide threats, recalled that she felt powerless to respond to his talk of suicide: 'It's a shock to your system. You just don't know what to do, or what to say, or how to help that person, so you turn a blind eye to it.' Recognition of suicidal potential poses the concomitant question: 'What are you going to do about it?' Few of us feel equipped to answer.

When someone threatens suicide, they offer others a chance to intervene: 'Suicide threats have important meanings. They are often attempts to check out the level of caring and responsiveness that exists out there for them in their world.'[16] If a threat elicits *no* response, a young person may conclude that no one cares much whether he or she lives or dies. Self-esteem takes a further battering and action appears, more than ever, to be the only option left. Tragically, many suicide warnings are only recognised as such *after* a death, a fact harrowing for the bereaved. As one mother recalled: 'Talk about warnings. Looking back *now* there were warnings.' But warnings may be oblique. A preoccupation with death may be expressed more, or less, overtly by such throwaway remarks as: 'I wish I was dead'; 'You'll be better off without me'; or 'I won't be around much longer.' However flippant or unwarranted such comments may initially seem, the only appropriate response is to explore them further (see Chapter 7).

Where a young person's suicidal hints, threats or ruminations are discounted he or she may conclude that talking is ineffective and that actions speak louder than words. A general suspicion of suicidal talk has, as Janice observed, hazardous implications for young people at risk:

Too many people are going round saying: 'People don't talk about suicide, they do it.' They're encouraging it. They might as well say: 'Well do it then.' People don't just go round saying they're going to kill themselves for a joke. It's their way of saying: 'Help me.' They don't really want to commit suicide` but they probably think: 'If no one's going to bloody help me I'll have to because that's the only way I can cope with my problem.'

We must discard the myth that young people who threaten suicide do not go on to attempt suicide, and indeed to die. For young suicide victims and those close to them the price paid for this misconception could not be higher. Routine scepticism towards talk of suicide is, quite simply, dangerous.

Three: If someone wants to kill themselves there's nothing you can do about it

This truism is misleading, because it misrepresents the nature of most suicidal crises. Implying that one must want *either* to live or die, since to want both is contradictory, it overlooks the play of conflicting desires in suicidal behaviour. Few young people who harm themselves are totally dedicated to ending their lives. Most feel highly ambivalent about life and death, not at all sure they want to die, but nevertheless unable to go on living life as it is.

Most suicidal crises are characterised by confusion and ambivalence. The desire to be dead can be a volatile longing, and often conflicts with a strong instinct to stay alive. Suicidal motives reflect this tension. 'I want to be dead' conflicts and coexists with 'Help me, I want to live.' The desire to interrupt, or end for ever, the conscious experience of living in the present makes death attractive. Yet the desire to live, if only life were more bearable, remains strong. Self-destructive behaviour may itself be part of the search for reasons to live, through its appeal to others – or fate – to intervene in a situation that has become intolerable.[17]

For those who feel they have little left to lose, this high-risk, self-destructive strategy can seem to offer the only prospect of escape from the impasse in which they find themselves. Karen was a 20-year-old student nurse when she took, and survived, an overdose. Her immediate and overwhelming fear at the time was her impending finals examinations. As the pressure of work and revision mounted she became trapped in a wearying cycle of anxiety and sleeplessness. One night, unable to sleep yet again, Karen reached for some pills and swallowed an overdose. Afterwards she became frightened, but was not prepared to go to hospital. Past caring, her attitude was, she recalled, 'If I have taken enough then tough shit really. If I die, I die and if I don't, I don't.' In fact Karen's wish to be 'out of it for good' was short-lived and her 'gamble with death' represented a turning-point. By releasing intolerable tension it diminished her fears. She slept properly for the first time in weeks, soothing the strain of exhaustion. And by symbolising her desperation, the overdose provided insight into how depressed she had become. Afterwards a solution, or at least the prospect of carrying on, became conceivable:

> *I don't know what happened that night, but something clicked.*
> *I think I just got things into perspective. It scared me that I'd*
> *got so depressed. I thought I've got to get on and sort myself*
> *out. If I fail finals, I fail. I can always take them again.*

Karen's experience illustrates a common feature of suicidal episodes – their brevity. Most individuals who wish to die, or at least not to live, do so only for a quite short period of time.[18] The vast majority who attempt suicide do not remain suicidal in the long term. This appears to be the case even for those whose suicidal crises have been so intense that they attempted suicide using methods perceived to be 100 per cent lethal. Of suicidal people restrained from throwing themselves from the Golden Gate Bridge in San Francisco, 94 per cent were alive, or had died from natural causes, a quarter of a century later.[19] Similarly, 90 per cent of those who survive suicide attempts on the London Underground do not subsequently kill themselves. The common presumption might be that rescuing these people would only delay the inevitable: those desperate enough to jump from bridges or under trains will subsequently find a way to end their lives.[20] But the common presumption is clearly wrong and the most formidable suicidal feelings can abate with time. Survival can, in itself, feel miraculous. Survivors of such potentially deadly attempts have often experienced a sense of spiritual rebirth. The favourable intervention of fate may restore hope and a sense of purpose, proving to be a highly critical personal turning-point. For some, the suicide attempt appears to function as a contemporary rite of passage, in a culture notably lacking in symbolic milestones.

The ambivalent and temporary nature of most suicidal crises makes a fatalistic approach to the needs of the suicidal unacceptable. In the vast majority of cases this is exceptionally inappropriate. When applied to the young, the idea that someone who *really* wants to kill themselves is beyond help seems particularly unpalatable. Negating responsibility for the suicidal, it justifies an approach that says: 'There's nothing we can do.' Similarly, if more subtly, absolute respect for an individual's 'right' to take their own life may convey much the same message:

> To say that a suicide is justifiable and understandable, that the individual should be allowed to decide, may seem on the face of it the ultimate enlightenment, avoiding as it does an unwarranted intrusion into another's autonomy which should remain sacrosanct. Paradoxically, however, suicidal persons so often see this as a form of final rejection whereby we merely confirm their loss of hope and their despair.[21]

In fact, suicidal feelings often fade, as those in crisis respond to rest, care and support. Respite from intolerable feelings and proof that others care may lift hopelessness just enough to make life seem possible again. As Edwin Schneidman, a long-time proponent of suicide prevention work in America, has emphasised: 'after a short time most individuals can go on, voluntarily and willingly, to live useful and creative lives'.[22] Much can and must be done to help the young through suicidal episodes.

Four: Talking about suicide encourages it

A widespread fear exists that talking about suicide may encourage it.[23] This fear which will clearly affect responses to children and adolescents who express suicidal thoughts or feelings, is a critical issue for suicide prevention. The frequency of hints, warnings and threats prior to suicides suggests that most victims would have divulged more about their suicidal feelings had they been encouraged with specific questions.

Because their thoughts are so disturbing and difficult to share, the suicidal often feels intensely isolated. The emotional resistance of others may confine the suicidal to silence for fear of rejection. Helen's brother Julian died from an overdose at 18:

> *You think afterwards: why couldn't he have come and asked for help rather than taken that very, very final step? And yet people who are suicidal know that it's incredibly hard for people to hear that they're feeling that bad. If you love someone it's very hard to hear that.*

Allowing a young person to talk through their worst fears and feelings may provide them with a lifeline. Yet as Helen suggests above, close relatives and friends of the suicidal find it especially hard to give this permission, because it is so personally threatening. Permission may be refused through silence or rebukes. When a preoccupation with death is expressed, others frequently find the cue to talk too daunting or improbable.

Isolation is a comfortless and dangerous position for the suicidal. As Lisa – who lost a sister and foster brother to suicide – reflected, the suicidal must feel emotionally, if not physically, isolated:

> *They probably think, 'If only you knew I'm thinking about killing myself.' I can imagine the more those thoughts flit*

163

through their head, the more it would alienate them and the more cut off from you they would feel.

Talking can reduce feelings of isolation and alienation. The intensity of a child or adolescent's mounting fear and tension may be relieved and their chaotic feelings explored.

A distinction may be drawn between talking to vulnerable individuals about suicidal feelings and a more general discussion of suicide. The fear that talking about suicide may encourage it has concerned teachers when suicide prevention programmes have been initiated in schools.[24] Such programmes are now common practice in schools in the United States, and have been piloted by The Samaritans in the United Kingdom. The general assumption behind teaching young people about suicide is that improved understanding and greater openness will help them to recognise suicide risk, in themselves or their peers. Yet there is a counter-concern that in encouraging understanding of suicide, such schemes make it appear an acceptable option.[25]

Caution is not misplaced. Representations of suicide *do* influence attitudes and *may* have an adverse effect on young people, as evidence of their imitative suicidal behaviour suggests. If relatives and friends, a news report or a film, can model suicidal actions, so too may an ill-conceived suicide prevention video (see pp. 62–63, 92–95). A sensitive approach is vital and it may be that suicide awareness is best promoted within a broader educational programme which teaches adolescents about emotions, depression and coping in general (see Chapter 4). Suicide taboos have a protective as well as a restrictive function. Ideally suicide prevention work would 'lessen the degree to which taboo interfered with the expressing and receiving of the cry for help, and at the same time support the portion of taboo which emphasised the value of life'.

Cries for help must be heard. A willingness to talk to suicidal young people and to promote awareness of suicide on a general level are both vital forms of dialogue. At the individual level, silence is neither a 'safe' nor a neutral response to

164

evidence of an adolescent's suicidal feelings. Not only does it deny a potentially therapeutic chance to talk about frightening feelings, but it is often experienced as a punishment by the suicidal, reinforcing their alienation.[26] In general, improved understanding of suicide risk will increase the chances that vulnerable young people are identified before they come to harm. Education about suicide risk is inevitably a sensitive issue, but none the less critical.

Five: Youth suicide cannot be prevented, because it is too impulsive

This is a myth that rests on a highly dangerous characteristic of youth suicide – its relative impulsiveness. Not all youth suicides are impulsive. Some are meticulously planned, others are contemplated for months and years in recurrent suicidal thoughts and fantasies. Yet compared to suicidal behaviour in older people, many youth suicides appear to occur 'out of the blue', driven by a fatal impulse and often happening shortly after a rejection, humiliation or disciplinary crisis (see Chapter 5). This quality can breed scepticism towards suicide prevention.[27] If young people's suicidal behaviour is so impulsive, and so often triggered by such unexceptional events, how is it possible, a sceptic would argue, to see it coming and to intercept it?

This important objection must first be dissociated from a tendency to trivialise the feelings and circumstances behind suicidal behaviour among the young. A perfunctory assumption that a suicide attempt was 'impulsive' functions, too often, as an evaluative short-cut. *En route* to hospital, after taking her overdose, Debbie was confronted with the judgement that she had indulged in a rash misdemeanour: 'The ambulance guy said "You need a good hiding." He just assumed I was being bullied or something, or I'd had a bad day.' The hostility in this response stung her at a time of intense distress and heightened vulnerability. Too often the 'impulsive' suicide attempt is interpreted as feckless, an act lacking a history and short of sufficient causes.

In general, young people will have less experience and

fewer resources to draw on in coping with stressful feelings and problems. The prevalence of suicidal behaviour in youth suggests that their emotional fuses are short. It fits neatly into a 'storm and stress' theory of adolescence which identifies this time of life as one of psychological turbulence and unpredictable behaviour. Yet impulses do not *explain* suicidal behaviour and it is vital to distinguish them from the underlying causes of despair.

Sometimes it clearly *is* the case that the explosive quality of a young person's behaviour makes it extremely difficult to anticipate a suicide attempt. Crises escalate quickly. Barry described the catastrophe of shame and panic that overtook him when, at 14, his peers confronted him about his being gay. 'I felt like a drowning man . . . Having hidden it all my life my first thought was suicide.' Barry found himself 'suddenly' out of his emotional depth and took an overdose. Yet the longer-term process which had exhausted Barry's resources, extinguished hopes and made suicide appear increasingly attractive was also evident. Barry had, in fact, been in considerable danger for years. Fearful of his attraction to other boys and isolated socially, he had experienced recurrent thoughts of suicide since the age of eight or nine. Barry's mother died when he was 13, after many years of illness. His father was remote and authoritarian, his older siblings had left home and Barry's teachers seemed oblivious to his misery. Disenchanted with the adult world, Barry relied increasingly on suicidal fantasies to cope. Being taunted and feeling exposed over his sexuality was the 'last straw'. A suicide attempt followed soon after. Barry may have attempted suicide in a hurry, but he had already struggled alone for years with anxiety, low self-esteem, 'black cloud' moods and suicidal thoughts. The most impulsive suicide attempt may represent the end-point in a process which has intensified over months and sometimes years.

The notion that youth suicides cannot be prevented because they are too impulsive suggests that suicide prevention is a 'last-minute' enterprise, confined to plucking the suicidal out of danger as their self-destructive feelings become evident.

Yet suicide prevention has to be a far broader endeavour than this. A growing body of knowledge about youth suicide is providing insight into its underlying causes and into the groups of young people who are unusually vulnerable, including those whose behaviour may be more impulsive, aggressive or explosive (see Chapter 2). Through promoting public awareness of suicidal potential and responding to young people's emotional and behaviour difficulties sooner rather than later, through developing well-resourced and acceptable mental health services and addressing the social pressures contributing to young people's despair, suicide prevention must follow this lead.

Six: Suicide prevention should be left to the professionals

> *I talked to one of my friends at school about feeling really suicidal, but not about why. Funnily enough he never asked me why. I don't think he took me that seriously because he never brought it up or questioned it.*
>
> (BARRY)

> *Why didn't she go to the headteacher and say, 'I've got a sixth-former who's suicidal – she's talking about killing herself'? Why couldn't she have told me? She never said a word. But her worst sin was inadequacy in the way she coped with it. It was just badly mismanaged.*
>
> (PATRICIA, ELAINE'S MOTHER)

Suicide prevention cannot be left to professionals for the simple reason that many young people who are in danger of suicide have no contact with them. Only half of youth suicide victims, according to American research, had been to see mental health professionals in the time leading up to their death.[28] Professionals are only consulted once problems are recognised. Suicidal information is first confided closer to home – to family, friends, teachers and workmates – and these confidences open up crucial opportunities for intervention. In an ideal world they would be recognised and handled sensitively, but in practice missed opportunities cost lives. Since the first aim of suicide prevention work must be to identify the vulnerable, public education in the wider community is essential.

Young people most frequently share suicidal feelings and plans with their peers.[29] Friends of adolescent suicide victims often know of their intentions, but refuse to betray their confidences.[30] Placing a high premium on confidentiality, the mutual loyalties of adolescent friendships provide a basis for intimacy, trust and support independent of adults. Friends may be seen as more suitable recipients of suicidal information because they promise not to pass it on, judge or interfere. They may also be the only confidantes available. Barry not only told his schoolfriend about his wish to die, but asked him to be there when he took an overdose: 'I wanted moral support in a strange way. He just accepted it, as if I'd said: "I'm going to the shop."' It is this promise of acceptance and confidentiality that make peers the most likely recipients of suicidal information. Sadly, where this loyalty prevails, it often incapacitates an adolescent's ability to ensure the safety of a suicidal friend.

Recipients of suicidal information are often ill-equipped to deal with it. Elaine's parents only learnt *after* her death that she had talked about suicide to a teacher. The teacher respected her pupil's confidence, but did *not* appreciate the urgency of Elaine's suicidal feelings. Before help could be arranged, the 17-year-old carried out her threat. Visiting schools after student suicides, the Director of a suicide prevention centre in California commented: 'We were struck by how often teachers recounted information that could have provided clues to the suicidal act – if they had been aware of its significance.'[31] Teachers are well placed to pick up clues of suicidal potential in their pupils, but are not naturally equipped to do so. More suicidal young people might be helped were teachers more aware of their needs and confident in their responses to suicidal information.

Relatives, friends, teachers and workmates frequently find themselves in the front line of suicide prevention; unprepared, anxious and with complicated feelings of their own. The help of mental health professionals may be essential to preventing suicide, but it is one step removed from a young person's day-to-day world. Most young people contemplating suicide confide *first* in members of their social network. Uniquely placed to recognise suicidal potential and avert a life-threatening crisis, these individuals are too often unable to do so. Any serious efforts at suicide prevention must accommodate this unpredictable reality.

Not long ago I was introduced to a 16-year-old whose younger sister had died. Talking about her death, he explained that she had had an accident with a belt in her bedroom. Despite the death of my own brother by suicide, I took this statement at face value. I wondered what could go so wrong with a belt as to be fatal. Somehow, the boy explained, the belt had got caught on a tall piece of furniture, and had strangled his sister. I struggled with the logistics of this in my mind's eye before it dawned on me that his sister, a 15-year-old, had hanged herself.

From then on it seemed a dubious 'accident'. The boy had not, it turned out, been allowed to attend the inquest into his sister's death, nor had he read the newspaper coverage. The inquest had attracted considerable publicity because the boy's father was a prominent local councillor. Instead his parents had obviously recounted to him what he now told me – that the 'open' verdict passed at his sister's inquest *proved* she had died accidentally. Suicide did not enter our conversation once. Its possibility seemed to loom just beyond his conscious grasp, waiting to emerge at some point in the future.

The psychological connotations of suicide *are* horrifying and, as in this case, denial may extend beyond the grave. As responses to the suicidal are explored more fully, it should not be forgotten how real are the anxieties of those whose child, sibling, friend or pupil is threatening suicide, and how isolated the young and suicidal may often be.

CHAPTER 7

Interrupting the Suicidal Process

Debbie recalled that in the time prior to her suicide attempt at 12, 'I was trying to see if there was any reason at all that I should live, and I couldn't find one.' As self-destructive thoughts and feelings intensify during the suicidal process, so too does the search for reasons to carry on. Suicidal talk, threats or self-harm – so often and dangerously dismissed as 'attention-seeking' – may play a part in this search by appealing for confirmation that someone else cares. For some young people this search will be more conscious than for others. Debbie was well aware that she needed help with her suicidal feelings and asked for it (see p. 103). For others, feelings may remain incomprehensible and self-destructiveness oblique. They are less likely to ask for help directly, though the care and attention of others will be no less crucial to them.

One of the most common influences on the suicidal process will be the responses a young person elicits from others. These may build up communication and introduce sources of reassurance and help. Or they may reinforce a young person's sense of isolation, worthlessness and rejection. To someone at risk of suicide, emotional isolation may prove extremely dangerous. Yet between a young person and the understanding and help of others lies a formidable communication barrier. It is a barrier that may be reinforced in a number of ways.

The Communication Barrier

'I can't explain'

I suppose I could have said I was pissed off instead of putting them through all that. But that was just it. I just couldn't. I couldn't work it out myself. If I couldn't put it into plain English myself it was a bit difficult.

(GARETH)

Children and adolescents may have particular difficulty in explaining their feelings and problems to others. Unable to express themselves in words, because they do not understand or have the vocabulary to describe their feelings and situation, young people may feel trapped. Without words, distress must be expressed and coped with in other ways. Often it is vented through behaviour. Gareth injured himself with knives on a number of occasions following attacks of anxiety and despair. Unable to explain these feelings to himself, there seemed little chance of him describing them to others. He had no *choice*, he reflected, between injuring himself and confiding in his parents. Without the insight or words to describe this tension and depression, he could not ask for help.

At a disadvantage in expressing their needs verbally, young people may be isolated further as others react negatively to their 'venting' behaviour. An imprecise form of communication, behaviour leaves ample scope for misunderstanding. Where it seems to others to be socially unacceptable – getting drunk or high on drugs; fighting and bullying others; stealing; staying away from school; 'sleeping around'; taking physical risks and attempting suicide – the risk of a young person being not only misunderstood but chastised and alienated will increase. Rejection and disapproval then cement the communication barrier.

Underestimating distress

*Sometimes I used to come home and say, 'I've got no friends.
Today they bullied me, took my things, threw me in the corner
and called me stupid names.' And my mum would say, 'Take
no notice. Ignore them.' But it's pretty hard ignoring these
things. And you can't really ignore being ignored.*

(SUSIE)

*They say they're the ones that have got the problems; they're
the ones paying the bills; they've got to clothe you and feed
you; they're worried about where the next pound's coming
from. They don't think their 16-year-old kid's got a problem.
They don't look no further than the end of their nose to see
what is bothering that child. For all they know their stepfather
could be raping them or they're getting bullied at school or
threatened or beat up.*

(JANICE, MARK'S SISTER)

Tensions between the perspectives of youth and adulthood are
notorious. Perhaps inevitably, the problems of growing up may
shrink in the minds of those who have survived their own
youth, grown into an adult role and accumulated years of life
experience. Adult life brings its own agenda and new problems
and stresses. Preoccupied with a working life and the demands
of nurturing and providing for their children, those older may
note the absence of these responsibilities in young people's
lives. Meanwhile, the pressures on children; the imperatives
and change of adolescence; the strains of simply growing up,
may be overlooked. The abuse, victimisation, hardship and loss
some children suffered early on in life often seem unthinkable.
And young people's mental health problems, which can make
coping with life so difficult, frequently go unrecognised. The
reality of serious mental suffering among children is often sub-
sumed by 'lay attitudes regarding the naivety, cuteness, and
simplicity of childhood'. By adolescence emotional difficulties
may readily be written off as teenage blues or growing pains.

When suffering becomes simply a nuance of age the assumption is that a young person will 'grow out of it'.

Whilst an angry young person may attribute these oversights to negligence, they are often far more complex. Incomprehension, which provides the communication barrier with strong foundations, is critical. Joan, whose son Jason was deeply depressed when he took his life, recalled that the severity of his depression was unfathomable to her:

> *You don't fully understand how they're feeling. You get your down days but you feel all right again the next day. You don't understand someone that's really depressed. How can you if you're not feeling like that yourself? It's difficult to think about someone being so down that they don't want to live any more. Although I worried about him I didn't realise this pain he was in.*

Those close to a vulnerable adolescent may not be familiar with the effects of depression: the deep sense of futility and worthlessness, the changed perceptions of relationships that once provided comfort and protection, and the emotional isolation this generates. As Joan suggested, it may be hard to recognise emotional states or problems which are beyond one's own experience. And without adequate support or information, those with no special interest in mental health issues are hard pressed to distinguish the signs of serious depression from teenage 'blues', an eating disorder from a diet, or a substance abuse problem from a recreational experiment. Research confirms that parents and teachers tend to overlook the seriousness of depression and other mental health problems in the children and adolescents close to them.[1] Even suicide attempts are often successfully concealed from parents.[2]

Such oversights entrench communication difficulties. The encouragement of relatives, friends, teachers or colleagues may be experienced by a depressed young person as a tyranny of optimism. Karen found it impossible, in the weeks prior to her suicide attempt, to communicate her mounting fears to others.

Overwhelmed by the pressure of work and impending exams, she had stopped sleeping at nights and was growing increasingly exhausted and desperate. Each time she tried to tell someone what she was feeling she was pre-empted by their assurances that she had nothing to worry about. This ready assumption trapped rather than reassured her. To Karen, it seemed to deny that her feelings were real or valid:

> No one said, 'Are you all right?' and really meant it. They would ask how I was and then not take my answer seriously. Nobody actually took it on board that I was terrified about my finals. No one ever said, 'Yeah, there is a problem.' They'd say, 'Of course you'll pass.' I was so isolated and scared and I felt like I couldn't talk about it.

The blanket optimism of others deprived Karen of the chance to talk her feelings through and put her situation in perspective. It did not allow for the possibility that without sleep and emotional support Karen might *not* feel able to go on and face the test that lay ahead of her. The assumption that she *would* cope erected a barrier between herself and others. As her exams drew nearer and panic mounted, she could no longer bear her feelings and took an overdose.

The isolation of young people who are finding it hard to cope is reinforced when others minimise their distress. The failure of others to 'see' what he or she is going through may fuel the sense of rejection and desperation. Unchecked, suicidal thinking may become more active (see Chapter 6). Yet as thoughts of death and suicide become more explicit and are revealed in hints and threats, the communication barrier may still stand firm.

Prohibitions and disbelief

> I used to trash my room and my mum would say, 'You're going to end up like your cousin', because I had a cousin in a mental hospital. I'd sit in my room and beat myself with a

hairbrush and scratch myself. Inflicting pain was a punish-
ment thing, because I hated myself and thought I was ugly
and really horrible. I'd say, 'I hate you' to myself. Out of sheer
frustration I used to bang my head against the wall. I thought
maybe I'd be able to damage my brain and end up as a cab-
bage. It'd get some tension and anger out. And when I was
really depressed I used to walk around the house saying, 'I
wish I was dead.' But my mum would say, 'You shouldn't say
that.'

(SUSIE)

Susie *did* express her suicidal feelings to those close to her. For her, adolescence was a tormented time fraught with tension between the social imperatives of her peers at school and the values of her fundamentalist Christian parents. She could nei-ther reconcile nor live up to either set of expectations. At school she was 'odd', singled out and bullied, and at home she feared catastrophic rejection by her parents and church as her religious doubts grew more sophisticated. Susie's worsening anxiety and depression nurtured self-abuse and suicidal thoughts. Her daughter's behaviour and talk of death clearly frightened Susie's mother who, helpless and alarmed, chided her and counselled more restraint. Yet the message that Susie's feelings were dangerous, unacceptable and would lead her to the men-tal hospital did nothing to resolve them. Ignoring the evidence of a young person's suicidal potential does *not* reduce it.

Statements that prohibit talk of suicide – 'You shouldn't talk like that' or, 'Don't say things like that' – may be an auto-matic response to the threat posed by someone else's suicidal feelings. Yet to a young person who has risked mentioning the unmentionable such responses confirm that their feelings are inadmissible and isolating. For her book *A Special Scar: The Experiences of People Bereaved by Suicide*, Alison Wertheimer inter-viewed many people bereaved through suicide. Of her dead husband one woman asked, 'How did he keep that to himself? But at the same time it's so awful how do you tell anyone?'[3] Her questions suggest the Catch-22 of suicidal states: those who are suicidal feel prohibited from expressing their thoughts about death, and yet have desperate needs with which they cannot cope alone.

Disbelief is another common response to suicidal communications. As suicidal talk is dismissed a young person may feel compelled to prove or act out feelings that words have failed to convey. Being dismissed and disbelieved may extinguish any hope of change. Action became inevitable, for Debbie, once words had failed:

The thing is that two weeks before when I said I was going to do it they didn't take me seriously. But I didn't do it out of spite because no one believed me. I just thought, what more can I do? They don't take you seriously. The only difference between before and after was that I did it.

(DEBBIE)

When suicidal talk is prohibited or disbelieved a young person is left alone to cope with frightening feelings. Since being cut short or disbelieved is demeaning, self-esteem may be more bruised than ever. Some may subsequently manage on their own or be redeemed by improved circumstances, but isolation will leave others more vulnerable to their self-destructive feelings.

Silence

When I got out of hospital it was like nothing had happened. Nothing was ever, ever said about it again. It was like I'd just come home from school for the day. Nobody asked if I was all right. I was in bed for a few days and they treated me like I'd got a sore throat or something. Just nothing was said. Which makes it quite hard when you're 12.

(DEBBIE)

When my mum and dad came to visit me in the hospital it was: 'How's things today? Did you see such and such in the

176

paper?' It was back to the same act as before as if nothing had
changed. I was obviously saying, 'Look, I am unhappy.
Something's not right in my life.' But they just carried on as
normal. It was never mentioned in my family at all, because
it's a shameful thing to do. You get the guilt tripping, because
it's as if I was putting them down in some way. I don't think
I'll ever be able to talk to them about it, because that's how
they feel.

(LORRAINE)

Although a suicide attempt has the potential to communicate what a young person has not managed to convey in words – that he or she is desperate and unable to cope – it often fails to do so. A young person's suicide attempt is often met with silence. Research suggests that following a child's overdose, parents rarely discuss what has happened once their adolescent returns home from hospital. Where the reasons behind a suicide attempt are never brought out into the open, communication is likely to remain blocked. The feelings that preceded the attempt may now be inflamed by the reaction of others to it. Interviews with those who have attempted suicide suggest that the ensuing silence of relatives and friends is often experienced as punishment.[4] Through evoking guilt and shame, and by refusing a young person the opportunity to express their most frightening feelings, silence is experienced as punitive. Those who have attempted suicide and are met with silence receive a further blow to their self-esteem.[5]

Such silence resonates with unexpressed feelings. Suicidal behaviour is extremely disturbing to *all* involved and evokes powerful emotions: shock, fear, concern, anger, a sense of rejection and betrayal. Freezing communication – by staying silent – can allow relatives and friends to cope with potentially overwhelming emotion. It also veils feelings which are often highly confused. At a time when sympathy may collide with rage, those close to a young suicide attempter, who frequently receive no support to cope with *their* feelings, may settle for silence. Fraught and desperate circumstances, with their undertow of fear, contort the need to feel safe. Joan recalled the evening on which she and her husband intercepted her son's suicide attempt. Her immense anxiety – this was not his first attempt – was assuaged by the hope that the suicidal threat was now under control: 'I was so strung up. All I was concerned about was that the storm was passing.'

It may, of course, be young people themselves who opt to remain silent after a suicide attempt. Like many others who harm themselves, Gareth remained confused and unable to explain his actions afterwards. Naturally his distraught parents wanted to understand why he had injured himself:

> *My parents were just gutted. They said, 'What have we done wrong?' I said, 'You haven't done anything wrong. It's just me. I don't know what's going on.' I couldn't explain. Everybody was saying, 'Why? Why? Why?' and I couldn't say.*

Gareth's inability to explain himself added to his sense of shame, guilt and humiliation. In the days that followed he longed for the questions to stop, the tension at home to fade and for things to get back to 'normal' as soon as possible:

> *I wanted everything to settle. I just wanted time to go by really quickly and for everybody to forget about it. Everybody was checking up on me. It was a bit of a strain – everybody wary of everybody else and treading on eggshells. Nobody was sure what to say.*

Silence, however tense, accommodates this uncertainty. What it does *not* do is address the ongoing distress and danger a young person may be in. Silence following suicidal talk *or* behaviour means that the opportunity to introduce change and address problems is often lost. If the difficulties that led to the attempt remain unresolved suicidal impulses are likely to resurface. When they do the communication barrier will be stronger than ever.

Recrimination and ridicule

> *When I was in hospital my mum used to write me letters*
> *telling me how I was breaking the family up and how I was*
> *doing it to hurt them. She'd say, 'Why are you doing this to*
> *us? Don't you think we've suffered enough?'*

> (CARRIE)

Reeling in the aftermath of a suicide attempt, other families may fall into a pattern of recrimination. The strain and anxiety induced by a young person's suicidal behaviour may explode in accusations and hostility (see Chapter 6). Yet when family or friends turn away from a young person in anger, he or she is left in considerable danger. This may well precipitate a final break-down of communication.

So too may hostility veiled by humour. The danger, for a vulnerable young person, of being ridiculed as a result of suici-dal communication or behaviour is self-evident. It is common to cope with anxiety through humour, yet this coping mechanism may inflict considerable damage. Feelings of humiliation and shame are common after a suicide attempt. At a time of height-ened vulnerability ridicule may feel damning, as Gareth found on his return to school:

> *They'd say: 'Are you going to the toilet for a slash?' Or they'd*
> *say: 'That was a cutting remark, wasn't it?' or, 'You're as*
> *sharp as a razor.' Stuff like that.*

Building Communication

Facing an intensely despairing, angry or disturbed young per-son about whom one cares, perhaps very deeply, can be distressing and threatening. Their self-destructive feelings, statements and behaviour may seem strange and frightening. And the threat that he or she will act creates tremendous anxi-ety and stress. Under pressure it is not always clear what response will best protect or help a suicidal young person. Concern and good intentions may turn quickly to fear, anger and defensiveness (see Chapter 5). Yet even young people who are deeply and consistently suicidal remain ambivalent about killing themselves. If the right opportunity arises to share suicidal ideas, the great majority will do so. Many will then feel more secure and may be willing to accept help with underlying problems.[6] Young people often offer others the chance – through verbal or non-verbal, direct or indirect warnings – to turn their suicidal process around. Yet even if others recognise this they often lack the confidence to broach the subject. Opportunities to talk about depressed and suicidal feelings must be grasped, and handled sensitively, if they are not to be lost. Where the responses of others confirm feelings of isolation or rejection, guilt or anger, fear or worthlessness, a young person is more likely than ever to perceive an answer in the 'suicide solution'.

Acceptance

You need the opportunity to speak. I never really felt that I could. I needed someone to appreciate that I felt how I felt, not to try and make these wonderful solutions, but to say: 'Yeah. I realise that you're feeling that bad.'

(CARRIE)

Many of the potentially damaging responses to suicidal communications already discussed – prohibitions, disbelief, recriminations – improvise on *non*-acceptance. For a young person to mention suicide is often regarded as unacceptable and talking about it dangerous. A number of misconceptions – that talking about suicide will encourage it; those who talk about suicide do not kill themselves – reinforce these assumptions. Negating the need to respond to suicidal communication, these misconceptions promote the idea that it is safer, for all concerned, to avoid the subject. The dangers of talking about it are strangely exaggerated, while the threat posed by the thoughts and feelings underlying suicidal talk is underestimated. This vigilance is illogical. It is suicidal feelings and thoughts that are dangerous to a vulnerable young person. Preoccupied with death and dying he or she will *already* be at risk. Verbalising these feelings in suicidal hints, references and threats merely expresses what is already going on in his or her head. The real danger will be isolation and lack of support.

The first step towards helping someone who is suicidal is to accept that they are and encourage them to share the burden of their feelings. Allowing a young person to admit what they feel, without fear of judgement, dismissal or recrimination, will be a valuable response. Carrie recalled that permission to talk about her suicidal state would, at the very least, have ended her isolation. But this permission was never given, and she continued to conceal her suicidal preoccupations. Because suicide is a forbidden subject, young people often feel trapped with their inadmissible thoughts and feelings.

Listening

> *I did all the talking. Never did I sit with my son and say, 'How are you feeling? What are your thoughts? Do you want to talk?' and wait for him to get it out. He was depressed and he needed desperately to talk to someone about his feelings so that he could understand them. He would come home from school and just lie on his bed and brood. I'd come home, run upstairs and try to cheer him up. I think he eventually built a wall around himself and his depression to hide it from me.*
> (Susan Bowden-White, Everything to Live For)[7]

Susan Bowden-White's 17-year-old son Jody shot himself after a period of depression. In her book, *Everything to Live For*, his mother recalls with some anguish the way in which she may have inadvertently reinforced her son's sense of isolation. In retrospect, she felt, her attempts to encourage her son and cheer him along may have been counterproductive: 'He probably thought I would be disappointed in him if he brought me his pain and problems. He might even have feared it would cause me also to reject him.' Her optimism, this mother suspected, may have heightened her depressed son's own sense of worthlessness.

Sadly, love and concern for a young person by no means guarantee insight into their feelings and problems. The only way to establish and sustain this understanding is through communication. The details of a young person's despair may inevitably be extremely painful to those who care for them. But distressing as it may be, the first step towards helping a young person who may be suicidal is relatively simple – listen to what they really feel.

An often underrated skill, listening plays a vital role in dismantling communication barriers and turning the suicidal process round. Listening in a way that conveys acceptance, concern and empathy may generate hope and help to establish trust. Listening in a way that does *not*, may quickly sabotage communication and reinforce their sense of aloneness. A young person at crisis point may be highly sensitive to the way others listen or fail to listen, and the interpretations they appear to make of what they hear. Hopes of being able to communicate with others may be low and young people defensive. The suicidal process will often have thrived on a young person's difficulties in making others aware of feelings and needs.

Common mistakes and defences confound good listening. Interruptions create a hurried atmosphere. Identifying problems on a young person's behalf, without offering them the chance to explain what they understand of their feelings and problems, undermines. Signs of boredom or impatience convey lack of interest. A yawn or a look at a watch may speak volumes to a young person sensitised to rejection. Instant interpretations, garrulous advice and magic solutions only alienate. Where others appear to have little time or inclination to listen, a young person is unlikely to reveal themselves:

The thing was, in the hospital, they asked me why I'd [taken an overdose] when it was obvious they only had two minutes to spare. They didn't have long. They were doing the rounds. I felt like they were dismissing me from the start.

(DEBBIE)

The kind of attention that builds trust and throws a human life-line to young people at risk of suicide cannot be cursory. Trust may well take time to establish and listening must form part of an ongoing process. If they perceive that their feelings are taken seriously and their point of view valued, young people are more likely to feel enough trust. Susie had fantasies about suicide throughout adolescence, and had many reservations about confiding how she felt to anyone outside her family. Bullied at school, set apart by her family's religious convictions and miserable with anxiety, Susie's problems did not go unnoticed by her teachers. Yet the opportunities created for her to talk about them did not come close to meeting her need for reassurance:

I was very shy. A couple of teachers they'd come up to me after lessons and say; 'Are you OK? Do you want to talk about anything?' It made me cross and I'd clam up. I'd say, 'I'm fine.' I didn't want to talk to them. I felt embarrassed.

The need for reassurance runs deep. It is important for a child or adolescent to know that someone is ready to listen, whenever he or she feels ready or able to talk. Susie was in her teens, with a suicide attempt behind her, when she finally approached The Samaritans for help. By this time she had a far clearer idea of her needs:

I just wanted someone to look at me and smile and just listen, really. I didn't want advice or someone to say, 'Do this do that.' I needed to feel trust and feel secure and not feel that I was being patronised. I wanted to be able to talk without feeling I was being judged, without being told what to do. I just wanted to be able to say, 'I have panic attacks on buses. I think I'm awful. I hate myself.'

Talking about feelings, identifying problems

I'd been lying so long and covering up that maybe I'd got to the point where I'd got nothing to lose – always feeling lonely, mixed up, afraid, really confused. After all those months of pretending, not having to pretend for once was really great. It was as if something lifted and I spoke; I spoke for ages.

(GARETH)

Talking breaks the ice. If they don't talk you don't know what the problem is, so you can't help them. If they don't talk maybe they don't know what the problem is because all their feelings are wrapped up. You've got to try and unravel it, to say, 'What's wrong? I want to know.' You've got to talk to find out what's wrong. Then you can try to sort the problems out.

(JANICE, MARK'S SISTER)

For a young person who has felt isolated with frightening feelings or impulses for some time, being allowed to talk can come as an immense relief. The immediate effect may be to diffuse anxiety and alleviate the strain of coping alone. As a student, Gareth struggled secretly for months to disguise both his feelings and the injuries he had sustained during a suicide attempt. When he finally found himself able to talk to a friend, the therapeutic effect was immediate. Talking may release pressure, reducing the explosiveness of previously pent-up emotion. Since this often builds up before a suicide attempt, intensifying the suicidal process with desperate feelings, talking may do the opposite. Combined with the concern and attention of another person, talking can help to reduce the suicidal feelings and impulses which are so often ambivalent and volatile.

Talking may take the edge off self-destructive feelings but the risk of suicide is unlikely to go away for long if underlying problems are not addressed. As Janice suggests (above), talking has the vital function of providing others with insight into what these pressures might be. At the time he took his life, her brother Mark was struggling to cope with pressures his family knew nothing about:

> His girlfriend was pregnant. I don't really think he wanted the child. He wasn't old enough. Neither was she. She was 15. So I suppose he thought, she's not even old enough to have sex let alone have a baby. And he didn't want to hurt our mum and dad. He didn't know how to tell them. And he didn't know if he was going to be able to support his girlfriend and the baby. I think he was looking into the future and thinking – What do I do? The only way he could sort it out was for him to kill himself so the problem would be all right.

The pressure on Mark mounted as his girlfriend's pregnancy advanced. Yet without knowing of his circumstances Mark's family could do little to reassure him or to alleviate this pressure. This escalation of pressure may be avoided where others gain insight into the immediate stresses a young person faces. Tactful and gentle questions – 'Is anything wrong?'; 'How are you feeling?'; 'Do you know why you feel like this?'; 'Is there a particular problem that you would like to tell me about?' – may enable a young person to reveal specific problems and feelings. As these become apparent to others, solutions too become discernible.

Exploring feelings and problems has another vital function – assessing the immediate risk of suicide. The need to address *suicidal* feelings may become apparent in a number of ways. Some young people may make the need explicit through suicidal talk or behaviour but others conceal suicidal feelings out of shame, guilt or fear. It is not safe to wait for a young person to initiate the subject. Signs that a young person is depressed, despairing and finding it difficult to cope with problems may make it necessary to ask about suicidal thoughts.

Exploring suicidal feelings and assessing danger

> I didn't actually say, 'I'm going to kill myself.' I said, 'I feel really bad, I feel like killing myself.' I think she appreciated

how bad I felt, but she didn't think I'd do anything about it.
She talked to me after I'd done it and said 'I didn't realise that
you'd planned to do it.'

(CARRIE)

Carrie was deeply suicidal when she warned her GP of her feelings. Soon after this she attempted suicide. The doctor had not realised that Carrie was actively thinking about suicide and had planned an attempt. She had not realised because she had not asked. When a young person is clearly disturbed, despairing or talking of suicide the only way to assess the immediate danger is to ask direct questions.

It is often wrongly assumed that young people will be unable to talk about suicidal feelings. In fact, even young children who are suicidal are capable of describing their thoughts and impulses.[8] Those who are attracted to death will be able, and often relieved, to talk about this preoccupation and their wish to be dead. Yet trust and confidence will be vital to any communication in this area. Ideally, suicidal feelings should be broached only after a young person has been given the fullest opportunity to talk about feelings and problems in general. In practice the subject of suicide may be pitched into conversation, by a desperate young person, when others are least alert and prepared. In either case, the issue should not be avoided. Questions asked plainly – 'Have you ever . . . wanted to die?; thought about hurting yourself? thought about how you might do it?; tried to kill yourself?' – will help to throw light on suicidal desires, thoughts, plans and behaviour (see Chapter 5). Enquiries that imply judgement – 'You're not going to do anything silly, are you?' – should be avoided.

Asking about suicidal feelings is a daunting prospect. It is important to try and keep anxiety under control. Whilst evidence that others care may reassure a young person, it is unlikely that he or she will be able to cope with their most intense emotions. It is essential to try to respond as calmly as possible to what is said, bearing in mind two things. Firstly, allowing a young person to describe suicidal feelings does not endanger him or her. It *does* introduce the prospect that their problems will be recognised. Being allowed to talk about their most frightening and despairing feelings, without feeling judged or rejected, may help to turn a young person's suicidal process around. Secondly, the pain and concern these feelings arouse in others can be shared. Just as he or she will need help to cope so too will the parents, siblings, friends and teachers of a young person who is suicidal. Listening makes special demands when suicidal feelings are being described, as will the details of despair and the evocation of hopelessness. Hearing one's child, sibling or friend expressing the view that there is nothing to live for, that they wish to be dead, that life has no meaning, may well be excruciating. Just as a young person will find it extremely stressful to cope in isolation with very frightening feelings, so too will relatives and friends. If a young person has already made a suicide attempt anxiety will often be acute. Sympathetic support and informed advice from people experienced in caring for the suicidal and for distressed young people is only a phone call away (see Chapters 8 and 9). With support for *their* needs, those close to a vulnerable young person are more likely to be able to help them through a suicidal crisis.

Finding help

> She would sit there and talk to me – pep talks. I would tell her how awful I felt and she would tell me there were all these things to live for. It used to reassure me for a couple of days and then I'd go back down again.
>
> (DEBBIE)

When a young person appears reassured, perhaps as a result of talking feelings through, it is vital not to overlook the underlying problems that may have contributed to despair. As a danger-ously depressed 12-year-old, Debbie found that the solace she gained from her teacher's attention was invariably short-lived. Depression swamped its palliative effects within days and self-destructive feelings returned. A young person who reveals that he or she is depressed, unable to cope and suicidal needs special care, not only from family, friends and teachers but often from the professionals and volunteers who have time, knowledge and experience to offer. Suicidal feelings tend to reflect complex problems. Helping a young person to develop alternatives to the suicide solution is likely to take time and commitment. Wherever possible a young person who has revealed suicidal feelings should be encouraged to seek additional support.

ON THE RECEIVING END

For those who come across suicidal talk or behaviour in young people close to them

- All suicidal ideas and actions in young people are serious and must be treated as such.
- Suicidal feelings and ideas may give way to suicidal plans and actions very rapidly.
- *Expect* to find it hard to believe that someone close to you is feeling suicidal.
- *Expect* to find it unnerving and threatening. Do not rely on 'intuitions' that tell you a young person is not in danger, is 'bluffing' or does not intend to act, when he or she is telling you otherwise.
- Find out more about these feelings. Talking with a young person about their suicidal feelings will not encourage them to act. Ignoring their overtures might.
- Listening to, accepting and taking a young person's feelings seriously is the best way to build trust. Trust makes it more likely that a young person will feel reassured and accept the possibility of help.
- *Get further help*. Unless the underlying causes of suicidal feelings are addressed the young person is unlikely to be out of danger, even if the immediate crisis has passed.

CHAPTER 8

Seeking Help: Obstacles and Fears

A wide range of professionals and non-professionals can offer help to a young person in crisis. However, many victims of youth suicide – who are feeling desperate – do not seek help from outside sources in the time before their death. It seems likely that young people in crisis may expect, and prefer, rescue to come from closer to home. Naturally a young person turns first to those to whom he or she feels closest. Appeals are often made to family, friends or teachers. The idea that 'a stranger' could help may be one that either does not occur or does not appeal. If those who know them best cannot see what is going on, a young person may conclude, how will anyone else be able to?

For many young people, the first contact they have with formal services follows a suicide attempt. The casualty department of a local hospital is a fraught starting point for any process of recovery. Many young people are surprised and extremely distressed to find themselves in an emergency ward after a suicide attempt, either because they assumed they would die or because they acted in too much confusion to predict the consequences.[1] The first priority of many in such a situation is to get out of hospital as soon as possible. Offers of professional support are often rejected.[2] Other young people are not offered any or adequate follow-up help when they leave hospital. All may subsequently be left extremely vulnerable. Struggling with the same feelings or problems that propelled them towards a suicide attempt in the first place, their hopelessness may now be confirmed by feelings of shock, disillusionment or fear over their brush with the health service.

The term 'help' in this chapter refers to support offered by professionals, volunteers and self-help groups beyond a young person's family and social network. The process of establishing and sustaining support from outside sources will be less than simple for a number of reasons. Lack of information about services on offer as well as the availability of these locally will clearly influence what happens to a young person in need of support (see Chapter 7). But so too will his or her feelings about seeking help. Firstly, many young people are hardly ready or able to acknowledge their difficulties and distress, let alone to anticipate that they may need help. Secondly, even a young person who agrees that support is a good idea may, in practice, feel threatened and ambivalent about involving others. Young people who are suicidal often feel less in control of the feelings and experiences in their lives than others. Seeking help from unfamiliar sources, with unknown implications, may seem to threaten a further loss of control. Unless the difficulties and fears that prevent young people from seeking help are appreciated, those at risk of suicide may remain isolated and vulnerable.

Not Recognising Problems

It was just a general pain. It was like a black cloud waking in it. I didn't see a future. I didn't even think about it. It happens very gradually. It's just a whole mental attitude. But at what point do you decide – 'Right, I'm not well. I need to go and see a psychiatrist?' I didn't think talking to someone would have helped. I didn't even think about it. I always think you go to see a psychiatrist once something's happened. You never think to go before, do you?

(LORRAINE)

190

It is rare to seek help before one has recognised a problem or acknowledged a need. At 18, Lorraine slipped gradually into a state of depression from which death seemed to offer the only prospect of relief. In the months leading up to her suicide attempt she could neither understand nor describe the emotional pain that built up within her. Certainly, she could find no reasons to explain it. With no insight into her own depression, Lorraine felt helpless, worthless and ashamed that she could not cope. The idea that professional help might alleviate these feelings simply did not occur to her. Lorraine struggled on alone, hiding her intolerable depression from those close to her, until she could no longer resist the temptation of suicide.

Young people are at a particular disadvantage in recognising their own problems and needs. Becoming more self-aware may depend not only on the insight developed with age but often on help received. By his early twenties, Ashley was able to look back on years of chemical dependence and casual sex and recognise hidden needs:

> All I ever felt were anxiety and fear . . . When I were pissed up and trying to cop off with people it weren't just me being an evil bastard. It was about me wanting some love – something nice.

With the support of Alcoholics Anonymous, whom he contacted when he was suicidal and desperate, and subsequent counselling, Ashley gradually developed an understanding of his own needs. Yet it was a slow dawning. It took Ashley years to recognise his alcoholism, longer to give up drink and drugs, and longer still to become conscious of his emotional needs. Meanwhile his had been a dangerous adolescence. Like many children and adolescents he expressed despair through behaviour not words, and ended up isolated. Young people who are not yet in a position to recognise their own problems and feelings are often hard to reach. Ashley spent his adolescence fiercely rejecting the adults around him, directing his anger outwards at his teachers, the police and assorted political injustices.

Externalising his anger and despair got him into plenty of trouble but attracted little help or sympathy. It took a lonely suicide attempt for Ashley to realise that he would need to change his life as well as the world, and that he would need support to do so.

Trusting Others

A lot of people keep shit inside of themselves because they're scared of what other people will do with it. I know I kept a lot of stuff to myself because I was scared of how people would ridicule it and use it against me.

(ASHLEY)

For many young people the idea of opening up to others may carry with it the threat of shame and humiliation. This fear may often be based in past experience. When Ashley was sexually abused at the age of 13 he confided in a friend at school: 'I suppose I wanted to tell somebody and I thought I could trust him.' Yet the confidence backfired: 'He told everybody. I was the laughing stock of the school.' Opening up to others became equated, for Ashley, with being humiliated. He was not in a hurry to expose his vulnerability again. For many young people, whose self-esteem is already fragile, revealing their feelings may seem to run the risk of rejection or ridicule.

The fear of insensitive responses is likely to stand between many people and help. Among those admitted to hospital following self-injury or overdoses, a common explanation as to why help was not sought before resorting to such action, is that problems were too personal.[3] Young people who are most vulnerable to suicide appear to experience particular difficulties in sharing their feelings with others and seeking professional help. One study found that young people who have attempted suicide are more likely than their peers to agree that: 'If depressed it is a good idea to keep these feelings to yourself.'[4] Another study of adolescents who had taken overdoses or injured themselves found that those who were *most* suicidal regarded seeking professional help as a more difficult option than those who were *less* suicidal.[5] Presumably the suicidal process intensifies unchecked in young people who have difficulty asking for help and trusting others.

Losing Control

> *I still use eating to control things. A lot of the time, things that happen in your life and family are out of your control. I suppose food is one of the only things that's totally in my control. If I don't eat for a day I'll feel better. Maybe that's my coping mechanism and it stops me from feeling really suicidal. My GP has suggested that I have help for my eating habits from a local mental health centre. But I'm really wary of going to see somebody every week and opening up things that I might not be able to cope with. Because it's all very calm at the moment and I just want to keep it like that for a while.*
>
> (CARRIE)

Maintaining control in private – perhaps through alcohol and drug use, eating, self-harm or suicidal thinking – will not solve underlying problems but it is a way of coping that feels reassuringly familiar. For Carrie her sense of control or 'calm' was preferable to opening up emotional areas with which she might not be able to cope. Talking about past experiences or confronting problems may well feel very threatening. Even when a young person wants to seek help he or she may fear the painful, perhaps overwhelming, emotions that might be aroused.

Karen sought counselling in late adolescence. At 13 an uncle had repeatedly raped her. Like many young victims of sexual abuse she experienced a sense of disbelief following the trauma but a few years later memories started surfacing. Karen, who had by now left home, began to experience serious difficulties coping. Going to work became difficult and she began to withdraw from people. Karen recognised that she was not coping

and would need support to do so. Even so, she was unprepared
for the emotional impact that facing the past would have on her:

> When I started counselling I was quite numb about what had
> happened and how I felt. Counselling opened it up and
> brought a lot of feelings up. I found it really threatening. There
> was stuff opening up that I didn't want to open up. For a
> while I just felt really vulnerable – like everybody knew what
> had happened and people were going to do it again. It was just
> horrible and a lot harder than I thought it was going to be. It
> felt hard just realising how it has affected my life and how it is
> going to affect my life and that it's always going to be there.
> But then that kind of worked through and it was OK. I think
> as I worked on it more and more I knew where I wanted to end
> up and what I wanted to do.

Many of the problems faced by young people may be painful to
confront and even in most secure, supportive situations losing
control emotionally may be disturbing. Young people's feelings
of safety, when seeking help, will be vital to its continuation
and success.

Confidentiality

> I went to see this woman at The Samaritans. I was really
> scared going along – absolutely terrified. I thought I might cry
> and that would be very embarrassing. I knew they'd got this
> confidentiality thing but I thought maybe behind my back
> they'd refer me to a doctor. I was really scared about that. I
> thought maybe someone, somewhere along the line will have
> something to do with my church. I was really paranoid . . . I
> said to her, I'm really scared to talk about really deep things
> because I don't feel safe. There are things that just go on in my
> head. She reassured me by saying no way would she tell any-
> body; a doctor or my parents. It took ages for me to believe her.
>
> (SUSIE)

Susie had to overcome considerable fears before she could cope with talking to a stranger about her problems. Confidentiality was essential to her feeling secure with the support she received. Many young people in need of help are likely to share Susie's 'paranoia' about confidentiality. Privacy may seem to provide vital protection; giving it up to threaten a tenuous sense of control. Anxiety and defensiveness will be natural until a young person feels safe. The reassurance Susie received from her early visits to The Samaritans gave her the confidence to go on and explore help from a number of other sources. Where a young person is not sure about what rules of confidentiality apply to which sources of help they may avoid seeking support. Maxine, an 18-year-old university student, was steering clear of her student counselling service: 'I don't know if I could talk to a counsellor. I know it sounds stupid but I'm scared it might go down on my academic record.'

Stigma and Fear

She said to me, 'How would you feel about going to a psychiatric day hospital?' I said, 'Does that mean I'm a classified loony now ?' She said, 'No, just think of it as getting some kind of help.' I went along expecting to make wicker baskets and do knitting but they had yoga and various discussion groups and assertiveness training. I thought it wasn't bad. Some of the things were really helpful but I felt uncomfortable at first. I thought – 'Oh, I'm a mental patient now.' I couldn't get this stereotype out of my head.

(SUSIE)

A number of professions offer help and support to people experiencing 'mental health problems', a phrase which covers a wide range of emotional and psychological difficulties of varying intensity. Mental health problems undoubtedly help to make young lives intolerable. Yet the stigma of visiting the mental hospital and being identified as a psychiatric patient appears to prevent some young people who take their lives from seeking help.[6] In the 1990s, negative public attitudes to those who experience mental health problems still prevail.[7] Mental illness attracts less public sympathy than physical illness. Assumptions of culpability add to feelings of personal failure and inadequacy. Maxine recalled bursting into tears to a friend and mentioning that she was going to visit her GP because she was feeling depressed. Her friend urged her to 'snap out of it', adding, 'I bet they give you electric shock treatment and put you in the electric chair. If you're going to be like this don't expect me to stay around.' Although mental health problems are common – one in ten young people suffers problems of some kind – stigma and stereotypes often induce a sense of shame in those who do. Naturally young people will fear seeking help for mental health problems if they anticipate that the move will subject them to new stresses. Carrie feared the effects of a psychiatric diagnosis: 'Once a person puts a label on you and people know that label, they just automatically see you as that no matter what you're like really.' A young person may seek to protect their self-image from this stigma by denying mental health problems or struggling to cope with them alone.

Lacking information about what to expect from a visit to mental health professionals, many young people fear the worst. Although help with emotional and psychological problems is increasingly being offered in community settings, mental health care still tends to be associated with psychiatrists working in large institutions: 'I thought maybe they'd cart me off to a mental institution. I thought I'd be sedated and strapped down'; 'I was too scared to go to the doctor's because I thought they'd bang me up in a loony-bin or put me on tranquillisers.' Such coercive phantoms make involving others a dangerous prospect rather than a helpful step. Young people who fear dramatic intervention once their suicidal feelings are revealed are likely to keep them hidden. Malign expectations of the psychiatric system provide powerful disincentives to seeking help from professional sources.

Such fears must be addressed and allayed if vulnerable

young people are to feel any confidence in the help available to them. In general, the British public appears to have little under-standing of the role of the different kinds of treatment that are available for mental health problems.[8] This leaves a vacuum in understanding in which anxieties easily proliferate. Drug treat-ment appears to be a source of particular concern.[9] Since the addictiveness of the minor tranquillisers came to light in the 1980s, public confidence in all psychotropic (mood-altering) drugs appears to have been damaged.[10] Nearly 80 per cent of the public now believe antidepressant tablets to be addictive, an obvious disincentive to taking them.[11] Joan recalled the distrust of her son, who was depressed for a long period before his eventual suicide:

> Jason wouldn't have any tablets. The doctor offered him anti-depressants, but Jason refused them. He thought they were addictive. But apparently antidepressants are not addictive, whereas if you're on Valium they are. Had he taken antide-pressants there might have been some improvement.

Antidepressants might or might not have helped to prevent Jason's death. What is clear is that his fears about these drugs were never properly addressed. Had Jason been offered more information he would have been able to make a more informed decision about the treatment he was offered.

Interpretations of Distress; Questions about Treatment

> They chastised me, saying how stupid I was because people were being rushed into casualty all the time. I was made to feel – 'You silly little girl. What did you do that for?' They minimise what's just happened: 'It wasn't serious. It was just a cry for help.' Minimise or chastise. They do it and you do it yourself. I came out with something stupid about my boyfriend because they want a reason, don't they? I couldn't

say: 'This is the sum total. This is the solution. I've thought about it before.'

Young people's feelings about seeking help will often be affected by the way others appear to interpret their problems. These interpretations are emotive because they involve feelings and experiences which are both intimate and threatening. Inevitably they feel, to a young person, like judgements. During a crisis, when he or she is most vulnerable, these interpretations are more threatening than ever. And yet it is often at crisis point that feelings and behaviour are exposed to others.

Each year, thousands of young people come in contact with helping services for the first time in the midst of an extreme personal crisis. Arriving in the casualty department of a hospital, having injured themselves or taken an overdose, they will be unaware that pumping stomachs and putting stitches in self-inflicted wounds is routine for the doctors and nurses there. The attitudes of staff in casualty departments towards young suicide attempters may be far from indulgent, as they struggle to cope with their own feelings and defences towards those who harm themselves. A significant tension is evident between the perspectives of young suicide attempters and casualty staff, notably in their views of what motivates overdoses and acts of self-injury. Whilst the majority of adolescents, in one study, reported that they had acted meaning to die, or not caring whether they lived or died, medical emergency room staff viewed their motives very differently. *They* felt that the majority of young people had acted with no intention – clear or ambivalent – of dying.[12] These differences in interpretation are particularly significant given that a young person's attitudes towards seeking professional help in future will be deeply affected by their experiences in casualty.

By suggesting the meaning of emotional or psychological difficulties, the interpretations of others may affect a young person's self-image very deeply. David was 16 when he was admitted to hospital having taken an overdose. He tried to explain why he had done so to a doctor in casualty:

*I told him I took it because I was bisexual. He just told me to
go and see a psychologist or take some antidepressants or
something because being bisexual wasn't enough reason to kill
yourself. I fucking thought it was. The world does not accommodate you. Sexuality is certainly a very big part of someone's
life.*

A clash of perspectives may be reinforced by the *kind* of help
offered. David's disenchantment was compounded when the
treatment he was offered made no sense to him: 'I was taking
antidepressants because I was bisexual.' To David drugs
denoted being 'ill'. He felt unable to cope alone in a world that
forbade him to love men – 'I thought I was some kind of freak' –
but he did not regard himself as ill. It was not long before David
broke off contact with the health services. He felt not only that
the stresses and isolation he had experienced as a gay teenager
had been discounted, but that the treatment he received was
inappropriate.

Both the origins of mental suffering and the acceptability of
different types of treatment are hotly contended within the
mental health debate. Young people in crisis are unlikely to be
familiar with the history of this debate and the different schools
of opinion within it regarding the causes and treatment of mental distress. Their intuitions about different professionals and
types of help may nevertheless reflect some of its central
themes. Since explanations of what causes a mental health problem – for example depression – vary considerably, and a
number of different types of help may be offered for the same
problem, it is important that a young person coming into contact with 'helping' professions does not fall victim to utter
confusion.

Three strands of explanation often seem to compete regarding the causes of mental distress. **Social explanations** point out
the social and environmental pressures that create stress in
people's lives. **Psychological explanations** look at the ways in
which we learn to think, feel, behave and cope with our life
experience. **Physical or biological explanations** consider the

hereditary and biochemical factors that may contribute to mental distress. Common sense suggests that all three will influence experience, but the balance will differ for each individual. Whilst the *causes* of emotional and psychological suffering are complex and sometimes disguised, the *symptoms* can often be more easily identified. 'Mental health problems' tend to be classified according to the presence of certain symptoms. Low mood, panic attacks, hearing voices, not eating or sleeping are among the 'symptoms' that may help professionals to *name or diagnose* a mental health problem. Yet this diagnosis may say little about what has caused or brought about these symptoms.

Understanding that one *is* depressed is not, of course, the same as understanding *why*. The medical tradition of mental health treatment – psychiatry – has often been criticised for identifying problems resulting from traumatic and stressful experiences as mental illness.[13] The process of medical classification may seem to distance the symptoms of distress from their more recognisable causes. Psychiatry stands accused of *pathologising* people: encouraging them to see themselves as mentally ill rather than to recognise the social and psychological stresses that have contributed to problems.[14] One British study, for example, found that nearly half of all women who visit a psychiatrist have been sexually abused as children.[15] Among women in special hospitals the experience of such abuse is even more common.[16] The long-term effects of sexual abuse may be profound, yet those who suffered it early on in life may not recognise the connection between current difficulties with eating, depression, anxiety or self-harm and the experiences they suffered as children.[17] When such problems are diagnosed simply as mental illnesses a vital element of personal experience and meaning is obscured. A disregard for the origins of mental distress leaves a young person with little sense of why he or she has reached crisis point. The feeling of hope that comes with being able to understand and help oneself is then denied.

Unfortunately psychotropic medication has too often been used as an easy substitute for other kinds of treatment. In the 1970s, when overdosing reached peak rates, a researcher investigating the phenomenon commented that 'more listening and perhaps less prescribing by physicians may have a greater role in the primary prevention of parasuicide than any other single measure'.[18] The same principle might be applied to preventing suicide. Psychotropic drugs may well save lives by alleviating intolerable feelings and thoughts, but they leave many other needs unmet:

> He didn't believe in the drugs and at the hospital they didn't seem to talk to him, which just seemed bizarre. How did they know what was going on in his mind – all the complexities; all the mass of experience; all the inheritance; all the relationships? He needed someone who could just listen to who he was; to what he was trying to say. When you're desperate what you need is love and support.

A pill neither removes the need for a distressed person to be heard and cared for nor justifies neglect of their emotional, social and economic problems.

'Help' can be offered to a young person in ways which leave him or her feeling misinterpreted, confused and uncared for. A young person's confidence may drain into hopelessness if his or her emotional perspective and life experience are neglected by those who offer help.

What Would You Know About It?

> I was never very keen on talking to men psychiatrists. I used to feel a bit on edge so I could never really tell him everything. I felt threatened. All the men I'd known in the church were very strong and powerful and condescended to you. They were like big male gods looking down on you.
>
> (SUSIE)

> I found the patients even more racist than the staff. One of them had a habit of calling me Sambo. I couldn't believe it.

Even mad people hate us. I told the nurse and she told me I
was imagining it all. I was so angry. I know the difference. It
was from that day that I decided to keep myself to myself. I
was so lonely. But I was too wary of all these white people and
the only black people I saw were cleaners. (John, in *Sadness in*
my Heart)[19]

Mental health professionals are predominantly white and middle class and their assumptions and perspectives will not reflect
those of many young people who come to them for help.
Unfortunately there is clear evidence of bias in the provision of
mental health care. Studies have found that the type of aftercare
received by those admitted to hospital after a suicide attempt is
related to their social class.[20] Rates of compulsory treatment,
police intervention, diagnoses of schizophrenia and the admin-
istering of powerful neuroleptic (nervous-system) drugs to
Black people within the mental health system have caused considerable concern.[21] The race of a patient influences the attitudes
of psychiatrists.[22] Working-class and Black women are more
rarely offered counselling than others.[23] Individual professionals still appear to visit their judgements on young gays and
lesbians.[24] Clearly, prejudices may too easily be passed off as
medical judgements. Young people need, with good reason, to
be reassured that the personal assumptions, beliefs and life
experience of individual professionals are not hostile or preju-
diced against them, in either overt or subtle ways.

Among young people, there is a general danger that professionals will be identified as authority figures, associated with
parents, teachers, the police. For some the professional may also
be associated with a social group or system – identified perhaps with gender, class, race, sexual orientation or religion –
that he or she experiences as oppressive or threatening. Young
people may feel particularly wary of seeking help from those
whose background, cultural heritage and life experiences are
very different to their own. For some young people this distance in experience and perspectives may challenge trust
considerably and inhibit communication and understanding:

'I'd feel very shy and embarrassed talking to a man about the problems I had. I found it easier in some of the discussion groups with women' (Susie); 'The trouble is the gay people won't believe that the counsellor knows what they're talking about if they're straight' (David). 'Separate' services – addressing particular needs – may supplement general mental health care, helping a young person to feel more confident that their life experience will be appreciated, and comfortable among others sharing common social and cultural ground. In a similar way a young person may value common experience in those he or she turns to for help with a specific problem, such as alcohol or drug dependence. Advice from a recovering drug addict may inspire more hope and confidence than the words of someone who has never 'been there'. Young people seeking help need to feel both that their individuality is respected and that their specific needs and social experiences are recognised.

Poor Practice

I had to see a psychiatrist. I felt a lot of fear because she was the first person I'd ever come out and said I was gay to. It was a really massive admission but I told her the truth and broke down. I don't know what I expected but she said almost nothing. No emotion registered with her at all. She could have helped me by talking about it. She could have told me things and put me in touch with helplines but she just said, 'You can go now. The interview is finished.' Maybe I couldn't articulate myself very well and didn't really convey how worthless and negative I felt. Afterwards, I was so scared because I didn't know what she was going to do with the information I'd just told her. I didn't know if it was going to go back to my school or my father. I was in hospital for a week after that and I told everyone who asked me why I'd done it a complete load of lies about getting a girl pregnant.

Having survived an overdose at 14, Barry was discharged from

203

hospital with his problems unresolved and no arrangement for follow-up help: 'As soon as I came out of hospital I just went back into exactly the same slot as before.' He remained unsupported and made a further suicide attempt later in adolescence. If an attempt to find help ends in disillusionment a young person may not try again, even though more suitable and appropriate help may have been within arm's reach. Although many young people receive sensitive and invaluable support from the mental health services, a textbook system of care should not be assumed. In reality the difficulties of very vulnerable young people may be exacerbated by cursory attention and inadequate resources in a mental health care system that is often severely strained. Bad experiences of mental health professionals may prove extremely damaging and bitterly disillusioning. If young people have felt let down in a past crisis, their residual feelings will present obstacles to seeking help in a fresh crisis.

High Hopes, Realistic Expectations

After struggling with feelings in isolation for some time, young people may have high expectations of those to whom they turn for help. The powers of the 'expert' may be hard for them to gauge. Barry first met a psychiatrist when he was 14: 'I thought the fact that she was a psychiatrist meant she would probably see through me, so I *had* to tell her the truth. I couldn't lie to this person.' Yet professionals fall far short of omniscience. They must get to know a young person through talking with them, and possibly with members of their family, gradually building a picture of the young person's problems, personality and circumstances. They cannot provide immediate solutions to the often complex problems that lead to suicidal feelings. A young person may naturally yearn for a quick solution, particularly as feelings become intolerable, but the process of change and recovery will be more gradual.

It is essential that young people are helped to build realistic expectations both of those they approach for help and of the pace of change. Illusions or false promises will lead to early disappointment, on which a dangerous sense of hopelessness may thrive. Choosing the right *kind* of help from the wide range of treatments and therapies on offer is also essential:

> *I went to hypnotherapy. I wanted to break the pattern of never having a relationship that goes further than two weeks. I only went twice. It wasn't very good. I didn't go under. But it didn't work for me at all. Which was a shame because I was at my very, very lowest ebb then. I was thinking about suicide almost every waking moment.*

Having made the difficult decision to see someone about emotional problems, a young person may not repeat the experiment if 'help' appears to have been ineffective. When help is discredited, the dangerous isolation of a suicidal young person is reaffirmed. Tracy observed that going to hypnotherapy gave her 'something to believe in' at a time when she despaired of finding the relationship she longed for. Yet this new hope was short-lived. Nothing happened at the hypnotherapy sessions; there were no emotional dividends. After two visits Tracy decided not to make another appointment. She was left alone with suicidal feelings and a sense of powerlessness to change her situation.

Appropriate expectations of professionals are vitally important when a young person has said he or she is feeling suicidal. Being a 'professional' does not remove someone's fear of their patient's self-destructive potential. Although mental health professionals are trained in the assessment of suicide risk and the care of the suicidal, they are not untouched by the fear and denial experienced by relatives and friends of the suicidal. Mental health professionals have also been reported to ignore and deny suicidal clues.[25] And observing that therapy cannot always prevent suicide, one therapist warned: 'People should not feel that "everything is taken care of" just because the suicidal adolescent has entered therapy.'[26] The idea that suicide prevention is the exclusive responsibility of any group of professionals is as unfortunate as it is unrealistic.

Despair

You can't ever see things getting better. I didn't even see a future. I didn't even think about it. I didn't want to be here. You could have said to me at the time, 'Things have got to get better.' But I couldn't see that at all.

(LORRAINE)

When a young person sees more reason to die than live they have exhausted hope. Months or years of trying to cope, of trying to find milder 'solutions' to painful problems, appear to have failed. From this vantage point the future is not merely unclear; it is often inconceivable. Despair builds a wall beyond which a young person cannot see. Lorraine's bleak vision had built up over months. When she came round after her overdose her despair was, at first, unremitting and her disappointment to be alive, bitter. Lorraine no longer believed that things could change. The hopelessness that nurtures frustration, despair and suicidal feelings will, by its very nature, make it less likely that a young person will seek help.

A young person who has *tried* to change their situation and 'failed' may be extremely vulnerable to a sense of powerlessness. To those already feeling fragile, disillusionment can feel acute:

When you've tried . . . and nothing changes then it feels as if there's nothing else you can do. You take stock and think: 'Nothing's changed. Not a damn thing's changed. What the fuck am I doing wrong?' Then it feels as if there's not really much left.

(CLAUDETTE)

Information and Understanding

The fears and difficulties faced by suicidal young people can only be exacerbated by lack of information and unclear expectations. Confusion heightens anxiety during a crisis and anxiety raises the emotional temperature. A range of services are available to help those feeling suicidal and unable to cope. It may actually be easier for a young person to talk to a stranger who has no connection with their family or wider social network. Unfortunately, many vulnerable young people know little about 'outside' sources of support or the roles of those who provide it. Knowing about the sources of help which exist and the types of support offered by various professionals, volunteers and self-help groups can help young people and those close to them to see a way forward. Confidence and trust are likely to be built on clear understanding.

CHAPTER 9

Sources of Help: A Quick Guide

Establishing support which is trusted, reliable and sustainable may be a matter of trial and error. Help that is acceptable and suitable to one young person may not be to another. Some understanding of the range and types of support available can help a young person to see that he or she has choices and to build realistic expectations.

The number of young suicide victims who have *not* sought support before their death suggests how many do not recognise or believe that help may be available. If they do, they may have considerable reservations about approaching professionals or volunteers for reasons already explored. A young person will often need to be reassured that having a 'mental health problem' and seeking professional help does not mean that he or she is 'mad' or 'sick'. Finding it difficult to cope with distressing feelings and thoughts is more common than many realise. So too is seeking outside help for emotional and mental health problems. Encouragement and approval will nevertheless be vital to a young person who is contemplating this possibility. If those close to him or her regard seeking help from outside sources as suspicious or as a sign of 'failure' or as a rejection of them, a young person may also see it this way and give up. More helpfully, a young person's attempts to find support can be seen as a brave step towards admitting that problems exist and addressing them.

Personalities will always play an important and unpredictable part in contact with outside sources of support. Rapport affects the success of any relationship, and in one intended to be supportive and therapeutic this basic quality is essential. A suicidal young person who gains no comfort and reassurance from a helping professional or volunteer may not reappear. False starts may need to be overcome. When one type of help, or particular relationship, has not worked out it is important to keep trying others. One poor response or bad connection is not worth a young life.

Susie suffered anxiety, isolation, low self-esteem and suicidal thoughts for years during adolescence. These difficulties intensified in late adolescence when she started work, left home and met her boyfriend. She felt utterly torn between her own needs and the approval of her parents, who were fundamentalist Christians. Swamped by guilt and anxiety when her relationship with her boyfriend became sexual, Susie found it increasingly hard to cope. Finally, after a suicide attempt, she contacted The Samaritans. This represented the starting point of a longer process. Her subsequent experiences of voluntary, professional and self-help suggest how persistence was vital during this process and helped her to find the type of support with which she, personally, felt comfortable:

> I didn't phone The Samaritans, because I was scared of telephones, but I wrote to them and told them about these feelings and what had happened. I thought I wouldn't get a reply but I did. This woman wrote and said: 'If you want to come and see me you can.' But it was really difficult. I made loads of excuses at first, saying: 'I'm ill. I can't come today.' Then I eventually plucked up the courage . . .
>
> Then I went to see this Samaritans woman every week – just to talk. It was like counselling, really. It really helped – just speaking to someone who didn't have anything to do with my family or their church – just a woman I'd never met before.

Being able to talk was something I'd never been able to do while I was at home. I got such a lot out of that. That was a start.

[Susie felt reassured by her contact with The Samaritans but some months later, when under stress at work, old feelings and thoughts resurfaced.]

I began to get these same thoughts back again. It was mainly the stress at work. I had just got over this religious business with the family. I wasn't very confident. I began to think: 'Well I must be inadequate then. I must be no good. I must be useless.' I started binge eating just for comfort. I got depressed about global warming. I went to the doctor. I asked them not to put me on any medication. They gave me relaxation tapes but I couldn't do them on my own. That's when they asked me how I felt about going to a psychiatric day hospital . . .

I thought going there was going to be awful. I felt really uncomfortable with the day hospital thing at first. I couldn't get this stereotype out of the back of my head – 'I'm a mental patient now.' I thought I'd be just another number on their files. But it was all right actually. Some of the things were really helpful.

I didn't fancy going on tablets. Even at my worst moments I want to get to the root of the problem, not drug it up. And I was scared in case I got hooked on them. I said to the psychiatrist, 'Don't put me on any drugs. I want to get to the root of the problem.' They were surprisingly all right about it. He said, 'Whatever you want but if you find it gets too bad it might be a good idea.'

I could never really tell [the psychiatrist] anything. I was never very keen on talking to men. I used to feel a bit on edge. All the men I'd known in the church were like big male gods looking down on you. I'd feel very shy and embarrassed talking to men about the problems I had. I found it easier in some of the discussion groups with women.

Then I went to a mental health survivors' group. Their philosophy was really good. There would be other people talking about similar things that had happened to them. They talked about all sorts of things that I'd kept quiet. Listening to other people you see how you got into your rut. And I was actually beginning to see why I was like I was and find reasons for what I was doing.

Here was this safe place, with people confidentiality, where I could talk about all the hurt from the past. It was somewhere where you could get rid of your emotions safely. They were saying emotions like anger and crying were normal – that's how babies get rid of their hurt and pain. That was really helpful. I'd always been told to be wary of my feelings in my upbringing. The idea was to get rid of the hurts and feelings and frustrations of the past – to discharge emotion. It doesn't suit everybody because some people say they don't like going over the past. But it suited me; it got it out of my head.

Types of Help

The types of help offered by professionals, volunteers and self-help groups vary considerably. Approaching social, emotional and mental health problems in their own ways, they often complement each other by tackling different aspects of a young person's problems. Practical support and intervention may be urgently needed – bullying may have to be stopped, abuse at home confronted, neighbourhood harassment interrupted, homelessness tackled, and so on. The immediate problems which are exerting pressure on a young person must be addressed. Suicidal feelings thrive in those who feel trapped in intolerable situations. The nature of this situation will obviously determine the types of response and support needed in individual cases.

Any young person who has reached suicidal despair will also require strong emotional support. Specific mental health problems such as depression, anxiety, eating problems and alcohol abuse need to be addressed. The types of therapy or treatment available for emotional and mental health problems divide between the psychological kind – based on talking – and physical treatments, usually involving psychotropic drugs. Although many people find their distress is alleviated by a combination of both approaches, they obviously work in quite different ways. Psychological therapies are broadly based on talking, in a supportive setting, in order to vent emotion and build an understanding of how we feel, think and act. The aim is usually to come to terms with personal experience and change patterns of feeling, thinking and behaving that may be causing great misery. Treatment with drugs aims to relieve mental suffering by changing or controlling its symptoms. Children and younger adolescents are rarely treated with drugs. But a young person who is exhausted by anxiety and sleeplessness, or suffering the intolerable emotional pain that depression can bring, or losing touch with reality may need the relief that drugs can bring.

The 'right' response to a young person's suicidal crisis, and the problems it reflects, will not always be clear. Confusion can be heightened when tensions emerge between the way in which different professions, voluntary organisations and self-help groups interpret distressing feelings and problems. Each group of professionals and volunteers tends to have its own framework for understanding emotional distress and a special commitment to a particular type of response or treatment. It is vitally important that these tensions do not add to the acute stress of a suicidal young person. Above all, a young person's own ideas and preferences about the type of help that is appropriate to his or her feelings and situation will play a vital role in its outcome. The types of advice, support and therapy that may be valuable in turning a suicidal crisis around are described briefly below. A young person in crisis may want to make use of a number of them.

Immediate emotional support

There are times when a young person will need immediate sympathy and support, especially when he or she is feeling lonely, unable to cope and despairing. This support is available at any time of day or night over the telephone. If a young person does not have access to a phone there may be places locally – such as a Samaritans branch – where he or she can drop in without an appointment. An appointment to see a GP will take a little longer but a GP can provide further support.

Counselling

Provides a chance to talk to someone who is trained to listen. A good counsellor will convey a sense of empathy and provide a safe environment, where feelings and experiences can be shared in confidence. Counselling often helps someone to address a specific event or issue in their life – such as bereavement or relationship difficulties. Counsellors will not give advice or tell a young person how to solve his or her problems. Instead they encourage a young person to explore and understand their own feelings, thoughts and behaviour and experience. With support, counselling aims to help individuals to come to terms with problems. Many people – professionals, voluntary workers, those who run self-help groups – train in counselling.

Psychotherapy

Like counselling, this is a talking therapy which aims to provide a supportive relationship within which feelings, thoughts and experience can be explored. The origins of current problems are considered to lie in the past, and psychotherapy usually involves talking about past experiences. Whereas counselling tends to address particular problems over a relatively short period of time, psychotherapy may involve regular meetings over a longer period, allowing the past as well as the present to be explored in more depth. Like counselling, psychotherapy aims to help individuals to come to terms with their problems and to learn how to cope effectively in future.

Family therapy

This offers support to the whole family rather than individuals. Because a child or adolescent's emotional problems may be related to stresses or difficulties at home, and will certainly affect everyone in the family, this kind of help can be very valuable. It does not involve *blaming* family members for each other's problems but offers a positive chance to build up communication and emotional support between them. Families may then be in a stronger position to cope with problems and stresses together.

Behaviour and cognitive therapy

This type of therapy can help a young person to learn new ways of seeing and responding to situations and stresses. This will be helpful if their current perceptions or behaviour are causing them distress. **Behaviour therapy** works by setting practical tasks which can help a young person to develop the confidence to do things and cope with situations that he or she is not able, at the moment, to manage. **Cognitive therapy** tries to help a young person overcome negative patterns of thinking which reinforce feeling bad and behaving in ways that do not help. A young person who becomes panicky in certain social situations for example or feels that others are scornful of him or her might find this kind of approach helpful.

Group therapy and self-help groups

Such groups bring together individuals who share a similar difficulty or experience – for example anxiety, eating problems, under-assertiveness. Listening to others talk about a particular problem may encourage young people to share their own experiences and to learn from others. Isolation may be reduced as feelings and fears are more openly expressed. A group operates on the understanding that what is said within it is confidential. Group therapy involves at least one therapist. Self-help groups are more likely to be organised by non-professionals. Many such groups now exist, and they address a range of problems.

Psychotropic drugs

Although these are rarely prescribed to children and younger adolescents, an older adolescent or young adult with an emotional or mental health problem may be offered medication.

214

Psychotropic drugs can be valuable in controlling depression, anxiety, manic energy, strange thoughts and so on. It is essential that a young person has information about the drug she or he is taking. Knowing how long it will take to work, what side-effects can be expected and the dangers of coming off the drug suddenly will all be important. Whilst some drugs work very quickly, others do not take effect for weeks. A young person who feels that drugs are not working and stops taking them one day, may be suffering withdrawal symptoms the next. Psychotropic drugs fall into four main categories: the major tranquillisers, minor tranquillisers, antidepressants and lithium. Information about these drugs is available from the mental health charity MIND, which also publishes the *Guide to Psychiatric Drugs* by Ron Lacey.

Support with alcohol or drug problems

Dependence on alcohol and drugs is a serious problem affecting growing numbers of young people. Those who experience suicidal feelings alongside an alcohol and/or drug problem will find it hard to change what they feel without also changing what they drink, smoke, swallow or inject and the lifestyle that may go with it. Since young people often use alcohol or drugs to escape unhappiness or cope with problems in the first place, coming off drink or drugs must be backed up by strong emotional support for underlying difficulties. Professionals, voluntary organisations and self-help groups can offer specialist help and support to young people trying to cope with dependency problems.

Support with other problems

The suicidal feelings of some young people are unlikely to go away if specific problems are not tackled head on. These problems will of course be very varied, but so too is the range of professionals, voluntary organisations and self-help groups who offer local help and support with specific difficulties. Some counsellors, for example, have received training in how to support a specific group of people – for example, the bereaved or

215

those who have been diagnosed HIV positive. Details of helplines or other forms of help for young people with a specific need are listed in 'An A–Z of Help' further on in this chapter.

Practical help

This may relieve immediate pressures and help the young person to see a way forward. Practical support and advice on, for example, current housing, employment, financial or legal problems may make a crucial difference to a vulnerable young person who feels unable to cope with mounting pressures.

Other therapeutic activities

Art, music and drama therapy may help some young people to express themselves. Yoga or relaxation techniques may allow others to learn ways of coping with anxiety. 'Alternative' treatments such as massage or homoeopathy may also be valuable. As individuals we all have our own 'therapies' – or ways to relax and wind down – some of them healthier than others. Running, swimming or climbing mountains maybe; writing and reading; dancing or listening to music may be positively therapeutic for some young people. But they may also be lonely. When a young person is suicidal these other therapeutic activities are *not* safe substitutes for the direct emotional support they will need.

Sources of Help

A young person who has expressed suicidal feelings or resorted to self-harm needs considerable care, empathy and support. Those close to him or her will also need support and advice in order to cope with their own feelings and respond with confidence to a young person at risk. It is important, for all concerned, to build up a picture of the kinds of help that are available locally. Some of these – a visit to the GP or a call to The Samaritans – will always be available. In practice, services for children and adolescents are often overburdened. Inadequate resources and growing demand can mean expanding waiting lists. The local situation will vary; services on offer in one area of the UK will be almost non-existent in another. Child psychotherapy provides a notably inequitable example. The vast majority of NHS child psychotherapists are concentrated in the counties of south-east England, cold comfort for children in need elsewhere. The role of voluntary and self-help services locally also varies considerably from region to region and place to place. It is vital for those seeking help to steel themselves for such variations. Try, if possible, to be persistent rather than disheartened when local help proves to be less than ideal.

Telephone Helplines

A number of telephone helplines offer support to young people who are in crisis or trying to cope with difficult problems or feelings. Some provide support whatever the problem. Others provide support and advice for a specific problem only. Telephone support is within easy reach and, for a young person who has not sought support before, making a phone call may seem less daunting than going to see someone face to face. Kaye, for example, found that an anonymous phone call offered the chance to rehearse 'coming out': 'I rang The Samaritans and said: "Ha, ha, I think I may be gay." And they took it really seriously. I was a bit gobsmacked because I thought I would get a bad reaction.'

The Samaritans

Will answer the phone at any time of the day or night, every day of the year. Their trained volunteers have considerable experience talking with suicidal and despairing callers. They will not be shocked to hear a young person describe their suicidal feelings but promise to listen sympathetically and without judging. A young person need not give a name and their call will be treated as absolutely confidential. The Samaritans do not aim to give advice but to support young callers for as long as they need to find their own solutions. They will, however, pass on information about sources of help that are available. A national organisation, The Samaritans have local branches throughout the UK. At some branches a young person may be able to call in during the day to talk to someone face to face. If a young person agrees, a friend or relative can contact The Samaritans on their behalf. A volunteer will then get back to them. **To contact: find the telephone number of your local branch under S in the phone directory.**

Childline

Offers support to children and adolescents who are suffering any kind of problem, including abuse, bullying, difficult relationships and suicidal feelings. Young people who are worried about a friend can also call. Those calling Childline will talk to a trained volunteer counsellor, who can help them to decide what to do or where to go for help next. Counsellors will be able to suggest other sources of help. Where someone is at risk Childline will contact social services or the police *but only with a young person's permission.* **To contact: Telephone 0800 1111. Calls are free and the number will not appear on itemised phone bills. You can also write to Freepost 1111, London N1 OBR.**

NSPCC Child Protection Helpline

Offers support and advice to children who feel they are being abused or who are worried about a friend. Parents and other adults who are concerned about a child's safety may also call. **To contact: Telephone 0800 800 500. Calls are free and will not appear on itemised phone bills.**

For other telephone helplines, which address specific needs and groups, see 'An A–Z of Help' (p. 227–232).

Professionals

Young people with thoughts and feelings so distressing that they are thinking about dying, will often need the support and skills of mental health professionals. 'Mental health profession-als' are those trained to help people suffering emotional and mental health problems. Depression, low self-esteem, bottled-up anger, hurt and guilt, swinging moods, anxiety, eating difficulties, flamboyant thinking and many other demoralising and painful problems are familiar to them. Unfortunately few young people have a very clear idea of who these professionals are and what types of help they offer.

Professionals often work as a team to make available a range of services, therapies and support. Psychiatrists, psychol-ogists, psychiatric nurses and counsellors work alongside mental health social workers, occupational therapists and art therapists. These professionals are based either in the local com-munity – at a local clinic or health centre, for example – or in a hospital. Some mental health professionals are trained to help children and adolescents in particular and may work closely with schools. Once over the age of 16 young people are usually referred to the adult services, although they sometimes stay with the adolescent services for a couple of years after this. Support may come from the following sources.

General practitioners (GPs)

A young person's willingness to visit their general practitioner will depend on a number of factors. The quality of a relation-ship that already exists between them is important. So too is a young person's view of the GP's role. This may be associated with physical health care only. In fact, GPs are – or certainly should be – concerned about their patients' emotional welfare and mental health. Even when a young person is aware of this, he or she may doubt that their GP will have the time to listen. A ten-minute appointment slot does not ease the disclosure of sui-cidal feelings. To some young people, the GP's close involvement with the whole family may also be offputting. For Kaye, a visit to her GP to discuss her feelings would have been far too risky: 'That would have been completely out of the ques-tion. I didn't think about it at all because it was the *family* doctor.'

Inevitably, the quality of the support a young person receives at their local surgery will depend on the GP's personal qualities and training. Some will have had no special training in how to help patients who are depressed and experiencing other mental health problems. They may even find it hard to cope with the evidence of a young person's suicidal state. Yet other GPs will know just how to react. Phyllis recalled the sensitive response her son Tommy received when he went, depressed and suicidal, to visit his GP: 'She was only young but she was so *kind*. He went in and explained that he'd tried to kill himself before. She asked him about troubles in the past, about home, if he got into bad tempers. She said she could get him in to see a psychiatrist and a counsellor and if he didn't click with this counsellor to tell her and she could arrange another one.' GPs can offer immediate support and treatment, advise young people about types and sources of further help and refer them to other professionals. Those who are worried about a young person close to them who is suicidal might also find it helpful to visit their GP to talk things through.

Psychiatrists (child, adolescent and adult)

These are doctors who have completed the usual medical training and have gone on to specialise in how to recognise and respond to people's emotional, behavioural and mental health problems. Some psychiatrists work solely with children and adolescents and have a greater understanding of their development, needs and stresses. Psychiatrists are trained to recognise the risk of suicide and have regular contact with people who are feeling suicidal.

Only a small proportion of the young people who see psychiatrists go into hospital. Most visit a psychiatrist at a health centre, clinic or hospital outpatients department, while carrying on their usual lives. At a first meeting a psychiatrist will need to spend time talking with a young person to establish the feelings, thoughts and problems that seem to be making life intolerable. The *type* of help or treatment that is then offered will be influenced by a number of factors including a young person's age, the apparent causes of distress and – in some cases – the preference of an individual psychiatrist or psychiatric department for certain kinds of treatment.

Psychiatrists have traditionally had the final say, within the mental health care team, on the care and treatment of individuals. As with GPs, a psychiatrist's medical training enables him or her to prescribe drugs. In this, they are alone amongst the other mental health professionals described here. But psychiatrists offer a lot more than drugs. In the treatment of children and adolescents with emotional and mental health problems the use of psychotropic drugs tends to be avoided. Child and adolescent psychiatrists in particular will often hope to involve families – perhaps through family therapy – in addressing why a young person has become suicidal. Following her depression and suicide attempt at 18, Lorraine's psychiatrist offered her both psychotherapy and medication:

Before [the overdose] I didn't realise that I needed to talk to someone about how I felt. But the psychiatrist did help. I saw him for a year. All they do is sit you down and you've to speak. It was probably a good thing because it got a lot of things out of my system. It's just a process you've got to work through. He gave me some answers. He seemed to think my sister's death had a lot to do with it whereas I thought I had got over that and it was just because I was a failure and I was going to let my boyfriend down and I wasn't going to get a good job. And I told him how my dad was a bastard to me when I was young. My dad always drank and he's a very violent man. He did a lot of bad things, which nobody really knew about. The psychiatrist would say, 'I'm sorry that happened to you', which I think was what I needed to hear. I needed some recognition that it was real. He also gave me some medication which seemed to help a lot. I'd take one if I was feeling stressed out. After a while I was feeling fine. So then he said – 'It's good that you don't want to be here any more but if anything happens, anything at all, phone up and we'll get you in here.'

221

To contact a psychiatrist: visit your GP to discuss the possibility. If an appointment with a psychiatrist seems appropriate the GP will write a letter of referral.

Psychiatric nurses and nurse therapists

Provide a great deal of support to people suffering from mental health problems. They work either in a hospital setting or are community based in local health centres and mental health units; they also visit people at home. After their full training in mental health care psychiatric nurses may also train in the skills needed to practise various kinds of therapy, such as family or group therapy. Community psychiatric nurses (CPNs) tend to be based in GPs' surgeries and local health centres, and may visit people at home. Registered mental nurses (RMNs) tend to work in psychiatric hospitals. **To contact a psychiatric nurse: visit your GP to discuss the possibility.**

Psychologists (clinical and educational)

All psychologists have a degree in psychology – the study of mind and behaviour – and further specialised training. Clinical psychologists develop their understanding of emotional and psychological problems, working within mental health teams. They are not medically qualified and do not prescribe drugs. The kinds of treatment or therapy they offer work through talking about feelings and addressing behaviour. Their work – like that of counsellors and psychotherapists – involves 'talking cures'. Carrie was deeply depressed when she explored her feelings and perceptions with a psychologist: 'She used to accept how I felt. She'd work through how I was actually feeling and the beliefs that I had about myself and the world, rather than just saying: "It will get better."' **To contact a clinical psychologist: visit your GP to discuss the possibility.**

Educational psychologists work with children and adolescents who are seen to be experiencing emotional, learning and behavioural difficulties at school or are refusing to attend. They have teaching experience as well as special training. Educational psychologists usually work in schools, bringing together children, parents and teachers to resolve problems. **To contact an educational psychologist: ask your school or local education authority.**

Counsellors and psychotherapists

It is not only 'counsellors' and 'psychotherapists' but psychiatrists, psychologists, nurse therapists and many others working in voluntary organisations who may offer a young person what is broadly referred to as a 'talking treatment'. This reflects the fact that the basic counselling skills of listening and empathy are likely to be fundamental to any supportive and healing relationship. Yet the wide array of people calling themselves 'counsellors' or 'psychotherapists' can also be highly confusing to someone looking for help. People train to be counsellors and psychotherapists in very different schools and contexts, and although regulation of their training is under way, counselling still takes many forms. It is therefore vital that a young person who is suicidal receives advice about where to go for counselling. A GP or an organisation such as Young Minds (see p. 232) should be able to provide this. Some GPs' surgeries and health centres have a counsellor/psychotherapist. However, some people are so disturbed or distressed that they need to be in hospital, either for their own safety, the safety of others or both. A young person who is in immediate danger of suicide and will not agree to enter hospital voluntarily may be detained under the Mental Health Act, although this is rare. Most of those who go into hospital do so voluntarily. Further advice about the Mental Health Act, compulsory treatment and young people's legal rights is available from MIND, Citizens' Advice Bureaux or the Children's Legal Centre.

Self-help and Voluntary Organisations

Self-help groups offer mutual support and understanding to those who share a similar problem or need. They work in a similar way to group therapy but self-help groups, as the name suggests, are often run without the involvement of a mental health professional or therapist. This may appeal to those who feel uncomfortable, as Susie did, with the dynamics of receiving professional help: 'Sometimes in the Day Hospital I felt very much the patient. They were the staff and you were the patient. It was like parent to child – them telling you what to do and giving advice.' By contrast she felt the equal of those she met in the self-help group she attended: 'In the "mental health survivors group" it was like supporting *each other* – listening to other people talking about similar things that have happened to them.' Many self-help organisations and groups have developed in recent decades, and they address a wide range of needs.

Voluntary organisations also provide a great deal of counselling and practical support to people in emotional crisis or suffering from mental health problems. Some services are provided specifically for young people – youth counselling services or drop-in information services among them. Young people and their parents can obtain information about the youth counselling, advice and befriending services that are available in their area by contacting Youthaccess (see p. 232).

Major voluntary mental health organisations exist in the UK (see p. 227). As well as campaigning for improved services they provide direct advice and support to those experiencing emotional and mental health difficulties. They will be able to advise young people, or those concerned about them, which local services, voluntary organisations and self-help groups are available in their area. Local branches sometimes employ professionals and recruit volunteers to provide a range of services, including counselling and other forms of therapy. Although professionals may suggest that young people contact self-help or voluntary organisations, these sources of support are independent and may be contacted directly. Some time after his suicide attempt, on a desperate and despairing afternoon, Ashley suddenly felt he had nothing to lose from reaching out for help:

I was living in a state of paranoia. I was like tripping all the

224

time. I was so anxious I was having panic attacks. Everything was crazy. I was very paranoid, really frightened. Wherever I walked I felt like I had a spotlight on me. I was self-conscious in a ridiculous way. One day I just went out in the afternoon, got drunk, then came back here and rang The Samaritans. I remember thinking: 'I thought I knew loads of people. I thought I had a lot of friends.' But I was turning to help outside of that because there felt such a gap between me and other people. And I realised that was part of the problem. I rang The Samaritans and said, 'I can't handle it.' I spurted out all this rubbish. They were really good. They put me in touch with Alcoholics Anonymous.

It was through talking to this bloke at AA that I realised I was an alcoholic. There was no fucking denying it. Everyone else knew. I was drinking from 13 to 21. I was quite relieved, to be honest. I was that down I wasn't bothered. I ended up going to an AA meeting. I met other people like me, who'd copped off with loads of people, hassled women, just generally made a fool of themselves thousands of times in public. Being an alcoholic you lose all your self-respect. In the end I began to feel OK. I realised I wasn't alone. I felt some solidarity and some love.

I was in AA for six months without a drink. I was so physically ill. I've had a thousand hangovers and it's like you've got to deal with them all at once. It is heavy. I had anxiety and mild hallucinations. After about four or five months it had gone but it took me about 18 months to get physically and mentally reasonable.

For the first six months I was in AA my head was in the same place. I went to meetings about once, twice, three times a week but I was still pretty scared. A lot of the stuff that was important to me I wouldn't have talked about. Then this guy turned up and I really related to what he was saying because he had been a junkie and a villain. He's an amazing bloke and he talked about sex and stuff and how he felt bad about it. I've been lucky to meet someone I could speak with without being judged.

A lot of it was about not running away. I took the alcohol away and after six months my head was killing me. So I realised I had to talk out all the pain inside me – all the things I'd never talked about; all the stuff I'd accumulated during my life. But I stayed in for 18 months. I didn't have any relationships. I had to spend a lot of time recovering, licking my wounds and coming down off this thing.

The more I've talked about my past the more I've made sense of it. It's an incredible feeling to realise you're not at fault – to understand what has made you the way you are. I really believe that counselling is a way forward for people that are depressed. For me it worked. I could actually talk out my life and realise I had it rough. When I were pissed up and trying to cop off with people it weren't just me being an evil bastard. It was about me wanting some love – something nice. All I've ever tasted were police stations, alcoholic families, insecure mates, rough pubs – that's the sort of environment I grew up in. But I've had to take responsibility for all that's gone on in my life. Through talking stuff out I've come to understand where I was at.

For further information about local self-help and voluntary organisations contact your GP, the Citizens' Advice Bureau, local library or Community Health Council. Information, support and advice are also available from MIND, the National Association for Mental Health (England and Wales) or the Scottish Association for Mental Health (SAMH) *or* the Northern Ireland Association for Mental Health (NIAMH) (see pp. 227–232 for their addresses).

Further advice and information about sources of help

Further advice and information about the mental health services may be helpful and reassuring. The organisation Young Minds (see p. 232) offers advice to young people and their relatives about the local and national mental health services that exist to help them.

AN A–Z OF HELP: *Sources of Support for Young People with Specific problems or Needs*

Acceptance – A helpline and support group for parents of lesbians and gay men Tel: 0795 661463 Tues.–Fri. 7–9p.m.

ADFAM National – Support and information about drugs and related services in the UK for drug users and their families. 1st Floor, Upworth house, 25 City Road London EC1Y. Tel: 0171 638 3700 (Helpline 10–5 weekdays)

Al-Anon Family Groups UK and Eire 61 Great Dover St, London SE1 4YF. Tel: 0171 403 0888 (24 hour helpline). Support for those (relatives/friends) affected by a problem drinker. 1,090 groups in UK. **Alateen** based at the same address offers help to teenagers affected by alcoholics, usually parents.

Alateen – Help for young people aged 12–20 who have relatives or friends with alcohol problems. Information about local groups is available from 61 Great Dover Street, London SE1 4YF. Tel: 0171 403 0888 (24 hours a day)

Alcohol Concern, Waterbridge House, 32–36 Loman Street, London SE1 0EE. Tel: 0171 833 3471

Alcohol Counselling Service, 34 Electric Lane, London SW9 8JT. Tel: 0171 928 7377

Alcoholics Anonymous General Service Office UK, PO Box 1, Stonebow House, York YO1 2NJ. Tel: 0904 644026. Help for those who want to stop drinking – a group therapy approach. (Local contacts/groups in phone book)

British Association of Counselling Referral agency: provides extensive list of organisations and practitioners by area; also information about self-help groups, free counselling services and how to apply for NHS treatment. 1 Regent Place, Rugby, Warwickshire CV21 2PJ. Tel: 0788 578 328.

British Association of Psychotherapists Psychoanalytical & psychotherapy service. 37 Mapesbury Road, London NW2 4HJ. Tel: 0181 452 9823

British Pregnancy Advisory Service Advice on pregnancy and contraception (see phone book for local numbers). 7 Belgrave Road, London SW1V 1QB. Tel: 0171 828 2484

Brook Advisory Centres Advice on pregnancy and contraception (see phone book for local numbers). 153a East St, London SE17 2SD. Tel: 0171 708 1234

Childline Telephone helpline for children and adolescents. Freepost 1111, London N1 0BR. Tel: 0800 1111. (Free 24-hour phone service which will not show up on itemised phone bills)

The Compassionate Friends Self-help organisation for bereaved parents, open to parents who have lost a child of any age, in whatever way. The Shadow of Suicide (SOS) group brings together parents who are similarly bereaved. A quarterly newsletter **SIBBS (Support in Bereavement for Brothers and Sisters)** and contact network is available for young people bereaved through the death of a sibling. The Compassionate Friends, 53 North Street, Bristol BS3 1EN. Tel: 0117 9539 639

CRUSE Bereavement Care Service of counselling, advice and opportunities for social contact to all bereaved people. Cruse House, 126 Sheen Road, Richmond, Surrey, TW9 1VR. Tel: 0181 332 7227

Families Anonymous – Helpline for those who are worried about a family member's use of drugs. May be able to put you in contact with a self-help group in your area. The Doddington and Rollo Community Association, Charlotte Despard Avenue, London SW11 5JE. Tel: 0171 498 4680

Family Planning Association Advice on pregnancy and contraception. 27 Mortimer St, London W1N 7RJ. Tel: 071 636 7866. See phone book for local numbers

Gay Bereavement Project Support and advice for people bereaved by death of same-sex partner. The Vaughan M Williams Centre, Colindale Hospital, Colindale Avenue, London NW9 5HG. Helpline: 0181 455 8894; admin. 0181 200 0511

Gingerbread A national network of local mutual aid groups providing emotional support, practical help and social activities for one-parent families. 35 Wellington Street, London WC2E 7BN. Tel: 0171 240 0953

Jewish Bereavement Counselling Service Counselling and support to members of the Jewish community who are bereaved (mainly operated in north-west and south-west London). 1 Cyprus Gardens, London N3 1SP (24-hour ansaphone: 0181 349 0839/ Office hours 0171 387 4300 ext. 277)

Lesbian & Gay switchboard 0171 837 7324

Lesbian Information Service (LIS) Information and help for lesbian women. Publish a 'coming-out' pack for young lesbians. PO Box 8, Todmorden, Lancs OL14 5TZ. Tel: 0706 817235

MIND (National Association of Mental Health) Includes an information and advice service. Granta House, 15–19 Broadway, Stratford, London E15 4BQ. Tel: 0181 519 2122

Mindlink MIND's network for those that use mental health services. Publishes a quarterly newsletter, *Mindwaves*.

NAFSIYAT (The Inter-Cultural Therapy Centre) An inter-cultural centre offering a range of different psychotherapies, working with individuals from many different ethnic groups (mostly Islington area) 278 Seven Sisters Road, London N4 2HY. Tel: 0171 263 4130.

Narcotics Anonymous Self-help organisation for those who have a problem with drugs, based on local meeting. Telephone advice given by recovering addicts. PO Box 1980, London N19 3LS. Tel: 0171 498 9005. (Advice line 10a.m.–10p.m. every day)

National AIDS Helpline 0800 567 123 (Free – 24 hour)

National Association of Bereavement Services Refers individuals to bereavement support services in their area. 20 Norton Folgate, London E1 6DB. Tel: 0171 247 0617.

National Children's Home Action for Children Offers support to young people with a range of problems and can give contact numbers for help with specific problems. Tel: 0171 226 2033. Some local numbers are available from this national number

NAYPCAS (The National Association of Young People's Counselling and Advisory Services) 17–23 Albion Street, Leicester LE1 6GD. Tel: 0553 558 763. Can put you in touch with local youth counselling service. Include SAE.

NORCAP (National Organisation of Counselling for Adoptees) 3 New High Street, Headington, Oxford OX3 7AJ. Tel: 0865 750 554 (10a.m.–4p.m. Mon, Wed, Fri)

Northern Ireland Association for Mental Health (NIAMH) Beacon House, 80 University Street, Belfast BT7 1HE. Tel: 0232 328 474

NSF Formerly called the National Schizophrenia Fellowship, NSF provides information, support and an advice-line to support those whose lives are affected by schizophrenia. Self-help groups exist. **NSF:** 28 Castle Street, Kingston-upon-Thames KT1 1SS. Advice line: 081 974 6814. **NSF (Scotland):** 40 Shandwick Place, Edinburgh EH2 4RT. Tel: 031 226 2025. **NSF (Northern Ireland):** 37–39 Queen Street, Belfast BT1 6EA. Tel: 0232 248006

NSPCC Child Protection Helpline Support and advice for young people who have been abused or for anyone worried about a young person's safety. Offers the chance to talk confidentially to trained social workers and receive advice on what to do next. Tel: 0800 800 500 24-hour service; free calls that will not appear on an itemised phone bill

PACE (Project for Advice, Counselling and Education) London Lesbian & Gay Centre, 34 Hartham Road, London N7. Tel: 0171 700 1323

Parents' Friend Helpline and support group for parents of lesbians and gay men. c/o 36 Newmarket, Otley, West Yorkshire LS21 3AE. Tel: 0532 674627 (7.30p.m.–11p.m.)

Positively Women Self-help group for women who are HIV positive or have AIDS. 5 Sebastian Street, London EC1V OHE. Tel: 0171 490 2327

Rape Crisis Rape Crisis centres are listed in local directory. They provide contact numbers for 'Action Against Incest' groups where these exist. Tel: 071 837 1600 (London) or 041 221 8448 (Glasgow)

Relate Specialises in helping people with relationship difficulties, whether married or single. London Office 76a New Cavendish St, London W1. Tel: 0171 580 1087. Local addresses in phone book.

RELEASE Advice on legal problems arising from drug misuse. 388 Old Street, London EC1V 9LT. Tel: 0171 729 5255. Emergency telephone: 0171 603 6854

RESOLV (The Society for the Prevention of Solvent and Volatile Substance Abuse) A charity solely concerned with solvent misuse. They publish leaflets, booklets and videos and know about local agencies who can help. 30A High Street, Stone, Staffordshire ST15 8AW. Tel: 0785 817 885

Saneline Trained volunteers provide information and support to those suffering serious mental health problems and to their relatives and friends. Advice is available about local services and organisations. SANE, 2nd Floor, 199–205 Old Marylebone Road, London NW1 5QP. SANELINE: 0171 724 8000 (2p.m.–midnight, every day)

Scottish Association for Mental Health (SAMH) Atlantic House, 38 Gardeners Crescent, Edinburgh EH3 8DG. Tel: 0450 371 694/031 229 9687

Terrence Higgins Trust Counselling, welfare and legal help for people with AIDS and their friends and families. Tel: 0171 831 0330 Helpline: 0171 242 1010 (12 noon–10p.m.)

Young Carers Project Supports research and development work for carers who are school age and below and produces the *Young Carers Link* newsletter. c/o Carers National Association, 20–25 Glasshouse Yard, London EC1A 4JS. Tel: 0171 490 8818: Carers Line 0171 490 8898.

Young Minds Provides information about the national and local services available to young people. This organisation is trying to establish a national telephone helpline for adults who are worried about a young person's feelings, thoughts or behaviour. 22A Boston Place, London NW1 6ER. Tel: 0171 724 7262

Youthaccess Provides help and information to young people and their parents about the youth counselling, advice and befriending services that are available in their local area. Magazine Business Centre, 11 Newark St, Leicester LE1 5SS. Tel: 0533 558763

South Africa: Some Support Organisations

Radio 702 Helpline Provide a helpline for all people within their listening area, the PWV Province. Tel: 011 884 8448 (10a.m.–5p.m., Monday to Friday).

Radio 702 Crisis Centre 85 Tudhope Avenue, Berea, Johannesburg. Tel: 011 642 4462/3 (5p.m.–10p.m., Monday to Friday).

Life Line Southern Africa (National Office) PO Box 81419, Parkhurst, 2121. Tel: 011 622 6880, Pamela Weir: National Secretary. Tel: 011 447 4084, Sue Thonell. Please also call for information about Life Line organisations in your area.

FAMSA (The Family Association of South Africa) National Council PO Box 2800, Kempton Park 1620. Tel: 011 975 7106/7. Fax: 975 7108. Tel: 011 972 2761, Dr A.J. van Rensburg (Home). PLease also call the first number for information about FAMSA offices in your area.

AFTERWORD

Those bereaved by suicide are frequently plagued by the question: 'Why?' The need to understand why a relative or friend chose to kill themselves, and why suicide happens in general, often involves a process of torturous questioning. This was my own need following the death of my brother John, who ended his life at 20. For the bereaved, the search for explanations probably reflects a desperate wish to make some 'sense' of a devastating event. If a suicide can be understood, and reasons for it found, the psychological threat of meaninglessness is contained. We may even retrieve a little meaning for ourselves, with which to go on living. Yet the apparent reasons are never sufficient. They certainly do little to salve the emotional wounds and terrible sense of waste that the suicide of someone we love leaves behind. With support and time, most of us must eventually come to live with incomplete answers to the question: 'Why?'

REFERENCES

Chapter 1   **(pp.13–35)**
NUMBERS

1. ALVAREZ, A. (1974) *The Savage God: A Study of Suicide*. London: Penguin.
2. CHAMBERS, D.R. (1989) The coroner, the inquest and the verdict of suicide. *Medicine Science and the Law*, **29**, 181.
3. KATZ, I. (1992) Open verdict avoids truth. *Guardian*, 10th August.
4. CHAMBERS, D.R. & HARVEY, J.G. (1989) Inner urban and national suicide rates: A simple comparative study. *Medicine, Science and the Law*, **29**, 182–185.
5. PLATT, S., BACKETT, S. & KREITMAN, N. (1988) Social construction or casual ascription: Distinguishing suicide from undetermined deaths. *Social Psychiatry and Psychiatric Epidemiology*, **23**, 217–221.
6. ADELSTEIN, A. & MARDON, C. (1975) Suicides 1961–74. *Population Trends*, **2**, 13–18.
7. CHAMBERS, D.R. & HARVEY, J.G. (1989) Inner urban and national suicide rates: A simple comparative study. *Medicine, Science and the Law*, **29**, 182–185.
8. Ibid.
9. MCCLURE, G.M.G. (1984) Recent trends in suicide among the young. *British Journal of Psychiatry*, **144**, 134–138.
10. OFFICE OF POPULATION CENSUSES AND SURVEYS. *Mortality Statistics for England and Wales, 1979–1990*. London: HMSO.
11. Ibid.
12. KATZ, I. (1992) Open verdict avoids truth. *Guardian*, 10th August.
13. ALCOHOL, DRUG ABUSE AND MENTAL HEALTH ADMINISTRATION (1989) *Report of the Secretary's Task Force on Youth Suicide, Volume 1: Overview and Recommendation*. DHHS, Pub.No. (Adm), Washington DC: US Government Print Office. Superintendent of Documents.

14. OFFICE OF POPULATION CENSUSES AND SURVEYS. *Mortality Statistics for England and Wales, 1979–1990.* London: HMSO.

15. HAWTON, K. (1986) *Suicide and Attempted Suicide Among Children and Adolescents.* Newbury Park, California: Sage.

16. SHAFFI, M. (1989) Completed suicide in children and adolescents: Methods of psychological autopsy. In *Suicide Among Youth: Perspectives on Risk and Prevention* (ed C.R. Pfeffer). Washington DC: American Psychiatric Press.

17. ADELSTEIN, L.A. & MARDON, C. (1975) Suicides 1961–74. *Population Trends,* **2**, 13–18.

18. WORLD HEALTH ORGANIZATION (1992) *The International Classification of Diseases and Related Health Problems: Tenth Revision.* Geneva: World Health Organization.

19. CHARLTON, J., KELLY, S., DUNNELL, K., *et al* (1992) Trends in suicide deaths in England and Wales. *Population Trends,* **69**, 10–16.

20. Ibid.

21. OFFICE OF POPULATION CENSUSES AND SURVEYS. *Mortality Statistics for England and Wales, 1979–1990.* London: HMSO.

22. (1993) *Independent,* 22nd January.

23. HAWTON, K., SIMKIN, S., FAGG, J., *et al.* Suicide in Oxford University students, 1976–1990. *British Journal of Psychiatry* (in press).

24. DEPARTMENT OF HEALTH (1993) *The Health of the Nation. Key Area Handbook: Mental Illness.* London: Department of Health.

25. Ibid.

26. ADELSTEIN, A. & MARDON, C. (1975) Suicides 1961–74. *Population Trends,* **2**, 13–18.

27. Combined mortality statistics from OFFICE OF POPULATION CENSUSES AND SURVEYS (England and Wales), GENERAL REGISTER OFFICE FOR SCOTLAND and GENERAL REGISTER OFFICE FOR NORTHERN IRELAND.

28. Ibid.

29. ADELSTEIN, A. & MARDON, C. (1975) Suicides 1961–74. *Population Trends,* **2**, 13–18.

30. Ibid.

31. CHARLTON, J., KELLY, S., DUNNELL, K., *et al* (1992) Trends in suicide deaths in England and Wales. *Population Trends,* **61**, 10–16.

32. PRITCHARD, C. (1990) Suicide, unemployment and gender variations in the western world, 1964–1986: Are women in Anglo-phone countries protected from suicide? *Social Psychiatry and Psychiatric Epidemiology,* **25**, 73–80.

33. OFFICE OF POPULATION CENSUSES AND SURVEYS. *Mortality Statistics for England and Wales, 1979–1990.* London: HMSO.

34. DIEKSTRA, R.F.W. (1991) Suicide and parasuicide: A global perspective. In *Suicide and Attempted Suicide: Risk Factors, Management and Prevention* (eds S.A. Montgomery & N.L.M. Goeting). Southampton: Duphar Laboratories.

35. DIEKSTRA, R.F.W. & MORITZ, B.J.M. (1987) Suicidal behaviour among adolescents: An overview. In *Suicide in Adolescence* (eds R.F.W. Diekstra & K. Hawton). Dordrecht: Martinus Nijhof.

36. CHARLTON, J., KELLY, S., DUNNELL, K., *et al* (1992) Trends in suicide deaths in England and Wales. *Population Trends*, **6**, 10–16.

37. MCCLURE, G.M.G. (1984) Recent trends in suicide among the young. *British Journal of Psychiatry*, **144**, 134–138.

38. Ibid.

39. Ibid.

40. DEPARTMENT OF HEALTH (1993) *The Health of the Nation. Key Area Handbook: Mental Illness*. London: Department of Health.

41. Ibid.

42. KREITMAN, N. (1976) The coal gas story: UK suicide rates 1960–71. *British Journal of Preventive and Social Medicine*, **50**, 86–93.

43. O'GRADY, J.G., WENDON, J., TAN, K.C., *et al* (1991) Liver transplantation after paracetamol overdose. *British Medical Journal*, **303**, 221–223.

44. BULUSU, L. & ALDERSON, M.R. (1984) Suicides 1950–82. *Population Trends*, **35**, 11–17.

45. HAWTON, K. Personal communication.

46. DIEKSTRA, R.F.W. (1991) Suicide and parasuicide: A global perspective. In *Suicide and Attempted Suicide: Risk Factors, Management and Prevention* (eds S.A. Montgomery & N.L.M. Goeting). Southampton: Duphar Laboratories.

47. HAWTON, K., O'GRADY, J., OSBORN, M., *et al* (1982) Adolescents who take overdoses: Their characteristics, problems and contacts with helping agencies. *British Journal of Psychiatry*, **140**, 118–123.

48. MCINTIRE, M.S. & ANGLE, C.R. (1973) Psychological 'biopsy' in self-poisoning of children and adolescents. *American Journal of Diseases of Children*, **126**, 42–46.

49. HAWTON, K. & FAGG, J. (1992) Deliberate self-poisoning and self-injury in adolescents: A study of characteristics and trends in Oxford, 1976–89. *British Journal of Psychiatry*, **161**, 816–823.

50. WHO: EURO PARASUICIDE STUDY (to be published).

51. WELLS, N. (1981) *Suicide and Deliberate Self-harm*. London: Office of Health Economics.

52. HAWTON, K. & CATALAN, J. (1987) *Attempted Suicide: A Practical Guide to its Nature and Management* (2nd edn). Oxford: Oxford University Press.

53. DIEKSTRA, R.F.W. (1991) Suicide and parasuicide: A global perspective. In *Current Approaches in Suicide and Attempted Suicide: Risk Factors, Management and Prevention* (eds S.A. Montgomery & N.L.M. Goeting). Southampton: Duphar Laboratories.

54. HAWTON, K. (1986). *Suicide and Attempted Suicide among Children and Adolescents*. Newbury Park, California: Sage.

55. HAWTON, K. & GOLDACRE, M. (1982) Hospital admission for adverse effects of medicinal agents (mainly self-poisoning) among adolescents in the Oxford region. *British Journal of Psychiatry*, **140**, 166–170.

56. PLATT, S., HAWTON, K., KREITMAN, N. *et al* (1988) Recent clinical and epidemiological trends in parasuicide in Edinburgh and Oxford: A tale of two cities. *Psychological Medicine*, **18**, 405–418.

57. HAWTON, K. (1986). *Suicide and Attempted Suicide among Children and Adolescents*. Newbury Park, California: Sage.

58. KREITMAN, N. & SCHREIBER, M. (1979) Parasuicide in young Edinburgh women, 1968–75. *Psychological Medicine*, **9**, 469–479.

59. HAWTON, K. & GOLDACRE, M. (1982) Hospital admission for adverse effects of medicinal agents (mainly self-poisoning) among adolescents in the Oxford region. *British Journal of Psychiatry*, **140**, 166–170.

60. PLATT, S., HAWTON, K., KREITMAN, N., *et al* (1988) A tale of two cities. *Psychological Medicine*, **18**, 405–418.

61. BREWER, C. & FARMER, R. (1985) Self-poisoning in 1984: A prediction that didn't come true. *British Medical Journal*, **290**, 391.

62. HAWTON, K. & FAGG, J. (1992) Trends in deliberate self-poisoning and self-injury in Oxford 1976–90. *British Medical Journal*, **304**, 1409–1411.

63. FOSTER, D.P. & FROST, C.E.B. (1985) Medicinal self-poisoning and prescription frequency. *Acta Psychiatrica Scandinavia*, **71**, 657–674.

64. DIEKSTRA, R.F.W. (1985) Suicide and suicide attempts in the European Economic Community: An analysis of trends, with special emphasis on trends among the young. *Suicide and Life Threatening Behavior*, **15**, 27–42.

65. HAWTON, K., FAGG, J., SIMKIN, S., *et al* (1994) The epidemiology of attempted suicide in the Oxford area, England, 1989–1992. *Crisis* (in press).

66. HAWTON, K. & FAGG, J. (1992) Trends in deliberate self-poisoning and self-injury in Oxford 1976–90. *British Medical Journal*, **304**, 1409–1411.

67. HAWTON, K. Personal communication.

68. OVENSTONE, I.M.K. & KREITMAN, N. (1974) Two syndromes of suicides. *British Journal of Psychiatry*, **124**, 336–345.

69. HAWTON, K. & FAGG, J. (1988) Suicide and other causes of death following attempted suicide. *British Journal of Psychiatry*, **152**, 359–366.

70. Ibid.

71. DIEKSTRA, R.F.W. (1991) Suicide and parasuicide: A global perspective. In *Current Approaches in Suicide and Attempted Suicide: Risk Factors, Management and Prevention* (eds S.A. Montgomery & N.L.M. Goeting). Southampton: Duphar Laboratories.

72. HAWTON, K., FAGG, J., SIMKIN, S., *et al* (1994) The epidemiology of attempted suicide in the Oxford area, England, 1989–1992. *Crisis* (in press).

73. DIEKSTRA, R.F.W. (1991) Suicide and parasuicide: A global perspective. In *Current Approaches in Suicide and Attempted Suicide: Risk Factors, Management and Prevention* (eds S.A. Montgomery & N.L.M. Goeting). Southampton: Duphar Laboratories.

74. HAWTON, K. (1987) Assessment of suicide risk. *British Journal of Psychiatry*, **150**, 145–153.

Chapter 2 (pp.36–65)
SOCIAL PATTERNS, PERSONAL PAIN

1. WEST, D.J. (1985) *Sexual Victimisation*. Aldershot: Gower.

2. NOLLER, P. & CALLAN, V. (1991) *The Adolescent in the Family*. London: Routledge.

3. HARRISON, H. (1993) Personal Interview.

4. JOHNSON, K. (1982) One small horrid word. *Girls are Powerful: Young women's writings from Spare Rib.* (ed S. Hemmings). London: Sheba Feminist Publishers.

5. DIEKSTRA, R.F.W. & MORITZ, B.J.M. (1987) Trends and Factors. In *Suicide in Adolescence* (eds R.F.W. Diekstra, & K. Hawton). Dordrecht. Martinus Nijhoff Publishers.

6. Ibid.

7. FURNHAM, A. & STACEY, B. (1991) Young People's Understanding of Society. In *Sex and Gender*. London: Routledge.

8. NOLLER, P. & CALLAN, V. (1991) *The Adolescent in the Family*. London: Routledge.

9. WEINREICH, H. (1978) Sex Role Socialisation. In *The Sex Role System. Psychological and Sociological Perspectives*. London: Routledge & Kegan.

10. BROOKS-GUN, J. & REITER, E.O. (1993) The Role of Pubertal Processes. In *At the Threshold: The developing adolescent* (eds S.S. Feldman & G.R. Elliott). Cambridge: Harvard University Press.

11. WEISSMAN, M.M. & KLERMAN, G.L. (1977) Sex differences in the epidemiology of depression. *Archives of General Psychiatry*, **34**, 98–111

12. HORWITZ, A. (1977) The pathways into psychiatric treatment: Some differences between men and women. *Journal of Health and Social Behaviour*. **18th June**, 169–178.

13. JACK, R. (1992) *Women and Attempted Suicide*. Hove: Lawrence Erlbaum Associates.

14. Ibid.

15. Ibid.

16. Ibid.

17. MULCOCK, D. (1955) Juvenile suicide: A study of suicide and attempted suicide over a 16 year period. *The Medical Officer*, 155–160.

18. RALEIGH, V.S. & BALARAJAN, R. (1992) Suicide and self-burning among Indians and West Indians in England and Wales. *British Journal of Psychiatry*, **161**, 365–368.

19. RALEIGH, V.S. & BALARAJAN, R. (1992) Suicide and self-burning among Indians and West Indians in England and Wales. *British Journal of Psychiatry*, **161**, 365–368.

20. BURKE, A.W. (1976) Sociocultural determinants of attempted suicide among West Indians in Birmingham: Ethnic origin and immigrant status. *British Journal of Psychiatry*, **129**, 261–266.

21. FERNANDO, S. (1991) *Mental Health, Race and Culture*. London: Macmillan Education Ltd.

22. WRIGHT (1981) Ethnic differences in self-poisoning. *Postgraduate Medical Journal*, **57**, 792–793.

23. RALEIGH, V.S. & BALARAJAN, R. (1992) Suicide and self-burning among Indians and West Indians in England and Wales. *British Journal of Psychiatry*, **161**, 365–368.

24. GIBSON, P. (1989) Gay male and lesbian youth suicide. In *Report of the Secretary's Task Force on Youth Suicide. Volume 3: Prevention and Interventions in Youth Suicide* (Alcohol, Drug Abuse and Mental Health Administration). Washington DC: US Government Print Office. Superintendent of Documents.

25. Ibid.

26. BELL, A. & WEINBERG, M. (1978) *Homosexualities: A Study of Diversity Among Men and Women*. New York: Simon and Schuster.

27. TRENCHARD, L. & WARREN, H. (1984) *Something to Tell You*. London: London Gay Teenage Group.

28. LESBIAN INFORMATION SERVICE (1993) *Coming Out – Young Lesbian Pack*. Todmorden: Lesbian Information Service.

29. HARRY, J. (1986) *Adolescent Suicide and Sexual Identity Issues*. Submitted to the National Institute of Mental Health for the Secretary's Conference on Adolescent Suicide. Washington DC. 8–9 May, 1986.

30. REMAFEDI, G. (1985) *Male Homosexuality: The adolescent's perspective*. Adolescent Health Program, University of Minnesota (unpublished).

31. SHELTER RESEARCH AND DEVELOPMENT UNIT (1990). Shelter Fact Sheet 2. *Young and Homeless*. London: Shelter.

32. GIBSON, P. (1989) Gay male and lesbian youth suicide in alcohol, drug abuse, and mental health administration. In *Report of the Secretary's Task Force on Youth Suicide. Volume 3: Prevention and Interventions in Youth Suicide* (Alcohol, Drug Abuse and Mental Health Administration). Washington DC: US Government Print Office. Superintendent of Documents.

33. SMITH, R. (1985) Occupationless health. 'I couldn't stand it any more': Suicide and unemployment. *British Medical Journal*, **291**, 1563–1566.

34. PRITCHARD, C. (1992) Is there a link between suicide in young men and unemployment? *British Journal of Psychiatry*, **160**, 750–756.

35. Ibid.

36. PLATT, S. (1986) Parasuicide and unemployment. *British Journal of Psychiatry*, **149**, 400–405.

37. PLATT, S. & KREITMAN, N. (1984) Trends in parasuicides and unemployment among men in Edinburgh 1968–82. *British Medical Journal*, **289**, 1029–1032.

38. WINEFIELD, A.H., TIGGEMANN, M., WINEFIELD, H.R., *et al* (1993) *Growing up with unemployment: A longitudinal study of its psychological impact*. London: Routledge.

39. Ibid.

40. CURRAN, D.K. (1987) *Adolescent Suicidal Behavior*. New York: Hemisphere Publishing Corporation.

41. MARTUNNEN, M. (1994) *Adolescent Suicide in Finland*. Helsinki: National Public Health Institute.

42. CHARLTON, J., KELLY, S., DUNNELL, K., *et al* (1993) Suicide deaths in England and Wales: Trends in factors connected with suicide deaths. *Population Trends*.

43. Ibid.

44. DALLOS, R. & MCLAUGHLIN, E. (eds) (1993) *Social Problems and the Family*. London: Sage.

45. PLATT, S., HAWTON, K., KREITMAN, N. *et al* (1988) Recent clinical and epidemiological trends in parasuicide in Edinburgh and

Oxford: A tale of two cities. *Psychological Medicine*, **18**, 405–418.

46. HAWTON, K., O'GRADY, J., OSBORN, M., *et al* (1982) Adolescents who take overdoses: Their characteristics, problem and contacts with helping agencies. *British Journal of Psychiatry*, **140**, 118–123.

47. HAWTON, K., SIMKIN, S., FAGG, J., *et al* (1994) Suicide in Oxford University students. *British Journal of Psychiatry* (in press).

48. KERKHOF, A. & KUNST, A. (1994) A European perspective on suicidal behaviour. In *The Prevention of Suicide* (eds R. Jenkins, S. Griffiths, I. Wylie, *et al*). London: HMSO.

49. DOOLEY, E. (1994) Prisons. In *The Prevention of Suicide* (eds R. Jenkins, S. Griffiths, I. Wylie, *et al*). London: HMSO.

50. Ibid.

51. HOME OFFICE. Suicides in Prison (1994). London: HMSO.

52. GRINDROD, H. & BLACK, G. (1989) *Suicides at Leeds Prison: An enquiry into the deaths of five teenagers during 1988–1989*. London: The Howard League for Penal Reform.

53. WOOL, R. & DOOLEY, E. (1987) A Study of Attempted Suicides in Prisons. *Medical Science and the Law*, **27**.

54. Ibid.

55. DOOLEY, E. (1994) Prisons. In *The Prevention of Suicide* (eds R. Jenkins, S. Griffiths, I. Wylie, *et al*). London: HMSO.

56. CASALE, S. & PLOTNIKOFF, J. (1990) *Regimes for Remand Prisoners*. London: The Prison Reform Trust.

57. DOOLEY, E. (1990) Prison Suicide. *British Journal of Psychiatry*, **156**, 40–45.

58. CARVEL, J. (1990) Teenage prisoners still waiting for lifeline. *Guardian*. 20th December.

59. THE HOWARD LEAGUE FOR PENAL REFORM (1992) Suicides in Feltham. London.

60. HAWTON, K. (1986) *Suicide and Attempted Suicide Among Children and Adolescents*. Newbury Park, California: Sage.

61. PFEFFER, C.R. (1987) Families of suicidal children. In *Suicide in Adolescence* (eds R.F.W. Diekstra & K. Hawton). Dordrecht: Martinus Nijhoff.

62. MARTUNNEN, M.J., HILLEVI, A.M. & LÖNNQVIST, J.K. (1993) Precipitant stressors in adolescent suicide. *Journal of the American Academy of Child and Adolescent Psychiatry*, **32**, 6, 1178–1183.

63. CURRAN, D.K. (1987) *Adolescent Suicidal Behavior*. New York: Hemisphere Publishing Corporation.

64. SHAFII, M., CARRIGAN, S., WHITTINGHILL, J.R., *et al* (1985) Psychological autopsy of completed suicide in children and adolescents. *American Journal of Psychiatry*, **142**, 1061–1064.

65. MRAZEK, P., LYNCH, M. & BENTOVIM, A. (1983) Sexual abuse of children in the United Kingdom. *Child Abuse and Neglect*, **7**, 147–153.

66. DEYKIN, E., ALPERT, J. & MCNAMARA, J. (1985) A pilot study of the effects of exposure to child abuse or neglect on adolescent suicidal behaviour. *American Journal of Psychiatry*, **142**, 1299–1303.

67. RENVOIZE, J. (1993) *Innocence Destroyed*. A Study of Child Sexual Abuse. London: Routledge.

68. PHILLIPS, A. (1993) *The Trouble with Boys*. London: Pandora.

69. NEWSOM, S. (1994) Put away childish things. *Sunday Times*, 1st May.

70. MCLAUGHLIN, C. (1992) Blacker than the teenage blues. *Independent*, 24th November.

71. KOLVIN, I., BARRETT, M.L., BHATE, S.R., *et al* (1991) The Newcastle Depression Project: Diagnosis and clarification of depression. *British Journal of Psychiatry*, **159** (supplement 11), 9–21.

72. MARTUNNEN, M.J., ARO, H.M. & LÖNNQVIST, J.K. (1993) Adolescence and suicide in a review of psychological autopsy studies. *European Child and Adolescent Psychiatry*, **2**, 10–18.

73. Ibid.

74. HARRINGTON, R.C. (1993) *Depression Disorder in Childhood and Adolescence*. Chichester: John Wiley.

75. Ibid.

76. GELDER, M., GATH, D. & MAYOU, R. (1989) *Oxford Textbook of Psychiatry* (second edition). Oxford: Oxford University Press.

77. Ibid.

78. DRAKE, R., GATES, C., WHITAKER, A. *et al* (1985) Suicide among schizophrenics: A review. *Comprehensive Psychiatry*, **26**, 91–100.

79. GELDER, M., GATH, D. & MAYOU, R. (1989) *Oxford Textbook of Psychiatry* (second edition). Oxford: Oxford University Press.

80. HAWTON, K., FAGG, J., PLATT, S., *et al* (1993) Factors associated with suicide after parasuicide in young people. *British Medical Journal*, **306**, 1641–1644.

81. BRENT, D., PERPER, J., MORITZ, G., *et al* (1993) Psychiatric risk factors for adolescent suicide: A case-control study. *Journal of the American Academy of Child and Adolescent Psychiatry*, **32**, 521–529.

82. MARTUNNEN, M.J., ARO, H.V. & LÖNNQVIST, J.K. (1993) Adolescence and suicide: A review of psychological autopsy studies. *European Child and Adolescent Psychiatry*, **2**, 10–18.

83. SHAFFER, D. (1974) Suicide in childhood and early adolescence. *Journal of Child Psychology and Psychiatry*, **15**, 275–291.

84. Ibid

85. SHAFII, M., CARRIGAN, S., WHITTINGHALL, J.R., *et al* (1985) Psychological autopsy of completed suicide in children and adolescents. *American Journal of Psychiatry*, **142**, 1061–1064.

86. PFEFFER, C.R. (1989) Life stress and family risk factors for youth fatal and non-fatal suicidal behaviour. In *Suicide Among Youth: Perspectives on Risk and Prevention* (ed C.R. Pfeffer). Washington DC: American Psychiatric Press.

87. DAVIDSON, L.E. (1989) Suicide clusters and youth. In *Suicide Among Youth: Perspectives on Risk and Prevention* (ed C.R. Pfeffer). Washington DC: American Psychiatric Press.

88. DAVIDSON, L. (1989) Suicide cluster and youth. In *Suicide Among Youth: Perspectives on Risk and Prevention* (ed C.R. Pfeffer). Washington DC: American Psychiatric Press.

89. SHAFII, M. (1989) Completed suicide in children and adolescents: Methods of psychological autopsy. In *Suicide Among Youth: Perspectives on Risk and Prevention* (ed C.R. Pfeffer). Washington DC: American Psychiatric Press.

Chapter 3   (pp. 66–98)
WHY HAS YOUTH SUICIDE INCREASED?

1. GIOVACCHINI, P. (1981) *The Urge to Die: Why Young People Commit Suicide*. New York: Penguin.

2. GIDDENS, A. (1993) *Sociology*. Cambridge: Polity Press.

3. Ibid.

4. BELL, ELSA University of Oxford Counselling Service, speaking on 'Woman's Hour'.

5. GIDDENS, A. (1993) *Sociology*. Cambridge: Polity Press.

6. KLERMAN, G.L. (1989) Suicide, depression and related problems among the baby boom cohort. In *Suicide Among Youth: Perspectives on Risk and Prevention* (ed C.R. Pfeffer). Washington DC: American Psychiatric Press.

7. KLERMAN, G.L. (1988) The current age of youthful melancholia: Evidence for increase in depression among adolescents and young adults. *British Journal of Psychiatry*, **152**, 4–14.

8. DEPARTMENT OF EMPLOYMENT (1993) *Labour Force Survey: Economic Activity by Age*. London: Department of Employment.

9. WINEFIELD, A., TIGGEMAN, M., WINEFIELD, H., *et al* (1993) *Growing Up With Unemployment: A longitudinal study of its psychological impact*. London: Routledge.

10. DEPARTMENT OF EMPLOYMENT (1993) *Labour Force Survey: Economic Activity by Age*. London: Department of Employment.

11. GIDDENS, A. (1993) *Sociology*. Cambridge: Polity Press.

12. Ibid.

13. DONOGHUE, B. (1992) *The Time of Your Life? The truth about being young in 90's Britain*. London: British Youth Council.
14. Ibid.
15. Ibid.
16. Ibid.
17. DEPARTMENT OF EMPLOYMENT (1990) *New Earnings Survey 1989*. London: Department of Employment.
18. SHELTER RESEARCH AND INFORMATION SECTION (1990). *Fact-sheet 2. Young and homeless*. London: Shelter.
19. GIDDENS, A. (1993) *Sociology*. Cambridge: Polity Press.
20. FURNHAM, A. & STACEY, B. (1991) *Young People's Understanding of Society*. London: Routledge.
21. JACK, R. (1992) *Women and Attempted Suicide*. Hove: Lawrence Erlbaum Associates.
22. COLEMAN, J.C. & HENDRY, L. (1991) *The Nature of Adolescence* (2nd edition). London: Routledge.
23. FURSTENBERG, F.F. (1993) Coming of age in a changing family system. In *At the Threshold: The Developing Adolescent* (eds S.S. Feldman & G.R. Elliott). Cambridge, Mass: Harvard University Press.
24. COLEMAN, J.C. & HENDRY, L. (1991) *The Nature of Adolescence* (2nd edition). London: Routledge.
25. FURSTENBERG, F.F. (1993) Coming of age in a changing family system. In *At the Threshold: The Developing Adolescent* (eds S.S. Feldman & G.R. Elliott). Cambridge, Mass: Harvard University Press.
26. Ibid.
27. Ibid.
28. SHAFII, M. (1989) Completed suicide in children and adolescents: Methods of psychological autopsy. In *Suicide Among Youth: Perspectives on Risk and Prevention* (ed C.R. Pfeffer). Washington DC: American Psychiatric Press.
29. DIEKSTRA, R.F.W. (1991) Suicide and parasuicide: A global perspective. In *Current Approaches in Suicide and Attempted Suicide: Risk Factors, Management and Prevention* (eds S.A. Montgomery & N.L.M. Goeting). Southampton: Duphar Laboratories.
30. BULUSU, L. & ALDERSON, M. (1984) Suicides 1950–1982. *Population Trends*, **35**, 11–17.
31. GELDER, M., GATH, D. & MAYOU, R. (1989) *Oxford Textbook of Psychiatry* (2nd edition). Oxford: Oxford University Press.
32. CHARLTON, J., KELLY, S., DUNNELL, K., *et al* (1993) Suicide deaths in England and Wales: Trends in factors associated with suicide deaths. *Population Trends*, **71**, 34–42.

33. WELLINGS, K., FIELD, J., JOHNSON, A.M., *et al* (1994) *Sexual Behaviour in Britain: The National Survey of Sexual Attitudes and Lifestyles*. London: Penguin.
34. HAWTON, K., O'GRADY, J., OSBORN, M., *et al* (1982) Adolescents who take overdoses: Their characteristics, problems and contact with helping agencies. *British Journal of Psychiatry*, **140**, 118–123.
35. KOSSOFF, J. (1994) Female Suicide: Shock Trend. *Time Out*, **No. 1222**, 19–26 January.
36. HALL, C. (1993) 'New Man' behind rise in suicide. *Independent*, 3rd November.
37. PHILLIPS, A. (1993) *The Trouble with Boys*. UK: Pandora.
38. DOOLEY, E. (1994) Prisons. In *The Prevention of Suicide* (eds R. Jenkins, S. Griffiths & I. Wylie). London: HMSO.
39. CASALE, S. & PLOTNIKOV, J. (1990) *Regimes for Remand Prisoners*. London: Prison Reform Trust.
40. GRINDROD, H. & BLACK, G. (1989) *Suicides at Leeds Prison: An enquiry into the deaths of five teenagers during 1988–1989*. London: The Howard League for Penal Reform.
41. LEIBLING, A. (1992) *Suicides in Prison*. London: Routledge.
42. CASALE, S. & PLOTNIKOV, J. (1990) *Regimes for Remand Prisoners*. London: The Prison Reform Trust.
43. SCRIVENER, A. (1992) *Suicides in Feltham*. London: Howard League for Penal Reform.
44. WOOL, R. & DOOLEY, E. (1987) A study of attempted suicide in prisons. *Medicine, Science and the Law*, **27**.
45. MIND open letter.
46. KLERMAN, G. (1988) The current age of youthful melancholia: Evidence for increase in depression among adolescents and young adults. *British Journal of Psychiatry*, **152**, 4–14.
47. CHEW, R. (1992) *Compendium of Health Statistics*. London: Office of Health Economics.
48. JOHNSTONE, L. (1989) *Users and Abusers of Psychiatry: A Critical Look at Traditional Psychiatric Practice*. London: Routledge.
49. CHEW, R. (1992) *Compendium of Health Statistics*. London: Office of Health Economics.
50. JACK, R. (1992) *Women and Attempted Suicide*. Hove: Lawrence Erlbaum Associates.
51. JOHNSTONE, L. (1989) *Users and Abusers of Psychiatry: A Critical Look at Traditional Psychiatric Practice*. London: Routledge.
52. Ibid.
53. Ibid.
54. ASHTON, H. (1991) Psychotropic drug prescribing for women. *British Journal of Psychiatry*, **158**, 30–35.

55. JACK, R. (1992) *Women and Attempted Suicide*. Hove: Lawrence Erlbaum Associates Ltd.

56. FOSTER, D. & FOSTER, C. (1985) Medical self-poisoning and prescription frequency. *Acta Psychiatrica Scandinavica*, **71**, 567–574.

57. SKEGG, G., DOLL, R. & PERRY, J. (1977) The use of medicines in general practice. *British Medical Journal*, **Vol 1 Jan–June**, 1561–1563.

58. HAWTON, K. & GOLDACRE, M. (1982) Hospital admissions for adverse effects of medicinal agents (mainly self-poisoning) among adolescents in the Oxford Region. *British Journal of Psychiatry*, **141**, 166–170.

59. DEPARTMENT OF HEALTH (1991) Personal communication cited in *National Audit of Drug Misuse in Britain 1992* (ed M. Ashton). London: Institute for the Study of Drug Dependence.

60. PLATT, S. (1992) Epidemiology of suicide and parasuicide. *Journal of Psychopharmacology*, **6**, 291–299.

61. JOHNSTONE, L. (1989) *Users and Abusers of Psychiatry: A Critical Look at Traditional Psychiatric Practice*. London: Routledge.

62. LACEY, R. (1991) *The MIND Complete Guide to Psychiatric Drugs: A Layman's Handbook*. London: Ebury Press.

63. JOHNSTONE, L. (1989) *Users and Abusers of Psychiatry: A Critical Look at Traditional Psychiatric Practice*. London: Routledge.

64. DIEKSTRA, R.F.W. (1991) Suicide and Parasuicide: A Global Perspective. In *Current Approaches in Suicide and Attempted Suicide: Risk Factors, Management and Prevention* (eds S.A. Montgomery & N.L.M. Goeting). Southampton: Duphar Laboratories.

65. PLANT, M.A. & PLANT, M. (1992) *Risk-takers: Alcohol, drugs, sex and youth*. London & New York: Tavistock/Routledge.

66. Ibid.

67. VELLEMAN, R. (1993) *Alcohol and the Family*. London: Institute of Alcohol Studies.

68. Ibid.

69. Ibid.

70. PLANT, M.A. & PLANT, M. (1992) *Risk-takers: Alcohol, drugs, sex and youth*. London & New York: Tavistock/Routledge.

71. THORLEY, A. (1982) The effects of alcohol. In *Drinking and Problem Drinking* (ed M.A. Plant). London: Junction Books.

72. PLANT, M.A. & PLANT, M. (1992) *Risk-takers: Alcohol, drugs, sex and youth*. London & New York: Tavistock/Routledge.

73. PLANT, M.A., BAGNALL, G. & FOSTER, J. (1990) Teenage heavy drinkers: Alcohol-related knowledge, beliefs, experiences, motivation and the social context of drinking. *Alcohol and Alcoholism*, **25**, 691–698.

74. GODDARD, E. (1991) *Drinking in England and Wales in the Late 1980s*. London: HMSO.

75. Ibid.

76. PLANT, M.A. & PLANT, M. (1992) *Risk-takers: Alcohol, drugs, sex and youth*. London & New York: Tavistock/Routledge.

77. Ibid.

78. PARRY, H.J. *et al* (1974). Increasing alcohol intake as a coping mechanism for psychic distress. In *Social Aspects of the Medical Use of Psychotropic Drugs* (ed R. Cooperstock). Toronto: Alcoholism and Drug Addiction Research Foundation of Ontario.

79. SHAFFER, D., VIELAND, B., GARLAND, A., *et al* (1990) Adolescent suicide attempters: Response to suicide-prevention programs. *Journal of the American Medical Association*, **264**, 3151–3155.

80. PLANT, M.A. & PLANT, M. (1992) *Risk-takers: Alcohol, drugs, sex and youth*. London & New York: Tavistock/Routledge.

81. GALLUP/WRANGLER (1992) *The Youth Report*.

82. RESEARCH BUREAU LIMITED (1989) *Anti-misuse of drugs campaign evaluation: Reports of findings of stages I-VII*. May 1989. London: RBL.

83. Ibid.

84. PIERCE, A. (1993) Raves threaten jobs in the drinks trade. *Times*, 27th October. Quoting report by Richard Woods (Henley Centre for Forecasting).

85. INSTITUTE FOR THE STUDY OF DRUG DEPENDENCE (1993) *National Audit of Drug Misuse in Britain 1992* (ed M. Ashton). London: Institute for the Study of Drug Dependence.

86. Ibid.

87. CURRAN, D.K. (1987) *Adolescent Suicidal Behavior*. New York: Hemisphere Publishing Corporation.

88. BOLDT, M. (1982) Normative evaluations of suicide and death: A cross generational study. *Omega*, **13**, 145–157.

89. DIEKSTRA, R.F.W. (1991) Suicide and Parasuicide: A Global Perspective. In *Current Approaches in Suicide and Attempted Suicide: Risk Factors, Management and Prevention* (eds S.A. Montgomery & N.L.M. Goeting). Southampton: Duphar Laboratories.

90. WARDEN, J. (1991) Euthanasia: New issue for conscience. *British Medical Journal*, **303**, 1422.

91. MACKINNON, I. (1992) Trial may advance demands for legal euthanasia. *Independent*, 21st September.

92. MARKS, K. (1992) Doctor's dilemma of pain or death. *Independent*, 21st September.

93. Ibid.

94. HUNT, L. (1992) Doctors welcome 'will' covering terminal illness. *Independent*, 8th September.

95. CHARATAN, F. (1991) Assisted Suicide: 1. America. *British Medical Journal*, **303**, 431.

96. JOHNSON, D., FITCH, D., ALSTON, J., *et al* (1980) Acceptance of conditional suicide and euthanasia among adult Americans. *Suicide and Life Threatening Behavior*, **10**, 157–166.

97. BERMAN, A.L. (1989) Mass Media and Youth Suicide Prevention. In *Report of the Secretary's Task Force on Youth Suicide, Volume 3: Prevention and Interventions in Youth Suicide* (Alcohol, Drug Abuse and Mental Health Administration). Washington DC: US Government Print Office, Superintendent of Documents.

98. STACK, S. (1987) Celebrities and suicide: A taxonomy and analysis 1948–1983. *American Sociological Review*, **52**, 401–412.

99. ANDERSON, F.S. (1977) TV violence and viewer aggression: Accumulation of study results 1956–1976. *Public Opinion Quarterly*, **41**.

100. PHILLIPS, D.P. (1974) The influence of suggestion on suicide: Substantive and theoretical implications of the Werther effect. *American Sociological Review*, **39**, 340–354.

101. ALVAREZ, A. (1971) *The Savage God: A Study of Suicide*. London: Penguin.

102. PHILLIPS, D.P. (1974) The influence of suggestion on suicide: Substantive and theoretical implications of the Werther effect. *American Sociological Review*, **39**, 340–354.

103. Ibid.

104. Ibid.

105. STACK, S. (1987) Celebrities and suicide: A taxonomy and analysis 1948–1983. *American Sociological Review*, **52**, 401–412.

106. PHILLIPS, D.P. & CARSTENSEN, L.L. (1986) Clustering of teenage suicides after television news stories about suicide. *New England Journal of Medicine*, **315**, 685–689.

107. CURRAN, D.K. (1987) *Adolescent Suicidal Behavior*. New York: Hemisphere Publishing Corporation.

108. WINTER, R. (1986) Medicine and the media. *British Medical Journal*, **292**, 1073.

109. SANDLER, D.A., CONNELL, P.A. & WELSH, K. (1986) Emotional crises imitating television. *Lancet* **(i)** 856.

110. PLATT, S. (1987) The aftermath of Angie's overdose: Is soap (opera) damaging to your health? *British Medical Journal*, **294**, 954–957.

111. COLLINS, S. (1993) Health prevention messages may have para-doxical effect. *British Medical Journal*, **306**, 926.
112. SCHMIDTKE, A. & HÄFNER, H. (1988) The Werther effect after tele-vision films: New evidence for an old hypothesis. *Psychological Medicine*, **18**, 665–676.
113. BREWER, C. (1993) Trying to change the British way of death. *Independent*, 16th February.
114. JACK, R. (1992) *Women and Attempted Suicide*. Hove: Lawrence Erlbaum Associates.
115. CHARLTON, J., KELLY, S., DUNNELL, K., *et al* (1992) Trends in suicide deaths in England and Wales. *Population Trends*, **69**, 10–16.
116. DIEKSTRA, R.F.W. (1991) Suicide and parasuicide: A global per-spective. In *Current Approaches in Suicide and Attempted Suicide: Risk Factors, Management and Prevention* (eds S.A. Montgomery & N.L.M. Goeting). Southampton: Duphar Laboratories.
117. CURRAN, D.K. (1987) *Adolescent Suicidal Behavior*. New York: Hemisphere Publishing Corporation.

Chapter 4   (pp. 99–121)
PREVENTING YOUNG DEATHS

1. KEIR, N. (1986) *I Can't Face Tomorrow: Help for Those with Thoughts of Suicide and Those who Counsel Them*. Wellingborough, Northants: Thorsons.
2. Secretary of State for Health (1992) *The Health of the Nation: A Strategy for Health in England*. London: HMSO.
3. Ibid.
4. ALCOHOL, DRUG ABUSE AND MENTAL HEALTH ADMINISTRATION (1989) *Report of the Secretary's Task Force on Youth Suicide. Volume 1: Overview and Recommendations*. DHSS Pub.No. (ADM) 89–1621. Washington DC: US Government Print Office. Super-intendent of Documents.
5. MARTUNNEN, M.J., ARO, H.M & LÖNNQVIST, J.K. (1993) Adolescence and suicide: A review of psychological autopsy studies. *European Child and Adolescent Psychiatry*, **2**, 10–18.
6. ALCOHOL, DRUG ABUSE AND MENTAL HEALTH ADMINISTRATION (1989) *Report of the Secretary's Task Force on Youth Suicide. Volume 1: Overview and Recommendations*. DHSS Pub.No. (ADM) 89–1621. Washington DC: US Government Print Office. Super-intendent of Documents.
7. SHAFFER, D., GARLAND, A., GOULD, M., *et al* (1988) Preventing teenage suicide: A critical review. *Journal of the American Academy of Child and Adolescent Psychiatry*, **27**, 675–687.

8. VASSILAS, C.A. & MORGAN, H.G. (1993) General practitioners' contact with the victims of suicide. *British Medical Journal*, **307**, 300–301.

9. GUNNELL, D. (1993) Recent studies of contacts with services prior to suicide – Somerset. In *The Prevention of Suicide* (eds R. Jenkins, S. Griffiths, I. Wylie, *et al*). London: HMSO.

10. ROYAL COLLEGE OF PSYCHIATRISTS AND ROYAL COLLEGE OF GENERAL PRACTITIONERS (1992) *Defeat Depression*. London: Royal College of Psychiatrists.

11. THE SAMARITANS (1992) *Reach out . . . we'll be there*. Slough: The Samaritans.

12. ROSS, C.P. (1987) School and suicide: Education for life and death. In *Suicide and Adolescence* (eds R.F.W. Diekstra & K. Hawton). Dordrecht: Martinus Nijhoff.

13. Ibid.

14. CURRAN, D.K. (1987) *Adolescent Suicidal Behavior*. New York: Hemisphere Publishing Corporation.

15. SHAFFER, D. (1993) Implications for education: Prevention of youth suicide. In *The Prevention of Suicide* (eds R. Jenkins, S. Griffiths, I. Wylie, *et al*). London: HMSO.

16. Ibid.

17. GILLET, R. (1987) *Overcoming Depression*. London: Dorling Kindersley.

18. ROSS, C.P. (1987) School and suicide: Education for life and death. In *Suicide and Adolescence* (eds R.F.W. Diekstra & K. Hawton). Dordrecht: Martinus Nijhoff.

19. DIEKSTRA, R.F.W. & HAWTON, K. (1987) *Suicide in Adolescence*. Dordrecht: Martinus Nijhoff.

20. OVERHULSER, R., EVANS, S. & SPIRITO, A. (1990) Sex differences and their relevance to primary prevention of adolescents. *Death Studies*, **14**, 391–402.

21. SHAFFER, D. (1993) Implications for education: Prevention of youth suicide. In *The Prevention of Suicide* (eds R. Jenkins, S. Griffiths, I. Wylie, *et al*). London: HMSO.

22. WATTS, J. (1992) Why must they be teenagers in love with death? *Observer*, 17th May.

23. HAWTON, K. (1992) By their own young hand. *British Medical Journal*, **304**, 1000.

24. PEREIRA GRAY, D. (1994) Primary Care. In *The Prevention of Suicide* (eds R. Jenkins, S. Griffiths, I. Wylie, *et al*). London: HMSO.

25. HAWTON, K. (1994) Causes and opportunities for prevention. In *The Prevention of Suicide* (eds R. Jenkins, S. Griffiths, I. Wylie, *et al*). London: HMSO.

26. PAYKEL, E.S. & PRIEST, R. (1992) Recognition and management of depression in general practice: Consensus statements. *British Medical Journal*, **305**, 1198–1202.

27. RICHMAN, J. & ROSENBAUM, M. (1970) The family doctor and the suicidal family. *Psychiatry in Medicine*, **1**, 27–35.

28. HAWTON, K., O'GRADY, J., OSBORN, M., *et al* (1982) Adolescents who take overdoses: Their characteristics, problems and contacts with helping agencies. *British Journal of Psychiatry*, **140**, 118–123.

29. RUTZ, W., VON KNORRING, L.M. & WALINDER, J. (1989) Frequency of suicide on Gottland after systematic postgraduate education of general practitioners. *Acta Psychiatrica Scandinavica*, **80**, 151–154.

30. VASSILAS, C.A. & MORGAN, H.G. (1993) General practitioners' contact with the victims of suicide. *British Medical Journal*, **307**, 300–301.

31. ROYAL COLLEGE OF PSYCHIATRISTS AND ROYAL COLLEGE OF GENERAL PRACTITIONERS (1992) *Defeat Depression*. London: Royal College of Psychiatrists.

32. VASSILAS, C.A. & MORGAN, H.G. (1993) General practitioners' contact with the victims of suicide. *British Medical Journal*, **307**, 300–301.

33. ALCOHOL, DRUG ABUSE AND MENTAL HEALTH ADMINISTRATION (1989) *Report of the Secretary's Task Force on Prevention of Youth Suicide, Volume 1: Overview and Recommendations*. DHSS Pub. No. (ADM) 89–1621. Washington DC: US Government Print Office. Superintendent of Documents..

34. HAWTON, K. (1994) Causes and opportunities for prevention. In *The Prevention of Suicide* (eds R. Jenkins, S. Griffiths, I. Wylie, *et al*). London: HMSO.

35. BBC (1993) *Producers' Guidelines*. London: BBC Publications.

36. EBBAGE, J., FARR, C., SKINNER, D.V., *et al* (1994) The psychosocial assessment of patients discharged from accident and emergency departments after deliberate self-poisoning. *Journal of the Royal Society of Medicine*, **87**, 515–516.

37. ARMSON, S. (1994) The Samaritans. In *The Prevention of Suicide* (eds R. Jenkins, S. Griffiths, I. Wylie, *et al*). London: HMSO.

38. MILLER, H., COOMBS, D., LEEPER, J., *et al* (1984) An analysis of the effects of suicide prevention facilities on the suicide rates in the United States. *American Journal of Public Health*, **74**, 340–343.

39. LESTER, D. (1972) The myth of suicide prevention. *Comprehensive Psychiatry*, **13**, 555–560.

40. KREITMAN, N. (1976) The coal-gas story: United Kingdom suicide rates 1960–71. *British Journal of Preventive Medicine*, **30**, 86–93.

41. Ibid.

42. BAGLEY, C.R. (1968) The evaluation of a suicide prevention scheme by an ecological method. *Social Science and Medicine*, **2**, 1–14.

43. KREITMAN, N. (1976) The coal-gas story: United Kingdom suicide rates 1960–71. *British Journal of Preventive Medicine*, **30**, 86–93.

44. CLARKE, R.V. & LESTER, D. (1989) *Suicide: Closing the Exits*. New York: Springer Verlag.

45. OFFICE OF HEALTH ECONOMICS (1981) *Suicide and Deliberate Self-harm*. London: Office of Health Economics.

46. SLOAN, J.H., RIVARA, F.P., & REAY, D.T. (1990) Firearm regulations and rates of suicide. A comparison of two metropolitan areas. *New England Journal of Medicine*, **322**, 369–373.

47. MARZUK, P.M., LEON, A.C. & TARDIFF, K. (1992) The effect of access to lethal methods of injury on suicide rates. *Archives of General Psychiatry*, **49**, 451–458.

48. HAWTON, K., COLE, D., O'GRADY, J., *et al* (1982) Motivational aspects of deliberate self-poisoning in adolescents. *British Journal of Psychiatry*, **141**, 286–291.

49. OFFICE OF HEALTH ECONOMICS (1981) *Suicide and Deliberate Self-harm*. London: Office of Health Economics.

50. BARRACLOUGH, B.M. (1974) Are there safer hypnotics than barbiturates? *Lancet*, **i**, 57–58.

51. OFFICE OF HEALTH ECONOMICS (1981) *Suicide and Deliberate Self-harm*. London: Office of Health Economics.

52. ROGERS, L. (1992) Doctors demand curbs on 'killer' paracetamol. *Sunday Times*, 14th November.

53. BRYAN, J. (1992) Help that can kill. *Guardian*, 22nd May.

54. ROGERS, L. (1992) Doctors demand curbs on 'killer' paracetamol. *Sunday Times*, 14th November.

55. HAWTON, K. Suicide and attempted suicide. In *Preventive Approaches in Psychiatry* (eds E. Paykel & R. Jenkins). London: Royal College of Psychiatrists.

56. CLARK, R. & LESTER, D. (1987) Toxicity of care exhaust and opportunity for suicide: Comparison between Britain and United States. *Journal of Epidemiology and Community Health*, **4**, 114–120.

57. MILLETT, K. (1991) *The Loony Bin Trip*. London: Virago.

58. RADICAL STATISTICS HEALTH GROUP (1992).

59. SHELTER (1991) *Community Care and Housing. Fact-sheet*. London: Shelter.

60. *Lancet*, December 1989.

61. Ibid.

62. MORGAN, H.G. (1992) Suicide prevention. Hazards on the fast lane to community care. *British Journal of Psychiatry*, **160**, 149–153.

63. GOLDACRE, M., SEAGROATT, V. & HAWTON, K. (1993) Suicide after discharge from psychiatric inpatient care. *Lancet*, **342**, 283–286.

64. Ibid.

65. MORGAN, G., JONES, R. & WILTSHIRE, J. (1994) Secondary Care. In *The Prevention of Suicide* (eds R. Jenkins, S. Griffiths, I. Wylie, *et al*). London: HMSO.

66. MORGAN, H.G. (1992) Suicide prevention. Hazards on the fast lane to community care. *British Journal of Psychiatry*, **160**, 149–153.

67. WHITE, E. (1991) *The 3rd Quinquennial National Community Psychiatric Nursing Survey*. University of Manchester: Department of Nursing.

68. CHARLTON, J., KELLY, S., DUNNELL, K., *et al* (1992) Trends in suicide deaths in England and Wales. *Population Trends*, **69**, 10–16.

69. LESTER, D. (1992) State initiatives in addressing youth suicide: Evidence for their effectiveness. *Social Psychiatry and Psychiatric Epidemiology*, **27**, 75–77.

Chapter 5   (pp.125–150)
ON THE SUICIDE THRESHOLD

1. SIMPSON, M.A. (1975) The phenomenology of self-mutilation in a general hospital setting. *Canadian Psychiatric Association Journal*, **20**, 429–434.

2. HARRISON, D. (1993) *Self Harm: The Visible Hurt*. South West MIND Newsletter, **No 18**.

3. HAWTON, K., COLE, D., O'GRADY, J., *et al* (1982) Motivational aspects of deliberate self-poisoning in adolescents. *British Journal of Psychiatry*, **141**, 286–291.

4. ELDRID, J. (1988) *Caring for the Suicidal*. London: Constable.

5. HAWTON, K., COLE, D., O'GRADY, J., *et al* (1982) Motivational aspects of deliberate self-poisoning in adolescents. *British Journal of Psychiatry*, **141**, 286–291.

6. WHITE, H. (1974) Self-poisoning in adolescents. *British Journal of Psychiatry*, **124**, 24–35.

7. HAWTON, K., COLE, D., O'GRADY, J., *et al* (1982) Motivational aspects of deliberate self-poisoning in adolescents. *British Journal of Psychiatry*, **141**, 286–291.

8. NAGY, M. (1948) The child's view of death. *Journal of Genetic Psychology*, **73**, 3–27.

9. STILLION, J. & WASS, H. (1979) Children and Death. In *Dying: Facing the Facts*. (ed H. Wass). Washington DC: Hemisphere Publishing Corporation.

10. ORBACH, I. (1988) *Children Who Don't Want to Live*. San Francisco: Jossey-Bass.

11. PIAGET, J. (1960) *The Child's Concept of the World*. Patterson, N.J: Littlefield Adams.

12. MCINTYRE, M.S., ANGLE, C.R. & STRUPPLER, L.J. (1972) The concept of death in mid-western children and youth. *American Journal of Diseases of Children*, **123**, 527–532.

13. ANTHONY, S. (1971) *The Discovery of Death in Childhood and After*. London: Penguin.

14. PFEFFER, C.R. (1986) *The Suicidal Child*. New York: Guildford Press.

15. CURRAN, D.K. (1987) *Adolescent Suicidal Behavior*. New York: Hemisphere Publishing Corporation.

16. PFEFFER, C.R. (1986) *The Suicidal Child*. New York: Guildford Press.

17. MCINTYRE, M.S., ANGLE, C.R. & STRUPPLER, L.J. (1972) The concept of death in mid-western children and youths. *American Journal of Diseases of Children*, **123**, 527–532.

18. FURNHAM, A. & GUNTER, B. (1989) *The Anatomy of Adolescence: Young People's Social Attitudes in Britain*. London: Routledge.

19. PFEFFER, C.R. (1986) *The Suicidal Child*. New York: Guildford Press.

20. Ibid.

21. MCINTYRE, M.S., ANGLE, C.R. & STRUPPLER, L. (1972) The concept of death in mid-western children and youths. *American Journal of Diseases of Children*, **123**, 527–532.

22. ORBACH, I. & GLAUBMAN, H. (1978) Suicidal, aggressive and normal children's perceptions of personal and impersonal death. *Journal of Clinical Psychology*, **34**, 850–857.

23. ORBACH, I. (1987) Assessment of suicidal behaviour in young children: Case demonstrations. In *Suicide in Adolescence* (eds R.F.W. Diekstra & K. Hawton). Dordrecht: Martinus Nijhoff.

24. PFEFFER, C.R. (1986) *The Suicidal Child*. New York: Guildford Press.

25. Ibid.

26. ORBACH, I. (1987) Assessment of suicidal behaviour in young children: Case demonstrations. In *Suicide in Adolescence* (eds R.F.W. Diekstra & K. Hawton). Dordrecht: Martinus Nijhoff.

27. PAYKEL, E.S., PRUSOFF, B.A. & MYERS, J.K. (1975) Suicide attempts and recent life events: A controlled comparison. *Archives of General Psychiatry*, **32**, 327–333.

28. HANSER, S.T. & BOWLDS, N.K. (1990) Stress, coping and adaptation. In *At the Threshold: The Developing Adolescent* (eds S.S.

Feldman & G.R. Elliott). Cambridge, Mass: Harvard University Press.

29. QUINNET, P. (1992) *Suicide: The Forever Decision*. New York: Continuum Publishing Company.
30. Ibid.
31. HAWTON, K. (1986) *Suicide and Attempted Suicide in Children and Adolescents*. Newbury Park, California: Sage.
32. ORBACH, I. (1988) *Children Who Don't Want to Live*. San Francisco: Jossey-Bass.
33. ROSS, C. (1986) School and suicide: Education for life and death. In *Suicide in Adolescence* (eds R.F.W. Diekstra & K. Hawton). Dordrecht: Martinus Nijhoff.
34. PFEFFER, C.R. (1986) *The Suicidal Child*. New York: Guildford Press.
35. HOBERMAN, H. & GARFUNKEL, B.D. (1989) Completed suicide in youth. In *Suicide Among Youth* (ed C.R. Pfeffer). Washington DC: American Psychiatric Press.
36. Ibid.
37. HAWTON, K., COLE, D., O'GRADY, J., *et al* (1982) Motivational aspects of deliberate self-poisoning in adolescents. *British Journal of Psychiatry*, **141**, 286–291.
38. Ibid.
39. KERFOOT, M. (1993) Personal communication.
40. HAWTON, K. (1986) *Suicide and Attempted Suicide in Children and Adolescents*. Newbury Park, California: Sage.
41. HARRINGTON, R.C. (1993) *Depressive Disorders in Childhood and Adolescence*. Chichester: John Wiley.
42. GOLDACRE, M., SEAGROATT, V. & HAWTON, K. (1993) Suicides after discharge from psychiatric inpatient care. *Lancet*, **342**, 283–286.
43. O'BRIEN, S. (1985) *The Negative Scream: A Story of Young People Who Took an Overdose*. London: Routledge and Kegan Paul.
44. GAZZARD, B.G., DAVIS, M., SPOONER, J., *et al* (1976) Why do people use paracetamol for suicide? *British Medical Journal*, **1**, 212–213.

Chapter 6   (pp. 151–169)
PERCEPTIONS OF THE SUICIDAL: UNTHINKABLE FEARS, COMFORTING MYTHS

1.   CURRAN, D.K. (1987) *Adolescent Suicidal Behavior*. New York: Hemisphere Publishing Corporation.
2.   ALVAREZ, A. (1971) *The Savage God: A Study of Suicide*. London: Penguin.
3.   STENGEL, E. (1973) *Suicide and Attempted Suicide*. (2nd Edition). Harmondsworth: Penguin.

4. WOLK-WASSERMAN, D. (1986) Suicidal communication of persons attempting suicide and responses of significant others. *Acta Psychiatrica Scandinavica*, **73**, 481–499.

5. Ibid.

6. ROSS, C.P. (1987) School and suicide: Education for life and death. In *Suicide in Adolescence* (eds R.F.W. Diekstra and K. Hawton). Dordrecht: Martinus Nijhoff.

7. GOODYER, I. (1993) Depression among pupils at school. *British Journal of Special Education*, **20**, 51–54.

8. Ibid.

9. ORBACH, I. (1987) Assessment of suicidal behaviour in young children: Case demonstrations. In *Suicide in Adolescence* (eds R.F.W. Diekstra and K. Hawton). Dordrecht: Martinus Nijhoff.

10. PFEFFER, C.R. (1987) Families of suicidal children. In *Suicide in Adolescence* (eds R.F.W. Diekstra and K. Hawton). Dordrecht: Martinus Nijhoff.

11. CURRAN, D.K. (1987) *Adolescent Suicidal Behavior*. New York: Hemisphere Publishing Corporation.

12. STENGEL, E. (1973) *Suicide and Attempted Suicide*. (2nd Edition). Harmondsworth: Penguin.

13. LITMAN, R. (1989) Psychological Autopsies of Youth Suicides. In *Report of the Secretary's Task Force on Youth Suicide. Volume 3: Prevention and Intervention in Youth Suicide*. (Alcohol, Drug Abuse, and Mental Health Administration). Washington DC: US Government Print Office, Superintendent of Documents.

14. Ibid.

15. WOLK-WASSERMAN, D. (1986) Suicidal communication of persons attempting suicide and responses of significant others. *Acta Psychiatrica Scandinavica*, **73**, 481–499.

16. WOLK-WASSERMAN, D. (1986) *Attempted suicide – the patient's family, social network and therapy*. Stockholm: Karolinska Institute.

17. BANCROFT, J.H.J., SKRIMSHIRE, A.M. & SIMKIN, S. (1976) The reasons people give for taking overdoses. *British Journal of Psychiatry*, **128**, 538–548.

18. ALVAREZ, A. (1971) *The Savage God: A Study of Suicide*. London: Penguin.

19. SEIDEN, R.H. (1978) Where are they now? A follow-up study of suicide attempters from the Golden Gate Bridge. *Suicide and Life Threatening Behavior*, **8**, 203–216.

20. O'DONNELL, I., ARTHUR, A.J. & FARMER, R.D.J. (1994) A follow-up study of attempted railway suicides. *Social Science and Medicine*, **38**, 437–442.

21. MORGAN, H.G. & OWEN, J.H. (1990) *Persons at Risk of Suicide:*

Guidelines on Good Clinical Practice. UK: Boots Company PLC.

22. SHNEIDMAN, E. (1970) Suicide as a taboo topic. In *The Psychology of Suicide* (eds E. Shneidman, N. Farberow & R. Litman). New York: Science House.

23. ROSS, C.P. (1987) School and suicide: Education for life and death. In *Suicide in Adolescence* (eds R.F.W. Diekstra and K. Hawton). Dordrecht: Martinus Nijhoff.

24. Ibid

25. SHAFFER, D. (1994) Implications for education: Prevention of youth suicide. In *The Prevention of Suicide* (eds R. Jenkins, S. Griffiths, I. Wylie, *et al*). London: HMSO.

26. WOLK-WASSERMAN, D. (1986) *Attempted suicide – the patient's family, social network and therapy*. Stockholm: Karolinska Institute.

27. HOBERMAN, H.M. & GARFINKEL, B.D. (1989) Completed suicide in youth. In *Suicide among Youth: Perspectives on Risk and Prevention* (ed C.R. Pfeffer). Washington DC: American Psychiatric Press.

28. SHAFFER, D., GARLAND, A., GOULD, M., *et al* (1988) Preventing teenage suicide: A critical review. *Journal of the American Academy of Child & Adolescent Psychiatry*, **27**, 675–687.

29. ROSS, C.P. (1987) School and suicide: Education for life and death. In *Suicide in Adolescence* (eds R.F.W. Diekstra and K. Hawton). Dordrecht: Martinus Nijhoff.

30. Ibid

31. Ibid.

Chapter 7   (pp. 170–188)
INTERRUPTING THE SUICIDAL PROCESS

1. HOBERMAN, H. & GARFINKEL, B.D. (1989) Completed suicide in youth. In *Suicide Among Youth* (ed C.R. Pfeffer). Washington DC: American Psychiatric Press.

2. WALKER, M., MOREAU, D. & WEISSMAN, M. (1990) Parents' awareness of children's suicide attempts. *American Journal of Psychiatry*, **147**, 10, 1364–1366.

3. WERTHEIMER, A. (1991) *A Special Scar: The experiences of people bereaved by suicide*. London: Routledge.

4. WOLK-WASSERMAN, D. (1986) *Attempted Suicide – the patient's family, social network and therapy*. Stockholm: Karolinska Institute.

5. Ibid.

6. MORGAN, H.G. & OWEN, J.H. (1990) *Persons at Risk of Suicide. Guidelines on Good Clinical Practice*. UK: Boots Company PLC.

7. BOWDEN-WHITE, S. (1985) *Everything to Live For*. USA: Simon & Shuster.

8. PFEFFER, C.R. (1986) *The Suicidal Child*. New York: Guildford Press.

258

Chapter 8   (pp. 189–207)
SEEKING HELP: OBSTACLES AND FEARS

1. WHITE, H.C. (1974) Self-poisoning in adolescents. *British Journal of Psychiatry*, **124**, 24–35.

2. HAWTON, K. (1986) *Suicide and Attempted Suicide Among Children and Adolescents*. Newbury Park, California: Sage.

3. KREITMAN, N. (ed) (1977) *Parasuicide*. London: Wiley.

4. SHAFFER, D., VIELAND, V., GARLAND, A., *et al* (1990) Adolescent suicide attempters: Response to suicide-prevention programs. *Journal of the American Medical Association*, **264**, 3151–3155.

5. PARKER, A. (1981) The meaning of attempted suicide to young parasuicides: A repertory grid study. *British Journal of Psychiatry*, **139**, 306–312.

6. RUNESON, B.S. (1992) Youth suicides unknown to psychiatric care providers. *Suicide and Life-Threatening Behavior*, **22 (4)**, 494–503.

7. PAYKEL, E.S. & PRIEST, R.G. (1992) Recognition and management of depression in general practice: Consensus statement. *British Medical Journal*, **305**, 1198–1202.

8. ROYAL COLLEGE OF PSYCHIATRISTS (1992) *Defeat Depression*. London: Royal College of Psychiatrists.

9. Ibid.

10. Ibid.

11. Ibid.

12. HAWTON, K., COLE, D., O'GRADY, J., *et al* (1982) Motivational aspects of deliberate self-poisoning in adolescents. *British Journal of Psychiatry*, **141**, 286–291.

13. JOHNSTONE, L. (1989) *Users and Abusers of Psychiatry: A Critical Look at Traditional Psychiatric Practice*. London: Routledge.

14. Ibid.

15. PALMER, R., CHALONER, D. & OPPENHEIMER, R. (1992) Childhood sexual experiences with adults reported by female patients. *British Journal of Psychiatry*, **160**, 261–265.

16. HMSO (1992) *Report of the Committee of Inquiry into Complaints About Ashworth Hospital*. London: HMSO.

17. WOOD, D. (1992) *Stress on Women: Policy paper on women and mental health*. London: MIND publications.

18. KREITMAN, N. (ed) (1977) *Parasuicide*. London: Wiley.

19. WESTWOOD, S., COULOUTE, J., DESAI, S., *et al* (1989) *Sadness in my Heart: Racism and mental health*. Leicester: Leicester Black Mental Health Group.

20. PLATT, S. (1991) Decisions about psychiatric aftercare for parasuicide patients: Is there a social class bias? In *Current Approaches*

in Suicide and attempted suicide: Risk factors, management and prevention (eds S.A. Montgomery & N.L.M. Goeting). Southampton: Duphar Laboratories.

21. WESTWOOD, S., COULOUTE, J., DESAI, S., *et al* (1989) *Sadness in my Heart: Racism and mental health*. Leicester: Leicester Black Mental Health Group.

22. FERNANDO, S. (1991) *Mental Health, Race and Culture* (Issues in mental health). London: Macmillan Education Ltd.

23. WOOD, D. (1992) *Stress on Women: Policy paper on women and mental health*. London: MIND publications.

24. GIBSON, P. (1989) Gay male and lesbian youth suicide. In *Report of the Secretary's Task Force on Youth Suicide. Volume 3: Prevention and Intervention in Youth Suicide*. (Alcohol, Drug Abuse, and Mental Health Administration). Washington DC: US Government Print Office, Superintendent of Documents.

25. LITMAN, R. (1989) Psychological Autopsies of Youth Suicides. In *Report of the Secretary's Task Force on Youth Suicide. Volume 3: Prevention and Intervention in Youth Suicide*. (Alcohol, Drug Abuse, and Mental Health Administration). Washington DC: US Government Print Office, Superintendent of Documents.

26. CURRAN, D.K. (1987) *Adolescent Suicidal Behavior*. New York: Hemisphere Publishing Corporation.

INDEX

GIRL, INTERRUPTED

By Susanna Kaysen

'Triumphantly funny . . . honest and moving . . . Susanna Kaysen's compelling and heart-breaking story shows how thin the line is between those society deems mad and those it deems sane' – **New York Times Book Review**

In 1967, eighteen-year-old Susanna Kaysen was sent to McLean Hospital in a taxi. For most of the next two years she was on the ward for teenage girls in a psychiatric institution renowned for its famous clientele, among them Sylvia Plath, Robert Lowell and James Taylor. *Girl, Interrupted*, a series of razor-sharp vignettes based on her experiences there, brilliantly evokes a 'parallel universe' set within the kaleidoscopically shifting landscape of the late sixties.

YOUNG PEOPLE UNDER STRESS
A Parent's Guide

By Sally Burningham

How do parents tell whether their child's moods or strange behaviour are simply part of adolescence, or signs that things are going wrong? This much-needed book explains many of the stresses and mental health problems that young people may experience, including family difficulties, bullying and severe depression. With information on approaching professionals, various treatments, the legal situation and helpful organisations, it encourages parents to make the best use of the services available as well as finding their own resources within the family and community. It also discusses parents' own feelings of anxiety and suggests ways in which they can get advice and support for themselves.

WHAT'S REALLY GOING ON HERE
Making Sense of Our Emotional Lives

By Susie Orbach

'A polemical blast against the brand of stiff-upper-lipped "emotional illiteracy" [Susie Orbach] sees as almost universal in westernised societies' – **New Statesman and Society**

Sex, war, anger, love, loss, holidays, food, politics, family relationships . . . In these brilliant articles from *The Guardian*, this highly accessible writer, and one of Britain's best-known psychotherapists, deftly leads us through the emotional minefields of our private and public lives. With an unerring ability to see what's really going on, Susie Orbach confronts our fears – 'we consider feelings to be a fearful genie, which, once released, will never return to the safe confines of its internal bottle' – and urges us to address 'the emotional illiteracy' that has become our way of life.